ENGINEERING

From Value Stream Mapping to Effective Action

STEVE PEREIRA & ANDREW DAVIS

FOREWORD BY KAREN MARTIN

COAUTHOR OF *VALUE STREAM MAPPING*

IT Revolution

Independent Publisher Since 2013

Portland, Oregon

25 NW 23rd Pl, Suite 6314
Portland, OR 97210

First Edition

Printed in the United States of America
30 29 28 27 26 25 24   1 2 3 4 5 6 7 8 9

Cover, book design, and illustrations by
Julianna Johnson and Kate Giambrone, Bologna Sandwich LLC.
Cover layout by Devon Smith.

Library of Congress Control Number: 2024931067

ISBN: 9781950508457
eBook ISBN: 9781950508464
Web PDF ISBN: 9781950508488
Audiobook ISBN: 9781950508471

For information about special discounts for bulk purchases or for information on booking authors for an event, please visit our website at www.ITRevolution.com.

FLOW ENGINEERING

Dedication

This book is dedicated to everyone brave enough
and idealistic enough to bring humanity
and flow back to the workplace.

Contents

List of Figures vii

Foreword by Karen Martin xiii

Introduction xvii

PART 1 The Flow Landscape

1 The Problem with Scale 3

2 Solutions to Scale 17

3 The Elements of Action 29

4 Flow Engineering 35

PART 2 Mapping the Landscape

5 Outcome Mapping 53

6 Current State Value Stream Mapping 77

7 Dependency Mapping 109

8 Future State Value Stream Mapping 129

9 The Flow Roadmap 145

PART 3 Navigating the Landscape

10 Principles of Flow Engineering 165

11 Leading Flow Engineering 185

12 Traps to Avoid 199

13 Value Stream Management 213

14 Scaling Flow Engineering 227

Conclusion 249

Appendix 253

Glossary 263

Bibliography 265

Notes 271

Acknowledgments 275

About the Authors 276

List of Figures

Introduction

FIG. 0.1 Bolt Global Current State Challenge   xxvi

Chapter 1

FIG. 1.1 The Three Human Costs of Scale   5
FIG. 1.2 Misalignment in Teams   7
FIG. 1.3 The Paradox of Scale Illustrated   9
FIG. 1.4 The Checkbox Project: Teams Involved   12

Chapter 2

FIG. 2.1 The Spectrum of Solution Approaches   18
FIG. 2.2 The Three Gaps to Enabling Large-Scale Collaboration   19
FIG. 2.3 The Iron Triangle of Constraints   20
FIG. 2.4 Cybernetic Feedback Loop   22
FIG. 2.5 A Siloed Organizational Structure   23
FIG. 2.6 Effects of Limited Visibility   23
FIG. 2.7 The Value Stream   24
FIG. 2.8 A Simple Value Stream Map   25
FIG. 2.9 The Toyota Production System's Improvement Kata   26
TBL. 2.1 Cybernetic Control Systems in Popular Decision Frameworks   27

Chapter 3

FIG. 3.1 Collective and Individual Flow   30
FIG. 3.2 Effects of the Three Elements of Action   30
FIG. 3.3 The Three Elements of Action   31
FIG. 3.4 Cybernetic Loop with the Elements of Actions   32
FIG. 3.5 The Elements of Action: Value, Clarity, and Flow   32

Chapter 4

FIG. 4.1 The Power of a Map   36

FIG. 4.2   Value, Clarity, and Flow Woven through all
            Flow Engineering Maps   38
FIG. 4.3   Five Maps of Flow Engineering   39
TBL. 4.1   Addressing the Three Gaps through Flow Engineering   40
TBL. 4.2   Each Map Serves at Least One of the Elements of Action   41
TBL. 4.3   General Facilitator Rules of Engagement   43
FIG. 4.4   A Segment of the Full Value Stream Map   46
TBL. 4.4   Purposes and Benefits of the Five Flow Engineering Exercises 48

Chapter 5

FIG. 5.1   Outcome Mapping Primarily Serves to Identify Value   54
FIG. 5.2   The Five Stages of Outcome Mapping   55
FIG. 5.3   A Rapid Outcome Map   56
TBL. 5.1   Common Situations That Can Be Transformed into
            Actionable Outcomes via Outcome Discovery   57
FIG. 5.4   Five Categories for Outcome Mapping   64
FIG. 5.5   Stages of Outcome Mapping   65
FIG. 5.6   Example of the Discovery Stage of Outcome Mapping   66
FIG. 5.7   Notes Organized into Themes   67
FIG. 5.8   Example of Voting Using Dots   67
FIG. 5.9   A Completed Outcome Map   70
FIG. 5.10 The Challenge Landscape within Sharon's Area of Responsibility 72
FIG. 5.11 The Bolt Global Outcome Mapping Process   73

Chapter 6

FIG. 6.1   Value Stream Mapping Primarily Serves to Build Clarity   77
FIG. 6.2   The Five Stages of Value Stream Mapping   81
FIG. 6.3   Simplified Value Stream Map   82
TBL. 6.1   Differences between Customer Journey Maps and
            Value Stream Maps   84
FIG. 6.4   Customer Journey vs. Value Stream   85
FIG. 6.5   The Traditional Form of Representing a Value Stream
            Map for Manufacturing   86
FIG. 6.6   A Simple Flow Engineering Value Stream Map   87
FIG. 6.7   Example of a Completed Value Stream Map   89

FIG. 6.8   Identifying a Constraint in the Value Stream   94

FIG. 6.9   Example Value Stream Map for Software Development   95

FIG. 6.10   Sample Value Stream Map Showing Cycle Timing and
            Wait Timing   96

FIG. 6.11   Annotated Value Stream Map   96

FIG. 6.12   Example Small-Scale Value Stream Map   97

FIG. 6.13   Identifying a Constraint on a Value Stream Map   98

FIG. 6.14   Value Stream Map with VAT and %C&A   102

FIG. 6.15   Sample Value Stream Map with Many Notes   104

Chapter 7

FIG. 7.1   Dependency Mapping Primarily Serves to Enhance the
            Clarity Built by Value Stream Mapping   109

FIG. 7.2   Dependency Mapping Targets Only Dependencies
            That Impact the Constraint   110

FIG. 7.3   Example of the Extent of Dependencies   111

FIG. 7.4   The Five Stages of Dependency Mapping   112

FIG. 7.5   Dependency Map of the Constraint: Environment Setup 117

FIG. 7.6   Gap between Sharon's Team and Karl's Team   118

FIG. 7.7   Three Assets for Collaboration   119

FIG. 7.8   The Dependency Map Jointly Created by Karl and Sharon 120

FIG. 7.9   Suspected Constraint Identified in Value Stream Mapping 122

FIG. 7.10   Example Sub–Value Stream Map   122

FIG. 7.11   A Sub–Value Stream Map to Illustrate the
            Dependent Workflow   123

FIG. 7.12   Direct Causes of Hot Spots   123

FIG. 7.13   Practice the Five Whys to Dig Deeper into the
            Suspected Constraint   124

FIG. 7.14   A Visualization of Dependencies across the Flow
            of the Checkbox Project   126

Chapter 8

FIG. 8.1   Future State Mapping Opens the Door to Enabling Flow 129

FIG. 8.2   Current, Ideal, and Future State Maps   130

FIG. 8.3   Flow Engineering Cycle of Mapping as an Improvement Kata 133

FIG. 8.4 The Four Stages of Future State Mapping   133
FIG. 8.5 Current State Map with Bottleneck Highlighted   139
FIG. 8.6 Future State Map with Improvement Areas Noted in Green   140
FIG. 8.7 Future State Map Reduced to Seven Serial Steps and
          One Parallel Step   140
FIG. 8.8 Future State Map with Cycle Timings   141
TBL. 8.1 Results of Mapping at a Travel Tech Company   143

Chapter 9

FIG. 9.1   The Flow Roadmap Primarily Serves to Enable Flow   145
FIG. 9.2   The Three Stages of a Flow Roadmap   146
TBL. 9.1   Issues Transformed into Actions/Experiments to Improve
           Flow at Bolt Global   148
FIG. 9.3   Sharon's Completed Flow Roadmap   149
FIG. 9.4   The Flow Roadmap Board   151
FIG. 9.5   The Future State Map Showing Improvement Areas   152
FIG. 9.6   Improvement Opportunities Broken Down into Actions   152
FIG. 9.7   Possible Improvements Ranked by Importance   153
FIG. 9.8   Plot Feasibility along the Horizontal Axis   154
FIG. 9.9   Indicate Dependencies between Activities   154
FIG. 9.10 Improvement Activities Categorized by Time Horizon
           (Now, Next, Later)   155
FIG. 9.11 Items Arranged in Sequential Order: Now, Next, Later   155
FIG. 9.12 Identified Measure of Progress   156
TBL. 9.2   Gartner's Flow Metrics Cover Technical, Product, and
           Business Concerns   156
FIG. 9.13 Example of Adding Assigned Owners   157
FIG. 9.14 Flow Roadmap Creation Progressing from Problem
           Areas and Concerns to Actions   160

Chapter 10

FIG. 10.1 The Five Principles of Lean   168
FIG. 10.2 A Simple Outcome Map Representing Diverse Concerns   170
FIG. 10.3 A Simple Flow Engineering Value Stream Map   172
FIG. 10.4 Value Stream Map Highlighting Wait Times   173

FIG. 10.5   The Efficiency Matrix   175

FIG. 10.6   Theory of Constraints Step 1: Identify the Constraint   176

FIG. 10.7   Theory of Constraints Step 2: Exploit the Constraint   176

FIG. 10.8   Theory of Constraints Step 3: Subordinate Everything
            Else to the Constraint   177

FIG. 10.9   Theory of Constraints Step 4: Elevate the Constraint   177

FIG. 10.10 Excess Work in Progress Is a Sign of Lacking Pull Systems   180

Chapter 11

FIG. 11.1   A Value Stream Map Depicts Multiple Feedback Loops   187

FIG. 11.2   Business Frameworks Are Templates for Management   189

FIG. 11.3   The Constraint on a Value Stream   191

TBL. 11.1   Examples of Enabling and Governing Constraints   192

Chapter 12

FIG. 12.1   Outcome Discovery and Outcome Mapping Help You
            Craft a Productive Narrative   201

FIG. 12.2   Outcome Mapping and Discovery Can Bridge Local
            Incentives by Establishing a Higher-Value Shared Target   203

FIG. 12.3   Limited Visibility Enables Limited Focus   205

FIG. 12.4   Example Value Stream Map with Irrelevant Downstream
            Precision   206

FIG. 12.5   The Current State Map Depicting the Full Agile Release
            Train (ART)   209

TBL. 12.1   Visual Activity Classification Legend, Depicting
            Non–Value-Adding, Testing, Value-Adding, and
            Coordinating Activities   209

FIG. 12.6   Example Future State Map Depicting Non-Critical and
            Non-Value Adding Activities   210

TBL. 12.2   Current State Flow Performance vs. Future State   211

Chapter 13

FIG. 13.1   Focus on Project Leads to Ignoring Longer Term Impact   214

FIG. 13.2   Each Cycle of Continuous Improvement Builds on the
            Previous One   214

FIG. 13.3 Current State Map: Steps, Timing, Roles, Tools, Artifacts   215

FIG. 13.4 Project or Product Orientation Lies on a Spectrum   216

TBL. 13.1 A Comparison of Value Stream Mapping and Value
Stream Management   217–218

FIG. 13.5 Phil's Journey at Parchment   221

TBL. 13.2 The Parchment Measurement Journey   222

FIG. 13.6 Waiting for Data Availability and Quality Means Uncertainty
Remains High for Longer and Outcomes are Later to Arrive   224

Chapter 14

FIG. 14.1 Value Streams Sharing a Common Constraint   228

FIG. 14.2 The Spectrum of Flow Investment   231

TBL. 14.1 Developmental and Operational Focus Implications   232

FIG. 14.3 Interdependence of Core and Supportive Value Streams   234

FIG. 14.4 A Value Stream Network Map   235

FIG. 14.5 The Y Axis of a Value Stream Network Map   236

FIG. 14.6 The X Axis of a Value Stream Network Map   237

FIG. 14.7 Connections Show Dependencies between Value Streams   237

FIG. 14.8 Example Value Stream Network Map Showing Shift
in Internal Dev Platform   238

FIG. 14.9 Example Value Stream Network Map Showing
Developmental Shift   238

FIG. 14.10 Flow Enabling Team Interactions with Product Streams   242

FIG. 14.11 The Flywheel of Flow Engineering   246

Appendix

FIG. A.1 Value, Clarity, and Flow   253

FIG. A.2 Calculating Speed: Lead, Wait, and Active Times   256

FIG. A.3 Cycle Time Includes All Value-Added and Non–Value-
Added Time Composing Each Stage   257

FIG. A.4 Calculating Quality: Percent Complete & Accurate   257

FIG. A.5 Example Map Board in Progress   259

TBL. A.1 Estimated Costs of Flow Engineering Exercises   261

Foreword

THE JOURNEY TOWARD ORGANIZATIONAL excellence demands commitment to value, clarity, and flow. This requires establishing a clear target, aligning stakeholders, and optimizing workflow. In my decades of experience with value stream mapping, I've seen countless examples of the impact this practice can have in empowering organizational change. I wrote *Value Stream Mapping* in 2013, and the practice continues to grow in popularity every year. Despite its recognized value, a gap exists between value stream mapping as an aspiration and real-world implementation. This book targets that gap, offering practical guidance for any organization.

I first met Steve through LinkedIn in 2020, and I met Andrew shortly after. We immediately recognized a shared passion for thinking of collaborative work in terms of value, clarity, and flow. We shared stories about incredible results achieved through value stream mapping in all sizes and types of organizations. We found that we shared a commitment to sharing those stories and what we've learned by using value streams as a model for work.

I was introduced to value stream mapping as a diagnostic, design, and prioritization tool for improving work systems. As I started working with clients to begin to "see" their work systems in a fact-based, data-driven way, I realized that value stream mapping was more than a "tool." It's an essential management practice with benefits far beyond creating flow across interconnected functions and work teams. It also addresses these common organizational problems:

- Siloed decision-making and work design that slows an organization's ability to deliver value to its customers, become agile and responsive, and create high-performing environments.
- Friction between leaders and entire branches of an organization due to misaligned strategic goals and priorities for improving how the organization operates.
- And not understanding how work flows—or, more commonly, doesn't flow—across the organization.

In an increasingly complex and interconnected business landscape, organizations of all sizes face myriad challenges as they strive to scale without losing their way in the process. The complexities of modern enterprises often lead to misalignment, inefficiencies, and a lack of clarity, hindering the organization's ability to effectively and efficiently deliver value to its customers. As we navigate these challenges, it becomes increasingly evident that a holistic approach to understanding and optimizing organizational workflow is essential but often missing.

The power of value stream mapping lies in its ability to provide a balance of both visual and data representations, constructing a useful representation that corresponds to a complete business workflow and layering on information about performance and effectiveness. This shared visual representation of the work process serves as a focal point for team discussions around performance improvement. Rapid implementations of value stream mapping serve as a quick and easy on-ramp for more detailed and comprehensive maps as buy-in increases. Davis and Pereira say: "Map quickly, show promise, go further." The goal is to create a visual, supported by data, that quickly reveals specific improvement opportunities.

Value stream mapping is not only a visualization exercise but also a method of communicating visually. It allows teams to collectively establish a shared mental model of the goal of their work and the method for carrying it out. This seemingly simple exercise provides individuals with the mental context needed to work effectively as a team. The apparent simplicity of a value stream map abstracts a complex collection of perspectives and data, yet this simplicity enables clear representation, conversation, and focus. Simple isn't easy, but this book provides step-by-step guidance to navigate the complexity of building these simple maps. Andrew and Steve have presented *Flow Engineering* as a clear set of practices that help to distill the complex reality of collaborative work into maps that make the invisible visible and reveal hidden insights on the most impactful improvements. This not only enables effective action but also teaches essential Lean and Agile principles by putting them into practice.

Flow Engineering offers approachable, flexible, and scalable practices to address the challenges of scale, visibility, and misalignment in modern organizations. By providing a simple, digital-native starting point on-ramp to effective action through value stream mapping, it meets teams where they are today: distributed, distracted, disoriented, and disconnected. With it, teams can gain a comprehensive understanding of their workflow, identify improvement opportunities, and align their efforts with the value they can deliver. The book serves as a guide to align stakeholders, identify opportunities, and implement performance improvement in complex organizations. The insights and practices shared within these pages will empower leaders to enable focus, clarity, and collaboration as catalysts for meaningful and sustainable action.

—**Karen Martin, 2024**
Author of *The Outstanding Organization*
and *Value Stream Mapping*

Introduction

WE'VE BECOME VICTIMS OF SUCCESS. Organizations are now so large and interconnected that digital dependencies tie us in knots. Across the organization, our understanding is fractured. We work in a hurricane of distraction, drowning in a sea of data, and we struggle to leverage it to make improvement decisions. We have hyper-optimized much of our work, and yet it can take months to make small business improvements. Organizations are tantalized by the promise of radical transformations (cultural, digital, Lean, Agile, DevOps), but these often devolve into rebranding and renaming the status quo rather than bringing about real change.

All of these challenges are amplified by the issue of scale. The scale of our organizations has grown dramatically as it has become easier to expand globally, to acquire new businesses, and to address new markets. While performance can be optimized in small autonomous teams, no team is an island. Enabling success at scale necessitates some kind of coupling across teams. These threads, which connect everyone and everything to everyone and everything else in the organization, inevitably get tangled in knots.

Effective action in organizations of any size depends on having coherent goals. But having coherent goals depends on having shared clarity. A lack of shared clarity sabotages improvement efforts. And scale makes achieving and maintaining shared clarity nearly impossible. Even at the scale of a "two-pizza team," clarity is often sacrificed at the altar of getting things done. And with the demise of clarity, our ability to get things done withers.

The default approach to addressing the problem of scale is to increase coordination. But the cost of attempting large-scale choreography across an organization is immense. Assembling all the stakeholders to work out their separate goals, incentives, perspectives, mandates, processes, dependencies, and challenges is neither efficient nor effective. Even with extensive collaboration efforts, the path to productivity isn't clear.

We've spoken to organizations that have spent $28 million and twelve months to add a single option to their billing system. We've seen organizations invest in automation that won't improve their time to market by a single percent. We've seen organizations with high-performing, multimillion-dollar "innovation centers" but no way to bring their improvements to market.

As scale increases, waste and delay grow exponentially, and interdependence exacts a massive tax on the business. Before we can descale, simplify, and disentangle our organizations, we need to make effective decisions about where to invest in improvements today within the context of our current state.

We need to be able to chip away at complexity. We need the capability to clearly set a target outcome, assess the current state landscape, and navigate decisions to address constraints and obstacles. We need to dismantle and decouple crippling dependencies and enable effective descaling to improve flow. And because collaboration is critical to this effort, we need effective ways to share perspectives, information, efforts, and ideas to disentangle the complexity.

All of this depends on a shared understanding of value, shared clarity, and a unified flow of activity in the right direction. And yet value, clarity, and flow are elusive within every business at scale. If you're looking to improve performance in a large-scale, complicated environment, this book is for you. It's a practical collection of exercises to help you improve flow across your organization quickly, visually, and collaboratively.

The Struggle for Value, Clarity, and Flow

The raw confusion that we have repeatedly seen in organizations and teams can feel like criminal waste. Enabling people to work toward a meaningful purpose demands a substantial amount of clarity. Teams need to see not only how their efforts contribute to valuable outcomes but also *how* the broader organization's activities are serving legitimate customer needs.

What orients a group of people into being a team is a sense of purpose that is shared rather than fragmented. Once the purpose is clear, the team can proceed to improve their understanding of how to reach shared goals.

Much has been said about having a shared sense of purpose and its power to inspire, engage, and direct. This sense of purpose can be outward looking or inward looking. The team can be focused on bringing benefit to others (benevolence and value delivery) or to the team itself (survival and value extraction). Maturation, whether as an individual, a team, or an organization, can be summarized as shifting our energy from survival to benevolence.

Org charts are, by nature, inward looking. In fact, the customer is nowhere on the org chart. Customer orientation requires a fundamentally different way of thinking about purpose within the organization. To enable an effective and sustainable flow of work, a team's shared purpose needs to be oriented around the customer.

The inward looking nature of the org chart makes it very difficult for teams to become clear on the purpose their work serves for customers and where they fit in the big picture of the organization. If you ask any two people on a team what the most important customer need is, it's a good bet they'll have surprisingly different answers. The larger the distance between efforts and outcomes, the harder it is to effectively connect what you're doing to what matters most. In the absence of a simple purpose oriented around the customer, teams default to acting in incoherent and self-serving ways.

Interestingly, the org chart is one of the only pieces of information in an organization that is kept meticulously up to date. The org chart is the simplest view of the internal power structures that underpin the organization. It is an explicit representation of power hierarchies, and the only obvious goal from looking at the org chart is to try to ascend it.

The power structures embodied in the org chart lead to another significant challenge. Because of organizational power structures and hierarchies, people are often nervous about expressing their real understanding and ideas. Contributors can be unsure about the value of their input and the consequences of sharing it with the group. Under these circumstances, sharing ideas constitutes a risk, especially when those ideas come from people who don't already have organizational power. The only safe ideas are those that are already widely shared.

If we optimize for only sharing what's safe, then new and potentially valuable ideas will never have an opportunity to take hold. This is why a culture of psychological safety is necessary for high information flow. Few organizations have created the visibility, psychological safety, and effective feedback loops required to support truly open information sharing. In the absence of these conditions, you're operating in an ineffective organization.

Attaining clarity depends on understanding the dynamics of group collaboration. In a team of eight people, you will have eight different sets of priorities, eight unique perspectives, and eight distinct behaviors. Being able to operate as a "team" is not something that's easy or automatic; it requires enormous trust and openness, as well as significant effort to keep the group's priorities, understanding, and activities in sync. That investment, however, is powerful since it imbues the group with a collective intelligence that enables effective collective action. As Ken Blanchard has said, "No one of us is as smart as all of us."[1]

The fastest path to clarity is visibility. Thirty percent of the human brain is dedicated exclusively to visual processing.[2] Making a group's most important priorities and understandings visible creates a common shared resource and keeps people's attention on that information by making it central to meetings and workspaces.

By contrast, the default in most organizations is meandering conversations and an endless sprawl of digital documents, spreadsheets, and slide decks. Any one document taken in isolation is easy to misunderstand, as they typically embody a single perspective and lack critical context. This fragmentation of information leads to a fragmentation of thinking and action.

Gaining shared clarity depends on creating a simple, visible, and shared representation of a team's purpose and activity. This view must be oriented around bringing benefit to customers, and teams must be able to pool their collective understanding honestly, openly, and without fear. Otherwise, it's impossible for teams to establish the key element of organizational success: the development of collective intelligence effectively applied to customer outcomes. Without that, you're not getting flow; you're not getting feedback; you're not getting smarter; you're just not getting it.

Unblocking the Stream and Finding Flow

Many contributors and leaders alike find themselves in large, "successful" organizations that still struggle to operate (and, more importantly, cooperate) at a high level of performance. These organizations may work with cutting-edge technology, aiming to optimize digital processes down to milliseconds, while at the same time taking months to deliver results.

The paradox of modern organizations is that the more specialized workers become, the more they struggle to understand the broader system in which they fit. Even the most capable contributors in these organizations—including coaches, team leads, and technical experts—are constrained by the limits of the system in which they work.

Silos are a natural consequence of specialization and scale. They exemplify the difficulty of maintaining clarity across large groups. As silos form, individuals and teams alike fall back to local operation and optimization rather than the big picture of sustained customer value delivery. The more complex the organization, the harder it is to see how localized activity contributes to the overall flow of work and the ultimate delivery of business value. This undermines motivation and makes an effective improvement strategy seem out of reach.

Many people study and admire high-performing organizations like Toyota and Amazon but struggle to understand how to catalyze performance across their own organizations. To catalyze and foster that performance, you need a system to enable effective action. You need to focus and align your efforts to a valuable target state, develop shared clarity on the current state, and establish a flow of activities toward delivering that outcome.

Collaborative mapping develops clarity throughout that process and aligns those involved while enabling understanding for anyone who's part of an improvement effort. Mapping equips changemakers with simple and safe tools to establish and expand pockets of clarity throughout the organization.

As more and more people in an organization build these skills, the organization becomes increasingly capable of high-performance collaboration. Profound change, such as building a Lean, Agile, or learning organization, depends on incremental change at the team and cross-team level. Mapping is a critical ingredient in building the enabling structure, architecture, and expertise of a high-performing technical organization.

Flow Engineering is a series of collaborative mapping exercises designed to connect the dots between an unclear current state and a clear path to a target state. It's an open, adaptive, and engaging series of practices that can take you from complexity to clarity, from friction to flow. The practical goal of this book is to provide you with scaffolding that allows you to confidently map for greater value, clarity, and flow without worrying about how to start or going off the rails.

Flow Engineering has been successfully applied across finance, health care, telecom, government, defense, retail, and education. It's been used to improve every type of workflow you'd find in an organization, from customer onboarding, product development, and hiring to sales, service engagements, and beyond. Some of the results of applying Flow Engineering include:

- $20 million of investment saved by targeting the correct constraint;
- eighteen months of development time saved by targeting key constraints;
- feature development reduced from sixteen weeks to two weeks;
- partner engagement reduced from a twelve-month process to three months;
- client engagement reduced from six weeks to two weeks;
- customer onboarding reduced from one week to one hour;
- customer onboarding (data/integration) reduced from six weeks to four days; and
- addressing a common dependency to unblock five teams with one intervention.

In most cases, these benefits came from just a few hours of mapping. Mapping reveals hidden opportunities that teams can address quickly by eliminating waste, aligning efforts, and adjusting their ways of working. The result is not only improved collective flow but also improved individual flow for everyone involved. (We'll discuss collective and individual flow in more detail later in the book.)

CASE STUDY | **Boeing Employees Credit Union (BECU)**

At the 2023 Flowtopia conference, Taryn Spingler and Doug Mathieu presented their progress after a year of engineering flow across Boeing Employees Credit Union (BECU). BECU started in 1935 to fund loans to support new hires during the Great Depression. Now, it has nearly 1.4 million members, 2,500 employees, and over $28 billion in assets.

In their presentation, they described the previous eighteen months, which brought three org changes, operating model changes, and a renewed focus on value and outcomes. Their story relays a transition from "mayhem" to "wins" enabled by their efforts with Flow Engineering.

Mayhem

- **Lack of Clear Priorities:** Value-based priorities were not clear across all levels.
- **Lack of Leadership Alignment:** Some leaders were adamant that money talks and outcomes without clear financial impact were not a priority.
- **Lack of Alignment across the Value Stream:** Misalignment led to frustration, factions, and pushback (optimization of the whole may seem suboptimal for the parts).
- **Outcomes vs. Tools:** "Roadmap organized around business outcomes? I already have a roadmap based on cool technology."
- **Inspect and Adapt?** Nope, lacking governance and time drove busywork rather than work on the highest-value items.
- **Outdated Project Management:** Their old project management approach made improvement efforts too complex, creating a waterfall flow and not allowing for iteration and delivery of value.
- **Not Enough Time:** Teams were too busy for traditional value stream mapping.

Wins

Flow Engineering allowed BECU to reveal and extract insights from the previously hidden work across the value stream.

The practice of Flow Engineering (Outcome Mapping, Value Stream Mapping, Dependency Mapping, Future State Mapping, and Flow Roadmapping) helped baseline a process to extract insights:

- Outcome Mapping was used to create alignment and shift focus away from implementation to the goal they were trying to accomplish.
- Dependency Mapping highlighted processes characterized by minimal value-added time.
- Now, Next, Later Flow Roadmaps helped drive strategy and prioritization.

- Value Stream Mapping empowered them to quickly (within one to four hours) establish clarity on flow and issues, and it made clear which leaders should volunteer to own each value stream and performance improvement.

Flow Engineering enabled alignment, visibility into dependencies, and a sense of ownership. Improvement projects were reframed in the context of the value stream, reducing their apparent complexity. This clarity and visibility created a demand for further Value Stream Mapping within the organization.

Experimenting with Flow Engineering led to a repeatable practice and a new way of working. Flow Engineering maps provided a templated approach to scale and sustain the practices as part of their business reference architecture and their standard implementation approach. As a result, their architecture organization now incorporates Value Stream Mapping into early governance activities, aligning all of their efforts for performance improvement to business outcomes and enabling flow as a core capability. Taryn and Doug courageously pioneered these activities based on early articles and presentations on Flow Engineering.

Who This Book Is For

We've written this book for our peers working in technology in large enterprises. However, we've applied and seen the techniques described in this book in contexts far beyond our immediate frame of reference. It's easy to adapt and tailor to varied situations. It's flexible enough to help teams of any skill level, and it's robust enough to be used for ambitious process improvements or day-to-day problem-solving.

We're specialists in digital product development and delivery, but we've seen the need for value, clarity, and flow throughout many roles, industry verticals, levels of seniority, and stages of growth and scale.

This book is written for professionals familiar with the basics of Lean and Agile but unclear how to start, restart, teach, or make measurable progress with confidence. This is a book for curious problem-solvers struggling to help their teams or organizations see the big picture. This is for those grappling with complicated frameworks and operating models and wondering, "How?"

We're aiming to help mid-level leadership in complicated enterprises, but we've applied and seen this material used in a broad range of roles and contexts, like product management, Agile coaching, technical leadership, architecture, marketing, sales, project management, design, customer success, and more. Why does it work in all these cases? It's a simple, flexible practice of building a path from where you are to where you want to go. Once you've grasped the concepts and techniques, you could find yourself applying Flow Engineering in contexts we've never imagined.

If you're looking for a clear, approachable, step-by-step system for building value, clarity, and flow across your organization, this book is written for you.

How This Book Is Organized

We'll begin this book by looking at the gaps that need to be bridged and why they have been so hard to cross in most organizations. We will ground the ideas in research, personal experience, and case studies. Specifically, we'll give additional background on the problem of scale and how it affects our ability to see, understand, and address performance issues.

We'll also introduce the hidden elements of effective action: value, clarity, and flow. Then we'll lay the foundation for Flow Engineering: how to work backward from a shared context and target, and how to connect dots from needs and goals to actionable insights.

Once the framework is set, we'll guide you through the practices of Flow Engineering—a series of quick, collaborative mapping exercises, each meant to bring you progressively closer to value, clarity, and flow. The process starts with Outcome Mapping to clarify a valuable target and potential obstacles for a team. We then use Value Stream Mapping to clarify the current workflow and possible improvements. To address the opportunities revealed in the value stream, we conduct Dependency Mapping and envision improvement opportunities to construct a Future State Value Stream Map. The understanding generated from these sessions is then synthesized into a Flow Roadmap that transforms insights into prioritized, measurable, and assigned actions.

Finally, we'll describe approaches to scale and sustain your progress with Flow Engineering beyond an initial pilot. We'll share how to launch your own Flow Engineering enabling team to expand impact and learning across your organization. Beyond mapping, we'll share how to implement large-scale, continuous, and automated Flow Engineering with Value Stream Management. We'll also share how Flow Engineering can help you navigate key inflection points, like acquisitions and reorgs, as you evolve.

Throughout the book, we'll use the fictional illustration of Bolt Global (see below) to help illustrate the practices of Flow Engineering.

BOLT GLOBAL │ **Introduction**

Sharon is VP of Engineering at a Global 2000 company that's struggled with digital transformation attempts over the past ten years. Sharon's case and organization, while fictional, represent an amalgamation of what we've seen broadly across large organizations in various industries.

Sharon's company, which we'll call Bolt Global, is facing a lot of market pressure. Competitive pressure is pushing them to make operational efficiency improvements and to open new lines of business. They've launched several improvement initiatives, which have created a lot of work. Sharon's team now has a massive backlog of changes they're tasked with delivering. She's under pressure to figure out how to deliver twice as fast as she's able to do today. The clear question is how. (See Figure 0.1.)

FIGURE 0.1: Bolt Global Current State Challenge

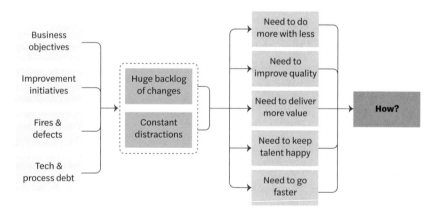

Every organization grapples with how to address current state
challenges in the face of increasing scale.

Although it's a fictional scenario, Sharon's situation is similar to lots of organizations around the world. Many of these massive IT initiatives and digital transformation projects end in failure. If we look at the literature about why many of these initiatives struggle to get off the ground or struggle to succeed, many sources[3] point to an underlying lack of clarity.[4] Either leadership fails to gain the clarity they need; or they fail to share that clarity across the organization, meaning individual contributors don't gain clarity; or the organization fails to collectively process concerns or dissenting opinions that could reveal flaws in the plan; or they fail to sustain clarity as the competitive landscape changes and technology evolves.

Throughout the book, we'll use Bolt Global's fictional situation as an aggregate of organizations we've worked with over the years to illustrate how the practices of Flow Engineering have helped alleviate these challenges.

PART 1

The Flow Landscape

CHAPTER 1

The Problem with Scale

> "... companies at all scales are classic complex adaptive systems."
>
> GEOFFREY WEST, from *Scale: The Universal Laws of Life, Growth, and Death in Organisms, Cities, and Companies*

SCALE UNDERMINES THE FOUNDATIONS of effective action. This is not news to anyone who works in a large organization and certainly not to anyone who works in government. The immediate and natural response to the problem of scale might be to quit your job, set out on your own or in a small team, and start enjoying a simpler and more productive life. But you would very quickly find that being a solopreneur brings with it innumerable headaches that were abstracted away when you were working in a larger organization.

Why We Scale

In the words of Peter Drucker, "The purpose of an organization is to enable ordinary human beings to do extraordinary things."[1] The fundamental reason organizations tend to grow is people desire to do ever more extraordinary things. This is made possible by *economies of scale*. This means that organizations that double in size don't necessarily need twice as many accountants or twice as many factories; great increases in output and revenue don't necessarily require great increases in the infrastructure needed to maintain them. Research by Geoffrey West, summarized in the book *Scale: The Universal Laws of Life, Growth, and Death in Organisms, Cities, and Companies*, estimates that organizations continue to benefit from economies of scale as they grow, gaining a 10% efficiency with every doubling in size.[2]

Organizations also scale to address opportunity and competition. With scale comes resiliency, influence, momentum, and attention. Amazon more than doubled its head count from 2019 to 1.6 million employees in 2021 to address increased demand and to leverage vertical integration.[3] Extreme scale requires extreme coordination but even scaling beyond a single individual demands care.

The Costs of Scale

While scale has clear benefits, there are clear challenges and costs as well. This book primarily addresses the challenge of how to enable teams to operate effectively in spite of the very real costs that scale imposes on effective action. To understand how teamwork is impeded by scale, we first need to understand the human costs of scale. The very purpose for which we assemble teams is undermined by the challenge of effectively coordinating them.

The Human Costs of Scale

Scale should enable increased capability and leverage, yet most organizations struggle to manage the scale they've created. We often hear things like:

- "We can't understand what's going on."
- "We can't understand where we should focus."
- "We need to do more with less."
- "We're not aligned."
- "We have too many tools, meetings, dependencies, and interruptions."
- "We have too much technical debt and work in progress (WIP)."
- "We spend too much time micromanaging or in the weeds."
- "We're always waiting for something out of our control to happen."
- "We can't retain/leverage/empower our talent."
- "We've always done it this way; that won't work here."

There are also indications that something deeper is eroding our ability to act effectively.

There are three specific human costs brought on by scale: *distraction*, *disorientation*, and *disengagement*. Distraction is a result of the constant interruptions, changing priorities, and demands on our attention. Disorientation occurs from a lack of clarity and alignment toward what matters most. Disengagement occurs when we resign ourselves to treading water without a clear connection to value. (See also Figure 1.1.)

FIGURE 1.1: The Three Human Costs of Scale

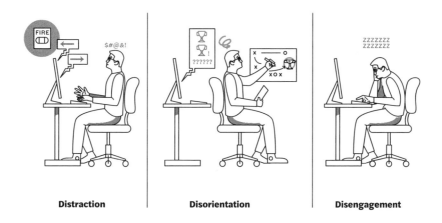

| Distraction | Disorientation | Disengagement |

Working in larger groups multiplies distraction, which exacts an enormous cost. According to the study "No Task Left Behind? Examining the Nature of Fragmented Work" by Gloria Mark, Victor Gonzalez, and Justin Harris, it takes roughly twenty-five minutes to refocus after interruption.[4]

If we're working on our own, we're distractible enough. But the more people we engage with, the greater the chances that one of them will disrupt our attention at any time. Our distractions also lead us to distract others, creating a cascade of interruptions that splinter across the organization like space debris from an exploded satellite. This has made focus one of the most endangered mental factors in the modern world. There's nothing more fatal to an organization's ability to get things done than a team that can't focus on its goal. Scale only exacerbates this problem.

While digital technologies enable coordination at far greater scale and speed, they can make it even harder to get and stay oriented to what matters most. The infinite profusion of information means that relevant details are easily lost. The fast pace of change lends itself to disorientation and to people moving at cross-purposes. Digital reality can be more transient and individual, where individuals decouple from each other far more easily than in physical reality. This means that special effort needs to be made to keep people's digital worlds in sync, especially at the enterprise scale.

Orientation is required for alignment. Every layer of interaction in an organization requires aligning the motivations, understandings, and behaviors of different people. A simple way of understanding this misalignment is shown in Figure 1.2. Even if a group of individuals are observing the same challenge, every observer will have a different perspective, leading to different perceptions, as is illustrated in Judy Katz and Frederick Miller's book *Opening Doors to Teamwork and Collaboration.*[5]

Because of our unique perspectives, we may possess or lack key information. Different people may also have different goals based on what they see to be most important at that time. We can also have different scopes of concern (wider or narrower, sooner or later, micro or macro, strategic or operational) that function like different zoom levels. Technologists are famous for zooming in on challenging technical details when making a decision. Those who are considering a situation from a greater distance may come to entirely different conclusions. All of these different perceptions can offer complementary points of view, but it takes effort to align.

The Gallup organization has tracked employee engagement metrics for thirty years and summarized many of their conclusions in *First, Break All the Rules.* As of their most recent surveys, engagement among US workers still hovers around 33%.[6] According to Gallup's *State of the Global Workplace: 2023 Report*, disengaged employees cost the world an unbelievable $8.8 trillion in lost productivity.[7] Worker disengagement means our innate motivation circuitry is not being activated by our work environment. This could be due to a lack of challenge, but more often it's due to a lack of purpose—or being too far removed from it. In these situations, it is not clear how our work serves a beneficial purpose, apart from a paycheck.

FIGURE 1.2 Misalignment in Teams

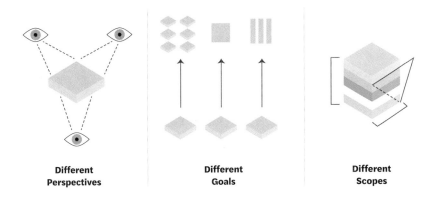

| Different Perspectives | Different Goals | Different Scopes |

Perspectives, goals, and scope vary widely across individuals, across groups, and over time.

Daniel Pink's bestselling book *Drive: The Surprising Truth about What Motivates Us* identifies autonomy, mastery, and purpose as key ingredients for maximum engagement.[8] And Google's Project Aristotle, a study conducted by Google to identify the key factors that make a successful team, found that sense of purpose was one of the five most important factors for high-performing teams.[9]

While it may be tempting to think that finding a sense of purpose requires changing jobs, the fastest and most powerful improvements come from simply understanding the purpose of the business you're in. Scale makes this difficult, since in a large process, the real beneficiaries of our work may be several steps removed from us.

The Organizational Costs of Scale

Scaling organizations brings with it special challenges. At an organizational level, the human challenges just mentioned manifest as misalignment. At scale, teams naturally become more distanced from the customer, from each other, from the purpose of their work, and from critical information. The critical feedback loop from customer need to team activity is stretched and broken.

Distance or closeness, whether physical or mental, is described as "proximity" by social scientists.[10] Empathy, or a worker's emotional connection to the challenges of a customer, is a function of *relational proximity*.[11] Having a shared understanding with coworkers is a function of *cognitive proximity*. These two kinds of proximity predict the likelihood of collaboration.

Coordinating an organization means navigating the invisible world of others' minds by trying to align incentives, forge trust, and clearly understand how to tackle the mountain of challenges and opportunities each team faces. Navigating an organizational ecosystem requires navigating an interdependent network of technical and social nodes (or interconnected components) and understanding that it's increasingly challenging to consider any component or area of the organization in isolation.

This invisible network is described in *Wiring the Winning Organization* by Gene Kim and Steven Spear as the:

> . . . social circuitry, the overlay of processes, procedures, routines, and norms that enable people to do their work easily and well. While individual specialists are focusing their attention on the problems immediately in front of them, this social circuitry establishes the patterns by which information, ideas, materials, and services flow, setting people up for success and integrating individual efforts for common purpose.[12]

This social circuitry is invisible and easily overlooked. As organizations scale, invisible gaps and misalignments become endemic. Avoiding or mitigating these costs of scale requires engineering this social circuitry to establish or reestablish a shared sense of purpose, orientation, and activity.

The Paradox of Scale

Even in simple coordination activities, like playing a game of tug-of-war, individual effort declines as group size grows. This loss of effort is known as the Ringelmann effect: as more people are involved in a task, their average performance decreases, with each participant tending to feel that their own effort is not critical to overall performance.[13]

Despite that inefficiency, in 2016 Microsoft and Facebook researchers conducted a study on forty-seven teams sized one to thirty-two people. They found that as team size increased, productivity of teams rose but collaboration costs and errors both increased. The study revealed valuable correlations between scale and performance: "We find that individuals in teams exerted lower overall effort than independent workers, in part by allocating their effort to less demanding (and less productive) sub-tasks; however, we also find that individuals in teams collaborated more with increasing team size."[14] In other words, large teams necessitate increased collaboration, yet the default effect is each contributor doing less.

In the end, the researchers found that "the largest teams outperformed an equivalent number of independent workers, suggesting that gains to collaboration dominated losses to effort."[15] To put it simply, collaborative work is best, but it's not our best work. The waste and cost of collaboration grow significantly at scales beyond the "two-pizza team" or "single-threaded team" popularized at Amazon[16] to address efficiency and scalability.[17]

FIGURE 1.3: The Paradox of Scale Illustrated

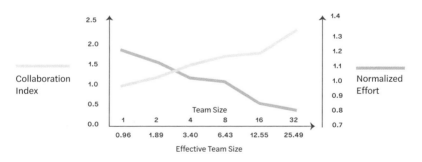

The graph shows the relative amount of effort by each individual declining and the prevalence of collaboration rising as the size of the team grows (more person-hours).

Adapted from Andrew Mao et al. "An Experimental Study of Team Size and Performance on a Complex Task." *PLoS ONE* 11, no. 4 (April 2016). https://doi.org/10.1371/journal.pone.0153048.

The study highlights a few aspects of scale we'll address later in the book with an approach to improve collaborative workflow:

1. As an organization grows larger, it will tend to become more inefficient. Effort is reduced and errors increase with scale unless care is
   taken to offset these risks.

2. These costs are hidden since economies of scale can bring gains that
   outpace the waste of poor coordination.

3. Cost and waste not only reduce company margins but also impact
   customer and employee experience.

These hidden inefficiencies also explain how large and established organizations can rapidly lose market share and crumble in the face of more agile
competitors. This is massively consequential when we consider modern
enterprise workflows comprising hundreds of teams and thousands of individuals as an interdependent network of collaboration at scale.

Challenges of Collaborating at Scale

Despite the enormous inefficiencies of trying to operate in organizations at
scale, the incredible opportunities of the modern world and the intensity of
competition push organizations to constantly strive for growth. Regardless of
the challenges and the waste of large-scale organizations, not acting is not an
option. And acting slowly or ineffectively is often as detrimental as not acting
at all.

Given these constraints, we must find ways of working together that are
effective for businesses, customers, and the workers themselves. Finding better ways of working together depends on finding a deeper understanding of
the systems we work in.

Organizations as Socio-Technical Systems

Modern businesses are best understood as socio-technical systems (the combination of social and technical systems). Thinking well and delivering value
are challenging even for individuals. Scale amplifies the challenge by com-
plicating communication, coordination, and collaboration. Several laws and
theories relating to scale help us understand organizational performance
across socio-technical boundaries:

- **Weick's Theory of Organizing:**[18] This theory suggests that organizations are essentially systems for coordinating interpretation and meaning. As organizations scale, the number of interpretations and meanings that need to be managed can become overwhelming, leading to communication challenges.
- **Complexity Theory:**[19] This theory illustrates how complexity will increase nonlinearly with scale, making predictability and control more challenging.
- **Attention Economics:**[20] Herbert Simon's theory states that as information becomes more plentiful, attention becomes scarcer. Attention is a prerequisite to clarity.
- **Transaction Cost Economics:**[21] This theory aims to explain how the costs of coordinating across a large organization can outweigh the benefits of scale, leading to inefficiencies.
- **Metcalfe's Law:**[22] This law implies that the value of a network is proportional to the square of the number of connected users. While it primarily refers to the value of the physical network, it follows that as a network grows, the complexity and cost of coordination within that network increases as the square of the network size.
- **Brooks's Law:**[23] This law posits that adding more people to a late software project only makes it later. It highlights the communication overhead that comes with each new team member, which can slow down a project rather than speed it up.
- **Conway's Law:** Organizations that design systems (including products and services) are constrained to produce designs that are a copy of the communication patterns within the organization. As organizations grow and diversify, maintaining coherent communication becomes a challenge. Incoherent communication patterns can result in incoherent systems that perform outdated functions or are misaligned with current goals. Conway's Law works in the other direction as well. Maintaining fragmented systems puts pressure on the organization to divide teams into specialists for those systems. Winston Churchill captured the spirit of this when he said, "We shape our buildings, and afterward our buildings shape us."[24]

The common thread here is that as scale increases, complex and consequential effects begin to threaten the performance of the organization. Communication, coordination, and collaboration suffer. This not only degrades operational performance but also begins to degrade the very products and services the organization produces.

CASE STUDY | **The Checkbox Project**

"The Checkbox Project" is a case study published in the Fall 2023 *DevOps Enterprise Journal.*[25] It describes a seemingly simple task of adding a single checkbox to customer billing that would fire an API call to resell a partner service and generate millions in revenue with practically zero operational expenditure. It seemed like a clear home run but turned out to be a painful exercise in the challenges of enterprise scale.

FIGURE 1.4 The Checkbox Project: Teams Involved

- - - - Line of Business (B2B, B2C)
- - - - Channel (In Store, Call Center, Digital)

Teams Involved

Delivery Teams	Shared Teams
Front End	Billing
Back End	Finance
Middleware Tier 2	PMO
Middleware Tier 1	Collections
Enterprise Data	Compliance
Marketing	Internal Council
Notifications	AppSec
Integration	Architecture
Networking	Procurement
Analytics	Accessibility

The effort spanned 10+ delivery teams for each of two lines of business (LOB) with three channels for each LOB, each heavily reliant on shared services.

Source: Kamran Kazempour et al., "The Checkbox Project: Learnings for Organizing for Outcomes," *The DevOps Enterprise Journal* 5, no. 2 (Fall 2023), https://itrevolution.com/product/the-checkbox-project/.

Implementing this change required navigating a complicated web of inter-dependencies: product development, IT, billing, global legal and compliance, and marketing, to name a few. All spanning and duplicated across multiple channels and lines of business.

Ultimately, delivery of the initiative required managed and close collaboration across over sixty teams in multiple organizational hierarchies across multiple channels and segments, including involvement from many coordination roles and shared services. In the end, the project took over twelve months from conception to completion and cost the company over $28 million to implement. Few stakeholders would consider it a success.

Managing the Invisible

We each understand value, clarity, and flow through our direct experience. We understand the experience of receiving something wonderful, deciphering some mystery, or having a feeling of progress. But all three of those experiences become harder to access when we're dealing with invisible things, especially at scale.

Dominica DeGrandis's book *Making Work Visible* helped popularize the challenge facing knowledge work organizations: our work is invisible. But even physical work benefits from making work visible.[26]

The famous time and motion studies pioneered by Frederick Taylor and Lillian and Frank Gilbreth were among the first efforts to track the way work is performed over time. Their analysis led to doubling productivity while also dramatically simplifying the work.[27]

While time and motion studies are largely focused on physical activity, our modern work demands human creativity, innovation, and dynamic collaboration. Even though they may have visible results, software development tasks themselves, for example, are invisible. Task management systems allow the work to be organized and visualized to a degree. Over time, we might notice trends in the number, duration, or allocation of these tickets. These can reveal patterns that are otherwise impossible to see. But just like the time and motion study can be misused to reduce human work to mechanistic and repetitive actions, misusing task management can lead to unintended consequences.

The most common mental model of work is that it's like a 100-meter race (not even a 100-meter relay race, just a race)—as if a team is a single runner and can just pick up the pace, improve their conditioning, or improve their technique. Comparing work to a race and your teams to independent athletes obscures the complexity of work and leads to proposed solutions that are little more than just hoping for magical improvements.

Collaborative work is more like a construction project. You can operate, even as a team, at peak performance and watch nothing improve. Until you address dependencies—the permitting process, the handoffs between trades, the supply chain for materials, the cost of inventory, the effects of weather—your efforts will be wasted.

Knowledge work is like a construction project in which the raw materials, the work being done, and the finished product are mostly invisible. As Frederick Brooks said in *The Mythical Man-Month*, "The programmer, like the poet, works only slightly removed from pure thought-stuff. He builds his castles in the air, from air, creating by exertion of the imagination."[28]

What a challenge! Working collectively to build "castles in the air," trying to coordinate invisible dependencies, and trying to understand and improve the invisible process that unfolds over time. No wonder most IT organizations are perceived as "black boxes" by those outside the department.

There are equivalent issues in every department. There are delays beyond our control, there are distractions and interruptions, there are queues and unfinished work, there are shared services, and there are approvals and standards. Until you leverage a paradigm that allows you to see and address constraints, the impact of those constraints will overpower any efforts you put into training, talent, tools, motivation, methodology, or anything else. Without the right paradigm for work, you could miss opportunities right under your nose.

Conclusion

Scale within socio-technical systems exacts a massive human cost through distraction, disorientation, and disengagement. Variations of perspectives, goals, and scope across individuals amplify these effects. Value, clarity, and flow become elusive, and our ability to collaborate and act effectively breaks down. We can't address issues we can't clearly see and understand. With a clear understanding of the specific impacts of scale and the importance of visibility to address them, it's time to talk about solutions. There are many common approaches to dealing with the challenges of scale. Let's look at the typical approaches with a fresh lens to identify the gaps that still exist in achieving effective action.

Key Takeaways

- Scale increases the distance between cause and effect; people's perspectives, priorities, and activities; and the ultimate value and purpose of their work.
- Distanced from the purpose of their work and from a shared view, people become disengaged, disoriented, and distracted.
- These human costs limit the ability of teams to effectively and efficiently deliver value.

CHAPTER 2

Solutions to Scale

"In this exquisitely connected world, it's never a question of 'critical mass.' It's always about critical connections."

GRACE LEE BOGGS

PERHAPS YOU FIND YOURSELF in the middle of an effort or system of work that feels slower, less clear, or less productive than it should. In the activity of daily work, it may be unclear how to resolve dependencies, align stakeholders, uncover constraints, measure performance, or focus investment. It's valuable to be able to quickly step back from the work to improve the work. It's important to check if the saw is dulled, if you're using the right tool, or if you're even cutting down the right tree.

A painful truth of enterprise-scale solutions is that what works in one case likely won't work in another. Despite its massive scale and complexity, Amazon stands as an example of an organization that dominates, pioneers, pivots, experiments, and, after nearly a quarter of a century, shows no signs of slowing down. But chances are your organization bears little resemblance to Amazon. It's also unlikely that, like Amazon, you can mandate a descaling effort to break your organization down into smaller, independent teams that can operate productively at scale.

Ever since childhood, we've been cautioned about the risks of trying to be like anyone else. The same holds true in business. Copy and paste is not a viable option. Existing solutions fall along a spectrum ranging from *prescriptive* to *generative*, as shown in Figure 2.1. Prescriptive methods take a centralized approach, relying on a small number of leaders or experts to define precise structures for how teams should be organized and interact. By contrast, generative methods take a distributed approach. They seek to bring together stakeholders throughout the organization and facilitate discussions and exercises in hopes of finding emergent solutions.

FIGURE 2.1: The Spectrum of Solution Approaches

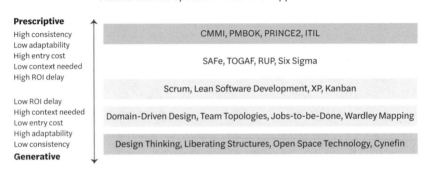

The power of the distributed approach used in generative methods is that you can engage everyone in the activity of cocreating solutions. When people are involved in creating a solution themselves, they are more invested in delivering the outcome. This is often called the "IKEA effect"—we value things we build ourselves more than things we receive preassembled.[1]

The risk of this distributed approach is that it might take longer, and it's difficult to guarantee what conclusions contributors will come to. While it's important to get buy-in, individual contributors can lack important context from looking at the business at a large scale in time or space. The generative end can seem to demand a trust fall into the unknown. These generative approaches can be challenging to convert into clear, actionable business value.

The power of a prescriptive or centralized approach is that it provides more clarity and direction. When insights are distributed across the organization, they become invisible to most people. Those in positions of power can make clear statements about goals, structure, and priorities and ensure that those messages are visible and amplified across the organization.

The main challenge with prescriptive methods, however, is that they tend to be so heavy and constraining that the overhead of applying them dramatically undermines the benefits. Prescriptive models like PRINCE2 have a considerable learning curve and training cost and require specially trained experts and up-front budget approval. It can seem like the prescriptive side demands "all or nothing" and requires massive investment in learning and structure to get started or to scale.

Ultimately, any approach that hopes to solve the challenges of scale must possess three characteristics to overcome the three *D*s of disengagement, disorientation, and distraction:

1. Like the generative methods mentioned, the solution you choose must engage all participants to ensure their perspectives are shared and that they feel committed to the solution. This addresses the risk of disengagement.

2. Like the prescriptive methods, the solution must be simple and aligned with the organization's strategic goals. This prevents the risk of disorientation.

3. But unlike typical prescriptive approaches, the solution must also be fast and easy to put into practice to quickly realize ROI. This avoids the risk of distraction.

We seek interventions that are short, focused, and can yield results before priorities change, keeping participants on a golden path toward their target outcome.

Gaps in Existing Solutions

The common approaches to enabling large-scale collaboration typically suffer from three gaps: an *alignment gap*, a *visibility gap*, and an *on-ramp gap*.

FIGURE 2.2: The Three Gaps to Enabling Large-Scale Collaboration

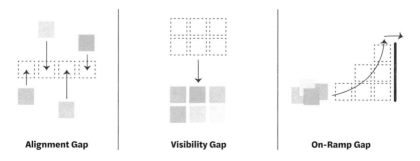

Alignment Gap   **Visibility Gap**   **On-Ramp Gap**

The *alignment gap* refers to the challenges of gathering support and enthusiasm, establishing business value, and connecting contributors to organizational needs and objectives. You can't do everything, so the organization needs to align its focus on what will deliver the results you need.

The *visibility gap* refers to the challenges of creating a shared picture of goals and the current state and making that picture accessible to everyone who's involved and affected. To assemble a complete view of your landscape, you must also include diverse, distributed perspectives. To navigate effectively, you also must be able to see where you're going. Creating a clear view from current to future state is essential to help everyone move together.

The *on-ramp gap* refers to the challenges of getting started, restarting, securing buy-in or investment, and building momentum. A key aspect of the on-ramp gap is the challenge of meeting organizations where they are based on their unique current state.

To truly hit a home run, any approach needs to accommodate the iron triangle of constraints in any large enterprise: budget, scope, and schedule. In other words, to satisfy the needs of a large, constrained, and inertia-bound enterprise, a solution must be inexpensive, minimal, and quick to pilot.

FIGURE 2.3: The Iron Triangle of Constraints

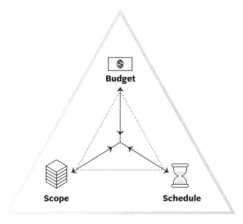

In today's landscape, most organizations lack an effective framework that achieves these things: quickly setting a valuable target, understanding the current state, and enabling effective action across a diverse group of individuals.

The Cybernetic Connection

Any effective remedy to the problems of scale must also be based on scale-free principles—i.e., principles that will hold true at any scale. Cybernetics is one of the most influential intellectual movements of the twentieth century and offers just such a scale-free explanation of how to accomplish goals.

Cybernetics introduced the idea that any attempt to navigate toward a goal depends on effective control systems. A control system is a system that uses feedback loops to continually adjust direction toward a target state. Cybernetics can be applied to understand systems as simple as a thermostat or as complex as a government. If your organization is like a plane, cybernetics is how you effectively fly that plane.

James Martin's 1995 book *The Great Transition* describes his vision for an enterprise of the future—a cybernetic corporation, or "cybercorp," incorporating two aspects of advanced performance: (1) technology enabling fast feedback, automation, scale, and new capabilities, and (2) employee empowerment enabling productivity, focus, collaboration, and autonomy. He decried the perils of separating "the business" and IT. Martin posited that for an organization to reach peak performance in the digital future, it needed to eliminate the gap between its people and its technology—across the enterprise—creating a single cybernetic system.[2]

Terms like "digital transformation" are thrown around casually in the media and in business discussions. It's helpful to reflect on what a profound change that implies: how much organizations already resemble cybercorps but also how much inefficiency remains in the way our organizations operate.

Thirty years ago, James Martin was among the last major authors to point to cybernetics as a way of describing a possible future of work. (A notable exception is Jeff Sussna's *Designing Delivery*.) Now that we're living in that future, it's worth stepping back to understand what's really happening.

From a cybernetic point of view, every activity an organization takes to keep moving in the right direction (whether management, training, IT systems, etc.) is part of a control system, a cybernetic feedback loop (see Figure 2.4 on page 22). (This loop echoes the elements of action loop we present in the next chapter.) None of this is new. None of this is controversial. But it *is* challenging to put into practice, especially in large groups.

FIGURE 2.4: Cybernetic Feedback Loop

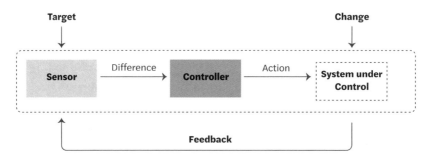

A cybernetic loop represents the flow of navigating change
through targeting, sensing, and response.

Everyone wants to feel like they have control over complex challenges. Dynamic activities, such as riding a mountain bike, are exercises in control. When we're riding down a mountain path, our target is staying on the trail and not wiping out. Our eyes, ears, and other senses are maximally engaged to maintain clarity about our current operating conditions. A skilled mountain biker will steer the front wheel and adjust their posture dozens of times per second. The experience of flow is undeniable.

Such a sense of progress, clarity, and focus may feel inaccessible at work. But perhaps that's because we've not yet built the cybernetic control systems needed to understand and act on the challenges at work. Our most important work goal should not be just to survive the next quarter. The most powerful goal is to engineer the experience of flow at work.

Understanding Work as a Flow

The primary challenge in business is how to enable a group of people to work together effectively to deliver value to customers. Value is defined as benefit compared with cost. Large organizations tend to organize people into functional groups and hand work across in a sort of relay race from customer need to customer satisfaction. The problem with these functional silos (see Figure 2.5) is they end up operating not as a single relay team but as entirely separate teams that train independently and may have differing goals.

FIGURE 2.5: A Siloed Organizational Structure

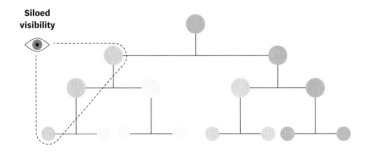

Silos are effective for personnel management but not for cross-organizational flow.

Imagine a relay race where each runner on the team trained alone and then showed up hoping for smooth handoffs mid-race. Not only is that relay team unlikely to perform well, but each racer on the team is also likely to focus mostly on their own performance. Training and measuring independently implies a lack of visibility into what everyone else is doing and how all the contributions come together to deliver value. Runners may spend many hours perfecting their stride but fumble the handoff, which is an order of magnitude more impactful on the ultimate performance of the team.

If we can only improve what we can see and we can only see a subset of the overall flow of work, all our effort could be wasted in comparison to addressing the weakest link in the chain of activities. If our visibility is limited to a subset of the work process, we will direct improvement efforts there. But if we fail to address the real constraint, our targeted improvements won't matter at best and could make things worse. (See Figure 2.6.)

FIGURE 2.6: Effects of Limited Visibility

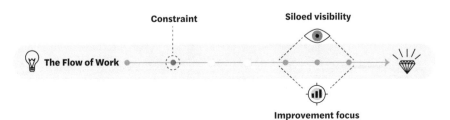

In *The Great Transition*, James Martin says, "A value stream is an end-to-end collection of activities that creates a result for a 'customer,' who may be the ultimate customer or an internal 'end user' of the value stream."[3] The scope of a value stream is the complete loop from customer need to customer satisfaction. A value stream represents a complete cybernetic control system, consisting of a customer target, a change implementation, and feedback processing.

Optimizing the value stream requires looking at this end-to-end work process to increase value delivery while reducing costs such as delay. By more effectively chaining together the work of each contributor, we approach a state where a single piece of work "flows" without interruption for the benefit of a customer.

Value stream optimization goes beyond optimization efforts that focus only on narrow segments of the workflow. For example, Agile principles and practices arose within the software development community to improve flow and customer centricity. Agile improved outcomes but put pressure on downstream deployment, infrastructure, and operations. DevOps later emerged as a solution to address that downstream handoff and accelerated delivery while improving outcomes.

Value stream optimization transcends DevOps to include the full process of delivering value to customers. Improving flow within a single value stream will shift the constraint elsewhere. Using the value stream as a model, we can see opportunities to accelerate and improve outcomes across the entire flow from customer need to customer satisfaction. (See Figure 2.7.)

FIGURE 2.7: The Value Stream

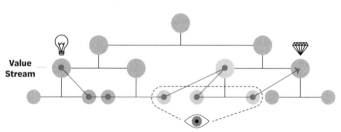

The value stream, the full scope of activity needed to satisfy customers,
passes through multiple functional groups.

Making Flow Visible

To manage and optimize the flow of work, we must first *see* the flow of work. To reason about work effectively, we need to create a simple model that represents this flow. In a large-scale working environment, no individual has the full picture. That means we need to pool data and our individual knowledge to create this model.

To do this, we engage in Value Stream Mapping, creating a visual representation of the value stream based on our collective understanding. By mapping the value stream (see Figure 2.8), we can measure performance and identify improvement opportunities. Effectively, we are building a representative model that is easy to see and understand so we can manage a process that is otherwise invisible.

FIGURE 2.8: A Simple Value Stream Map

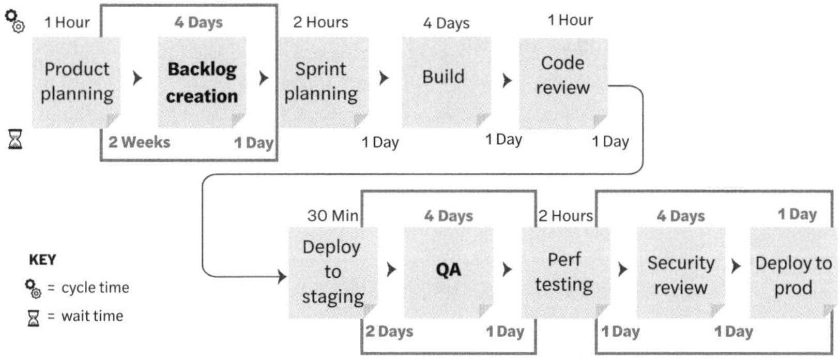

In cybernetic terms, this is the act of creating a control system, a concept we'll return to later. On this basis, we can learn and adapt to improve value delivery over time.

The classic Value Stream Map originated as a "Material and Information Flow" diagram within the Toyota Production System (TPS). TPS is a revolutionary approach to running an organization that led Toyota to dominate the auto industry beginning in the 1980s. Central to TPS is the idea of kaizen, or continuous improvement. This practice was summarized by Mike Rother as the Improvement Kata in his seminal book *Toyota Kata: Managing People for Improvement, Adaptiveness, and Superior Results,*[4] as shown in Figure 2.9.

The Improvement Kata is a four-step pattern of establishing a target condition, grasping the current condition, establishing the next target, and iteratively working toward that target. The Improvement Kata itself is a cybernetic loop, focused on continuous adjustment while navigating toward a target goal.

FIGURE 2.9: The Toyota Production System's Improvement Kata

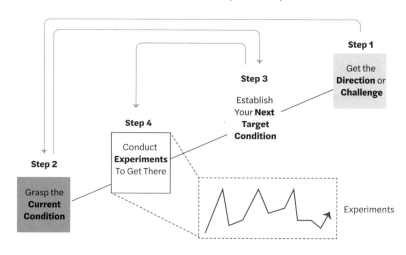

Source: Mike Rother, *Toyota Kata: Managing People for Improvement, Adaptiveness, and Superior Results* (New York: McGraw-Hill, 2009).

This pattern is repeated in some of the most influential frameworks of the modern day, as shown in Table 2.1.

Flow Engineering is a set of practices that builds on the foundations of cybernetics and the Toyota Production System to provide a lightweight and iterative way of building value, clarity, and flow. Armed with these techniques for groups of people to externalize and evolve their understandings, we can develop clear focus to facilitate collective action.

In the next chapter, we'll introduce the three elements of effective action (value, clarity, and flow) as a cybernetic model that forms the foundation for a better approach to enable effective action at scale.

TABLE 2.1: Cybernetic Control Systems in Popular Decision Frameworks

Framework/ Methodology	Target	Sense	Compare	Compute	Act
Lean Startup	Set hypothesis	Measure	Learn	Build	Build
OKRs	Objectives	Monitor key results	Compare to objectives	Compute adjustments	Act on adjustments
V2MOM	Vision	Obstacles	Values	Measures	Methods
Scrum	Sprint goal	Standup	Retrospective	Identified improvements	Improvement
Balanced Scorecard	Strategic objectives	Monitor perspectives	Compare to objectives	Compute strategy	Act on strategy
DMAIC	Define goal	Measure	Analyze	Improve	Control
Lean	Define value	Map the value stream	Measure the value stream against target outcome	Identify constraint & causes	Create flow/ establish pull/strive for perfection
TQM	Quality objectives	Monitor metrics	Compare to objectives	Compute corrective measures	Implement measures
OODA	Mission aim	Observe	Orient	Decide	Act
PDSA/PDCA	Plan	Do/observe	Check/study	Check/study	Act/adapt
Toyota Production System	Operational excellence	Observe (Gemba walks, Andon)	Identify waste (muda, mura, muri)	Kaizen bursts	Implement changes (jidoka, just-in-time, continuous improvement)

Key Takeaways

- Common solutions often suffer from an alignment gap, a visibility gap, and an on-ramp gap.
- Value streams provide a model for cross-organizational performance visibility, measurement, and management.
- Cybernetics provides a model for effective action to drive performance improvement.
- Our best methods for driving effective action leverage the cybernetic loop of targeting, sensing, and responding.
- We must leverage the learning of other organizations, but we can't copy success or experience.

CHAPTER 3

The Elements of Action

"Do what you can, with what you have, where you are."

Theodore Roosevelt

SCALE BRINGS MANY CHALLENGES. But perhaps the most insidious are the difficulties of developing and sustaining value, clarity, and flow, the fundamental elements of effective individual and collective action. *Value* informs direction, *clarity* provides understanding, and *flow* lets us get things done. When these elements are present, effective action is possible. When any are missing, effective action is difficult or impossible. These three elements are critical for establishing and maintaining effective collective action at scale.

Value broadly describes our individual and shared preferences for some outcomes over others. Essentially, it's why we're in business. Value drives the behavior of organizations on a macroscale and of individuals on a microscale. Value sets the target to be reached by our actions. Value is the pleasant experience of something that solves a problem or fulfills a wish.

Clarity describes the ability to accurately understand the key aspects of our situation. To have clarity means that our mental models align correctly with our observations. Because each of our perspectives and mental models is limited, building shared clarity in a group enables a more reliable perception.

Flow means unobstructed action that emerges from the effective pursuit of value. It refers to smooth, steady, sustainable activity that is both predictable and satisfying. Flow is the delicate balance between execution and adaptation, allowing us to circumvent obstacles and continually experience progress. Individuals are at their best when they can sustain a state of psychological flow, and teams are at their best when handoffs from one person to the next lead smoothly to the creation of value for the customer.

While our target is collective flow, the same factors apply at both a collective and individual level. (See Figure 3.1.) It's impossible to achieve individual flow in a collective environment full of friction, delays, and interruptions. One of the principles of cybernetics is that similar patterns can be seen at every scale. This book is aimed at providing you with clear practices to improve collective flow across individuals and teams and enable individual flow as a by-product of that effort.

FIGURE 3.1: Collective and Individual Flow

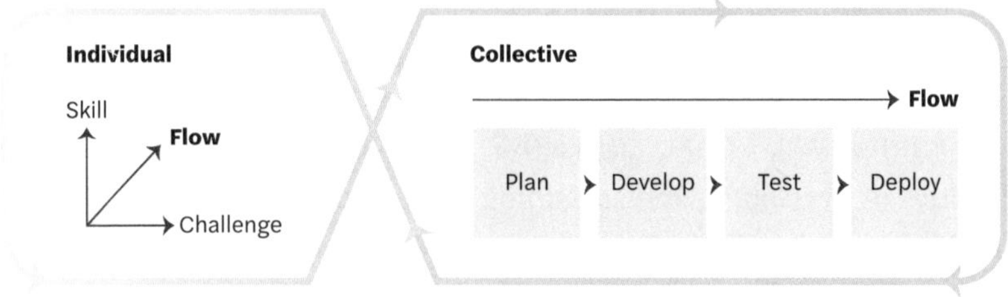

Flow exists across collective activities and within individual work.
The two levels are interdependent.

FIGURE 3.2 Effects of the Three Elements of Action

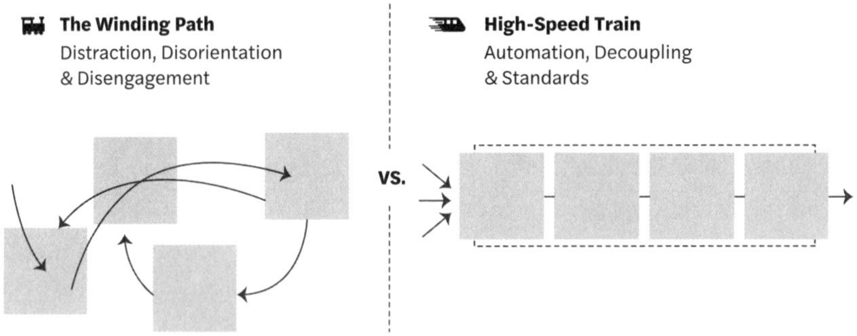

Flow without direction or clarity leads us on a winding path
full of waste and confusion. Value and clarity enable you to
build high-speed railways for flow.

These three qualities (value, clarity, and flow), while common in our language, are often hard to establish. And once gained, they are easily lost. The connection to value may fade over time. Clarity can become muddied. Flow can become blocked or slowed as conditions change. A problem with any one of these three qualities can spell disaster for a team or an organization. And these problems are exacerbated with scale. (See Figure 3.2 for more.)

How Value, Clarity, and Flow Interrelate

Value, clarity, and flow are mutually dependent. Our orientation or sense of value dictates what information we seek and how we interpret what we see. Thus, value is preliminary to building clarity. Clarity, in turn, allows us to see where we have opportunities or constraints and thus enables action. In particular, a high degree of clarity is required to achieve the skillful and continually adapting type of action we describe as flow. Flow makes optimal use of our energy to develop value, which unlocks new possibilities as we receive feedback. Flow enables the cycle to continue or accelerate. This mutually supportive relationship is shown in Figure 3.3.

FIGURE 3.3: The Three Elements of Action

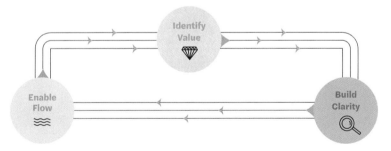

The elements of action—value, clarity, and flow—
are interdependent and feed each other.

A key aspect of the three elements of action is that they apply at any scale. As individuals, we must go through the loop of identifying value, building clarity, and enabling flow on an ongoing basis, shown in Figure 3.4 (see page 32). At larger scales, both teams and entire organizations must do the same:

set a target, understand their current state, and take action collectively. The problem of scale emerges when teams or individuals move in separate directions without establishing shared value, clarity, and flow.

FIGURE 3.4: Cybernetic Loop with the Elements of Action

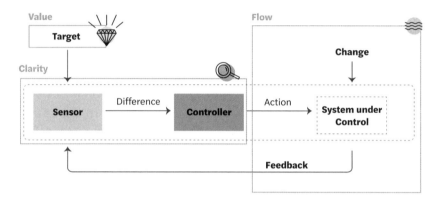

Value, clarity, and flow summarize the cybernetic loop.

As is represented in Figure 3.5, value, clarity, and flow help to align teams for collective action. Value represents the shared goal of the team or organization, clarity allows the team to understand a path to that goal, and flow reveals the optimum path to that goal.

FIGURE 3.5: The Elements of Action: Value, Clarity, and Flow

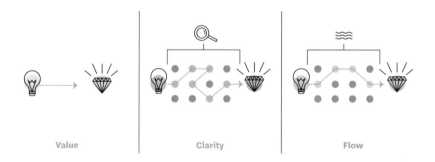

Value is our target; clarity allows us to understand a path to that target; and flow is about optimizing that path.

Conclusion

Effective action depends on value, clarity, and flow. And effective action at scale requires those elements to be shared across individuals and teams. Human collaboration doesn't scale naturally. Varied perspectives, goals, and contexts breed too much confusion when trying to work toward a common purpose. Confusion, waste, and friction are the leading causes of transformation failures.

Organizations rise or fall depending on their systems of collaboration. Systems of collaboration require a foundation of value, clarity, and flow. As we'll see in the upcoming chapter, mapping is a lightweight superpower for building the three elements of action. Different types of mapping can be used to clarify challenges with goals, processes, or dependencies. And mapping can be scaled and repeated to meet the demand for change.

Mapping in the form of Flow Engineering is ideal for effective collaboration and is the process for developing value, clarity, and flow. In the next chapter, we'll demonstrate how a clear sequence of collaborative mapping activities can identify value, create clarity, and enable flow.

Key Takeaways

- The elements of action (value, clarity, and flow) are invisible factors that are missing in considerations of business in the digital age.
- Because organizations rise or fall depending on their systems for effective action, value, clarity, and flow are critical factors for organizational performance.
- Collaborating on making work (and obstacles to work) visible is a powerful method for building value, clarity, and flow.

CHAPTER 4

Flow Engineering

> "In a dialogue, each person does not attempt to make common certain ideas or items of information that are already known to him. [They are] creating something new together."
>
> DAVID BOHM, *On Dialogue*

WE DISCUSSED IN CHAPTER 2 that the distance inherent in scaled organizations leads to disengagement, disorientation, and distraction. We looked at how tackling the gaps in solutions requires a rapid start, alignment from leadership to contributors, and visibility from start to finish. In this chapter, we take a look at collaborative mapping as a superpower to counteract the costs of scale.

Mapping can be highly effective in gaining alignment and action in teams. It's visual, interactive, and collaborative, which makes it highly engaging. It provides a space to pull together contributors and context, which allows a team to orient themselves as a group. It gives you a platform to distill many perspectives into something well-defined, focused, and shared, which enables clear next steps. The act of mapping enables you to learn by doing. Armed with the right methods for mapping, you can counteract disengagement, disorientation, and distraction. Additionally, with the right series of maps, you can develop value, clarity, and flow and quickly enable effective action.

The Abilene Paradox[1] describes a situation where a group collectively decides on a course of action that is counter to the preferences of most or all of the individuals in the group. It's based on a story of a family who collectively decides to take a long, uncomfortable trip to Abilene—despite none of them individually wanting to go—because each mistakenly believes the others want to go. The paradox occurs when members incorrectly believe their own preferences are contrary to the group's and, therefore, do not raise objections. This results in a situation where no one is happy with the outcomes, even though everyone believes it's what the group wants. In collaborative environments, a lack of clarity and alignment can take you places nobody wants to go.

Maps as Rosetta Stones

Maps can function as a Rosetta Stone, translating the distinct languages in an organization, such as "business" and "tech". The map bridges the perspectives of each side, serving almost as a mediator. Typically, when two people are looking at the same problem or the same set of data, they are perceiving different things based on their perspectives, their backgrounds, and so forth.

FIGURE 4.1: The Power of a Map

Business Focus
I see your concern for capacity, focus, technical debt, and investment.

Tech Focus
I see your concern for meeting OKRs, roadmap, cost, & talent targets.

We see the data revealing a constraint that affects us both.

Maps allow individuals to have higher-quality conversations on specific areas of focus.

But when they jointly build maps, two individuals can construct a mental model that synthesizes both of their views. The map allows them to decode each other's language, pointing them both toward the same understanding

(Figure 4.1). The maps in Flow Engineering aim to address the gaps in understanding that arise from silos of activity, concern, and visibility.

Value Stream Mapping is an extremely powerful technique for driving performance improvement in organizations. It's even easy to start. So why isn't everyone doing it all the time?

We often hear some version of the same complaint when Value Stream Mapping is brought up in enterprises: "We want to do it. We know we have to do it, but we're not ready for it." Despite the value, many leaders don't feel they can take the time, secure commitment or budget, learn the techniques, or try something new. Some leaders who are familiar with Value Stream Mapping associate the practice only with manufacturing or feel it can't be adapted to their complex environment.

It's easy to put off adoption of this technique in favor of the status quo. You may be convinced you can't do it yourself because traditional Value Stream Mapping has highly specialized language, symbols, and an official ISO standard. It can be challenging to connect a mapping exercise to higher-level objectives to establish alignment and justify the effort. These challenges are some of the primary reasons for creating a simple, sequential mapping approach for organizations that need to act, not just map.

Introducing Flow Engineering

Based on the need to enable effective collective action, we've developed a series of mapping practices to help teams arrive at shared clarity that we call Flow Engineering. Flow Engineering embodies these activities as a structured set of visual mapping exercises that draw out insights and align the efforts of a group of collaborators. If you can host a board game, you can host these mapping exercises.

Flow Engineering builds upon mapping's benefits to go beyond engagement, alignment, and focus. It enables effective collective *action*. Flow Engineering allows us to identify value by connecting current state context to a clear target outcome. It connects that outcome to specific benefits for customers and stakeholders. It keeps that value present as a north star so that contributors can make the best decisions about what will help boost and uncover value through their efforts.

Flow Engineering allows us to build clarity by making it easy for contributors to connect the dots from efforts, activities, and improvements to the most critical focus for the organization. Based on a more complete and holistic view of the full system of work, everyone can grasp their place in improving the system. The minimal design enhances clarity by avoiding a lot of less valuable context and noise.

Finally, Flow Engineering allows us to enable flow not only by uncovering the constraint most affecting the flow of work but also by building relationships, which unblock conversational and informational flow across stakeholders and contributors. By aligning everyone to one target outcome, one stream, and one constraint, everyone can move forward together rather than against or away from each other. The concise format makes it easier for teams to step away from daily distractions and gain clarity, so they can come back to daily work with renewed energy, awareness, and focus.

Five key Flow Engineering maps enable the three elements of action:

1. **Outcome Map**: To identify your target outcome.
2. **Current State Value Stream Map**: To reveal the current state and constraints of your workflow.
3. **Dependency Map**: To identify dependencies by studying constraints.
4. **Future State Value Stream Map**: To create a future state definition of flow.
5. **Flow Roadmap**: To organize insights, actions, and ownership into an improvement roadmap.

You can see how each map supports value, clarity, and flow in Figure 4.2.

FIGURE 4.2: Value, Clarity, and Flow Woven through all Flow Engineering Maps

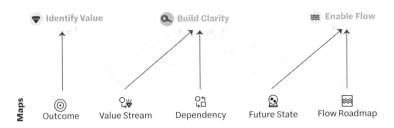

Solid lines indicate a direct contribution, dotted lines indicate indirect contribution.

These mapping exercises are designed to guide you through the essential steps to establishing team flow. They're adaptable and extendable to meet the unique needs of your team(s). And importantly, they are quick, clear, and easy to execute, allowing teams to remain agile and move at the speed of change.

FIGURE 4.3: Five Maps of Flow Engineering

Maps	Purpose	Simplified Diagram of Maps
Outcome Map	Discover and align on value	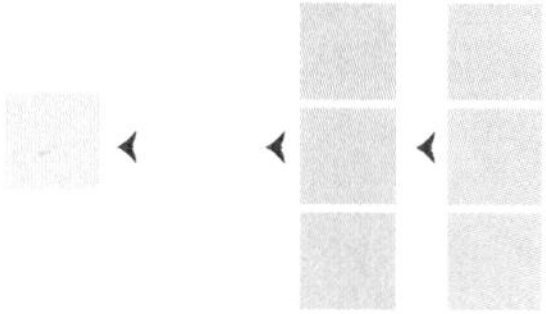
Value Stream Map	Find and measure key constraints	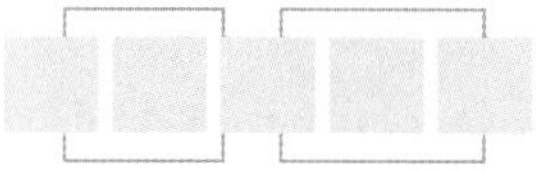
Dependency Map	Connect constraints to dependencies	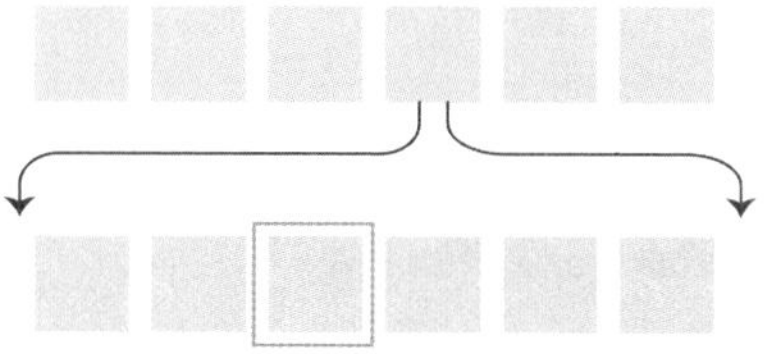
Future State Map	Design improved flow	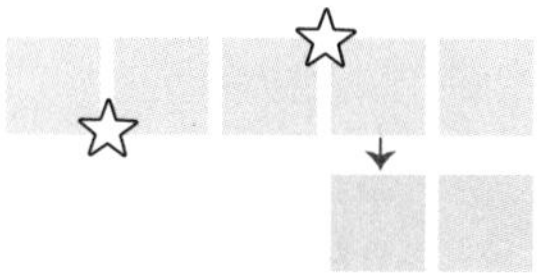
Flow Roadmap	Create and plot clear next steps	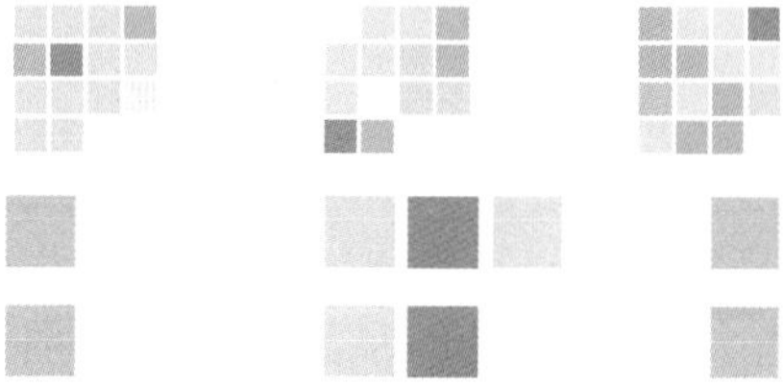

The full set of Flow Engineering exercises involves creating five maps:
an Outcome Map, a Current State Value Stream Map, a Dependency Map,
a Future State Value Stream Map, and a Flow Roadmap.

Filling the Three Gaps

Flow Engineering addresses the challenges presented by the alignment, on-ramp, and visibility gaps, as seen in Table 4.1:

TABLE 4.1: Addressing the Three Gaps through Flow Engineering

Need	Gaps		
	Alignment	On-Ramp	Visibility
Establish and maintain focus on a valuable target	✔	✔	✔
Visual and collaborative in real time	✔	✔	✔
Flexible and easily integrated into current practices	✔	✔	
Accessible to aspiring and novice facilitators		✔	
Inclusive and equitable	✔	✔	✔
Remote friendly	✔	✔	✔
Simple, quick, and affordable	✔	✔	✔
Scalable from pilot to enterprise-wide	✔	✔	✔
Complete program to address flow challenges	✔	✔	✔
Has its own flow (obviously)		✔	

With the goal of fostering the three elements of action, the maps of Flow Engineering each specifically serve one of the three elements but also support the others as a secondary benefit (as shown in Table 4.2). As we introduce each map in later chapters, we'll share which practices they're based on and viable substitutes for each should you have an existing practice in place or a substitute you'd like to employ instead.

TABLE 4.2: Each Map Serves at Least One of the Elements of Action

Map	Primary goal	Secondary benefits
Outcome Map	Assemble context and identify value	Provide clarity and alignment across multiple perspectives
Current State Value Stream Map	Clearly identify the most impactful constraint	Build clarity on current state workflow and performance
Dependency Map	Build clarity on causal factors	Build an artifact to share with external stakeholders
Future State Value Stream Map	Define improved flow	Identify valuable experiments and actions to improve flow
Flow Roadmap	Prioritize and plan flow improvements	Provide clarity on next steps and flow from today to future goals

Next, we'll look at each of the five maps of Flow Engineering, go over how to get started, and show you how to facilitate your team's progress through value, clarity, and flow.

The five mapping exercises in this book are presented as Liberating Structures. Liberating Structures are microstructures or patterns of interaction that can be used by groups to engage and enable all participants. They are based on principles of complexity science and follow a consistent format to make them easy to facilitate and engaging for participants. You can find more information in the book *The Surprising Power of Liberating Structures* by Henri Lipmanowicz and Keith McCandless or at liberatingstructures.com.

When to Start Flow Engineering

If you find yourself in a large-scale enterprise environment, at any moment it's likely you're faced with at least one of the following circumstances:

- You need to cut costs, boost efficiency, or improve time to market.
- You're planning in the midst of or recovering from a reorg.
- Your calendar is being eaten up by meetings.
- You're acquiring or have been acquired.
- You need to onboard staff into a complicated workflow.
- You just need to figure out what's going on, where to focus, and what to do.

Each one of these is a great opportunity to map, so let's look at how we can make it work.

Where Flow Engineering Happens

Steve started mapping with clients before work was shifted to remote-first, when groups could routinely be present in the same room to map. The energy, sense of connection, and tangibility of an in-person workshop can't be matched in a virtual space. But virtual mapping has many advantages. It's far easier for everyone to work at once, there's no facilitator blocking the board, and handwriting is never a problem. It's also far easier to start than booking a conference room with the ideal equipment. With virtual mapping, you can easily export, share, preserve, and update the results. You can save a lot of time working across teams and sessions by using templates. Even if you have a fully colocated team, you might consider virtual mapping to capture all of those benefits along with the advantages of in-person activity.

Flow Engineering Tools and Timeline

Any collaborative visual tool will work well for these maps in a virtual or hybrid environment. There are dozens of free tools that allow for real-time collaboration, and many offer anonymous voting and other powerful facilitation capabilities.

The important part is to build the maps collaboratively or at least get fast and varied feedback from everyone involved and affected. These days that means online, but this is all possible with a dry-erase board, paper, sticky notes, or almost anything you can write on together. For each map, you'll likely need two hours for an extremely skilled facilitator with prior experience or three hours for a new attempt.

Who's Involved in Flow Engineering

It's important to involve representation from at least the responsible and accountable parties within a given value stream. That means if design is part of the stream, someone from design should be present during mapping. That also means that leadership and those who are able to change the system, workflow, and team must be present and involved. Once you identify your key bottlenecks, you can narrow the involved parties to those who are critical to those areas. In general, it's good to include as many voices and perspectives as possible, but we find that twelve people is the maximum manageable size.

Facilitators are essential for collaboration. They can alleviate participants' fears, encourage creativity, and create a safe space for sharing ideas. They have the ability to open up and expand discussions while also narrowing down and refining them. Ideally, the facilitator has no skin in the game. They're neutral and supportive of the group's process. This helps move activity forward and keep it out of the weeds. An easy guide for facilitators is shared in Table 4.3.

TABLE 4.3: General Facilitator Rules of Engagement

✓	Facilitators talk as little as possible outside of guiding the mechanics of the process; they let the participants own most of the dialogue.
✓	Facilitators should caution any individual from talking too long; aim to stay within the duration of an elevator ride. In a larger group, a single sentence constraint can keep the effort moving.
✓	Promote a standard, non-disruptive interruption method (i.e., hand raise) to provide participants a way to voice their thoughts.
✓	Encourage participants to reach out to other participants who haven't spoken to ensure we hear from everyone.
✓	Keep participants comfortable with ranges and guesses; trust but verify with the group.
✓	Facilitators emphasize the need to stay focused on the time horizon in question. If we're looking at the current state, avoid talking about solutions or how things ought to be.

With all that said, you're ready to dive in. It's worth noting here that once you have completed the full Flow Engineering mapping sequence, you can remap maps individually depending on your need. Say, for example, your team still doesn't seem like it's aligned on a target outcome, you can revisit Outcome Mapping. Or, if you feel that maybe you're missing a dependency, you can go back to Dependency Mapping.

CASE STUDY	**What Flow Engineering Enables**

One of Steve's earliest clients was a Fortune 100 company with massive scale and resources. They could execute any initiative they focused on and deploy incredible amounts of support to achieve their desired outcomes. The only challenge was choosing the right focal point and aligning all of the stakeholders toward that objective. This is no small feat, especially with the complexity we face with modern knowledge work.

This organization had tens of millions of dollars to spend on improvements and automation with the aim of reducing time to market. The department leader hired some new staff to assess what they were doing differently than other successful organizations like Google and Facebook. They discovered that deployment automation was common among all these big players but was something they didn't have. Reasonably enough, they formed the hypothesis that they would go to the board and ask for the budget to roll it out.

They were about to follow the typical enterprise path and deploy millions of dollars toward automating deployments, the stage in the value stream when new packaged code is distributed to servers to be enabled for use by customers. Sounds like a great idea if you believe deployment will be improved through further automation. It would surely make the release process faster and simpler and perhaps even improve quality. What's not to love?

But step back a moment and consider the larger picture. If they pick deployment automation as their primary focus, they're making an assumption that it represents the best opportunity for improvement. How do they know that?

The budgetary process in the organization required that they make a case for any large investment, which is typically sponsored by a key stakeholder. In the past, they would point to industry best practices, aspirational examples, models and frameworks, and other resources outside the organization. They'd also compile opinions from trusted advisers who leveraged the same resources, as well as their own perspectives from within the organization. Typically, this doesn't follow a formal structure or process. This means they have no way of truly inspecting how the decision is made. They're not able to check the math and ensure the recommendation is the best one, given all the information available. They're operating on assumption and opinion.

On this occasion, the leadership team wanted to make a data-driven case to their board for funding. They wanted to be sure. They wanted to build and foster trust between the business and technology groups involved to reach a higher level of collaboration. The mandate was to collect data on the release process to support the proposal for automating deployment.

Consider yourself in the situation of our large, Fortune 100 enterprise. If you were able to ask for resources to spend in a few areas to tackle your most critical opportunities for the next year, what would you want to have at your disposal? How would you answer questions like "Why this?" or "Why now?" with confidence?

To address these questions in advance and ensure they had, in fact, picked the highest-priority opportunities for investment, the client engaged Steve to facilitate Value Stream Mapping their release process. Within a few hours of collaborative workshopping, it became clear that not only was artifact deployment a minor portion of the overall value stream, but there were also two other big bottlenecks waiting nearby.

The actual bottlenecks were in environment updates and acceptance testing. The bottleneck in acceptance testing was a surprise to everybody. The QA process had been operating in a stable state for a very long time. Nobody had been paying attention to it. Of course, it hadn't gone entirely unnoticed; some people had been talking about this "environment update" thing for ages, but they couldn't convince anybody to spend any time on it because they didn't have a way of describing it properly. They did have a visual method of showing the data to make their case; they were just arguing.

When you're just arguing, you're only as good as your negotiation skills, your role power, your experience, your credibility, your social capital, all these things that have nothing to do with the facts—making it a waste of time, in most instances. However, with Value Stream Mapping, all of a sudden these people who had been complaining about environment updates for years felt vindicated. They felt empowered knowing that now everyone could clearly see what they'd been trying to say for years.

FIGURE 4.4: A Segment of the Full Value Stream Map

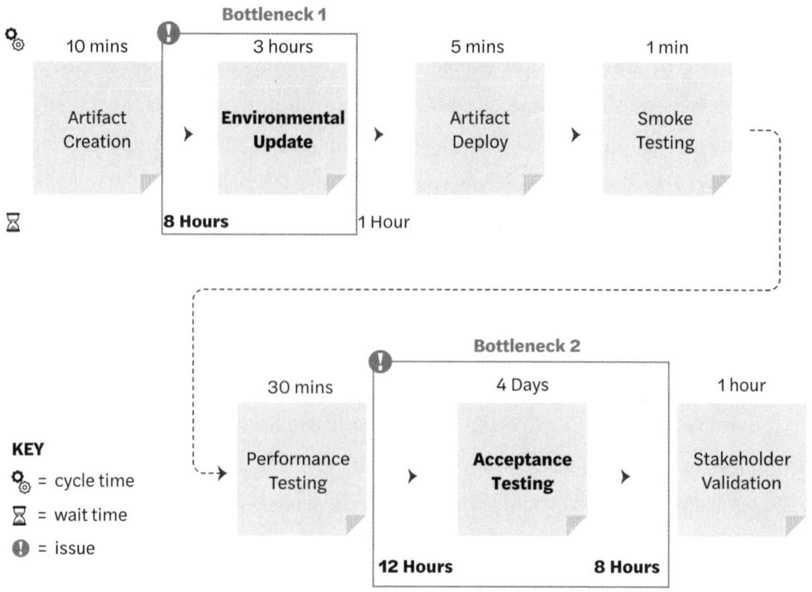

This mapping exercise disproved the assumption that automating artifact deployment would make a meaningful improvement. Two other bottlenecks were found instead.

By collecting the data across the value stream, three major opportunities for improvement were revealed, with the smallest being an order of magnitude more impactful than deployment automation. All of the stakeholders involved could see the same picture, the same data, and the same insight. Not only could they see the data pointing to three major opportunities within the value stream, but these opportunities could also be easily prioritized based on data collected on timing, quality, and value.

Let's review the outcomes of this investment, which took only a few hours of mapping:

- Twenty million dollars of investment rerouted to where it would have a dramatic impact.
- Eighteen months of time wasted on the wrong improvement was avoided.
- Stakeholders and contributors who had never met (yet worked in the same value stream) built relationships and understanding.
- The data enabled clear prioritization based on the relative investment and trade-offs.
- The department lead avoided an embarrassing, wasteful misstep and could instead present a clear and data-backed case for a preferable alternative.
- Not only leadership but each stakeholder and contributor inside and beyond the value stream had a visual artifact to aid common understanding and productive dialogue.
- The organization gained a new tool to understand their environment, make valuable decisions, and build trust across business and technology groups.

One stakeholder, a program manager overseeing their transformation efforts, described the value of the exercise with a shocking statement: "I've been here for nineteen years, and this is the first time I've seen our process from start to finish!" This case illustrates a number of benefits provided by a mapping-first approach to improvement. A fresh, minimal approach to mapping fit the need in terms of not only speed of creation but also simpler understanding and clearer insight.

Conclusion

The mapping practices in Flow Engineering are not a one-size-fits-all approach. And Flow Engineering is not a copy-and-paste methodology, which we know doesn't work. It's not a heavy framework that imposes a specific structure or operating model onto your company. Instead, it involves creating clarity with a particular team for that team and based on their unique situation. In the process of discovery, mapping, and definition, each team learns about how to improve performance by connecting their unique target outcome to the actual work that will deliver it. They reveal the constraints, obstacles, and insights that often stay hidden behind the scenes. And key information can be made visible, including the diverse perspectives across the value stream.

This process of choosing direction, mapping the business landscape, and navigating is at the heart of Flow Engineering. The ultimate goal of these efforts is to sustainably improve the flow of value to customers.

In the chapters that follow in Part 2, we introduce the five maps, which each serve a distinct purpose. The purpose of these five mapping exercises is summarized in Table 4.4. It's important to understand the underlying purpose of each exercise and what it seeks to overcome. Once we understand the purpose, we can adapt the mapping process or substitute a comparable process to meet the needs of our teams.

TABLE 4.4: Purposes and Benefits of the Five Flow Engineering Exercises

Mapping Exercise	Purpose	Risk It Averts
Outcome Mapping	Align all members of a team around the value they need to deliver.	Investing in irrelevant improvements.
Current State Value Stream Mapping	Clarify the most likely constraints in an end-to-end workflow.	Optimizing a process that is not the constraint.
Dependency Mapping	Enhance the team's clarity around likely constraints.	Inadequate understanding of the constraint.
Future State Mapping	Jointly envision a value stream with improved flow.	Failing to create a visible target for change.
Flow Roadmapping	Define the minimum set of steps to achieving improved flow.	Failing to effectively act on insights.

Flow Engineering can also include other visualizations and practices beyond these five maps if they help organizations understand what will deliver their target outcome.

Flow Engineering is about improving flow via collaborative mapping. You can create and customize your own unique version for your organization and its needs based on the goals, principles, and practices described in this book. In Part 2, we'll go through the details and instructions for each of the five maps of Flow Engineering, beginning with the Outcome Map.

Key Takeaways

- Collaborative, visual mapping is a superpower for knowledge work. It's remote-friendly, persistent, and easily shared.
- Flow Engineering is not a one-size-fits-all approach but rather involves designing improved flow within a particular value stream or team for their situation based on their unique target outcome.
- Flow Engineering was designed to address alignment, on-ramp, and visibility gaps and to reduce disengagement, disorientation, and distraction.
- Flow Engineering is easy to start, justify, and apply, so you can start doing it today.

PART 2

Mapping the Landscape

CHAPTER 5

Outcome Mapping

"To begin with the end in mind means to start with a clear understanding of your destination."

STEPHEN R. COVEY

WHEN WE START ANY JOURNEY, we need to know what our destination is before we can effectively navigate. Similarly, the first challenge to tackle in the process of Flow Engineering is clearly defining our desired outcome.

An outcome in the scope of Flow Engineering is the future state you want to be in within a set amount of time. Typically, we prefer to look six months into the future. This generally allows us enough time to implement a change and means minimal risk that conditions may change and disengage, disorient, or distract the group. A possible outcome could be, "We are delivering value to customers twice as often." Or, "We have cut production defects by 50%." We define our desired outcome and the path to achieving it by inviting team members to build an Outcome Map.

Envisioning a desired future is a technique for setting direction that's been a key aspect of strategy since Teleology emerged under Aristotle.[1] Norbert Wiener describes cybernetics as based on "teleological mechanisms."[2] Outcome Mapping is a structured practice that brings a team or group of colleagues together to identify value (i.e., their most important goal) and how to move toward it together.

Outcome Mapping primes the team for thinking in terms of outcomes (a desired future state) and delivering customer value. Mapping the desired outcome from the outset gives context and purpose to all the subsequent mapping exercises. If teams dive into later maps without this preparation, improvement activities will tend to be unfocused and fail to yield a meaningful impact for the organization.

A 2020 research report by Boston Consulting Group highlighted three key questions that companies need to ask when attempting a digital (or any other) transformation:[3]

1. Why are we doing this?
2. What should we do?
3. How do we implement the transformation?

As shown in Figure 5.1, Outcome Mapping establishes value by answering the question, "Why are we doing this?" while building the foundation for clarity and flow. In future chapters, we'll take a look at how Value Stream and Dependency Maps bring clarity by tackling the issue of "What should we do?" Finally, Future State Maps and Flow Roadmaps open the door to flow by asking, "How do we implement the transformation?"

FIGURE 5.1: Outcome Mapping Primarily Serves to Identify Value

What Is Outcome Mapping?

Outcome Mapping is a collaborative workshop to help a group of stakeholders clarify value (i.e., their primary goal and direction). Its goal is to focus the team while surfacing doubts, testing assumptions, and enabling the emergence of new insights. Just like with the other maps in Flow Engineering, Outcome Mapping accelerates change efforts with only a modest investment of time and forethought. Outcome Mapping helps the team start to define a clear roadmap toward the value they seek. It answers the following questions:

- Does everyone clearly understand our target objective?
- If another issue disrupts our focus, is it clear how to prioritize?

When you make your primary outcome clear, teams understand what's safe to ignore. This helps teams clarify what's in or out of scope, how much detail is needed, and, most importantly, how everyone can contribute to making the target outcome a reality.

As shown in Figure 5.2, there are five stages to Outcome Mapping:

1. Outcome Discovery: *What is our target?*
2. Defining the Target Outcome: *What goal(s) do we want to achieve?*
3. Defining Benefits: *Why does this outcome matter?*
4. Defining Obstacles: *What could get in the way?*
5. Defining Next Steps: *How are we going to proceed?*

FIGURE 5.2: The Five Stages of Outcome Mapping

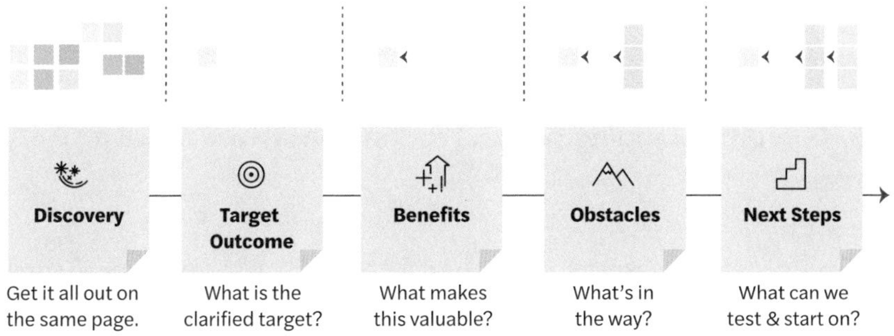

Discovery	Target Outcome	Benefits	Obstacles	Next Steps
Get it all out on the same page.	What is the clarified target?	What makes this valuable?	What's in the way?	What can we test & start on?

It's possible to create an Outcome Map within a quick conversation to clarify, align, and drive action. The map in Figure 5.3 (see page 56) was created during a ten-minute conversation and produced an artifact that could be shared, referenced, and evolved over time. A rough Outcome Map could be expanded into a more detailed map at a later date; it's a living document that over time individuals can (and will) edit, comment on, or vote on.

FIGURE 5.3: A Rapid Outcome Map

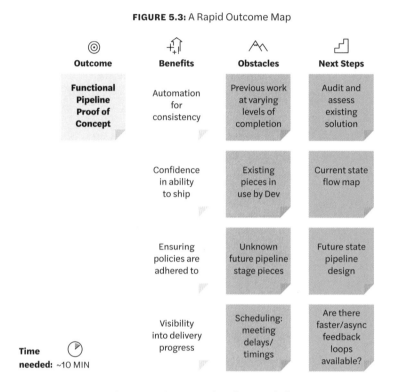

Outcome	Benefits	Obstacles	Next Steps
Functional Pipeline Proof of Concept	Automation for consistency	Previous work at varying levels of completion	Audit and assess existing solution
	Confidence in ability to ship	Existing pieces in use by Dev	Current state flow map
	Ensuring policies are adhered to	Unknown future pipeline stage pieces	Future state pipeline design
	Visibility into delivery progress	Scheduling: meeting delays/ timings	Are there faster/async feedback loops available?

Time needed: ~10 MIN

Est. time: Ten minutes to value, clarity, and what's next.

Why Outcome Mapping Works: Working Backward to Leap Forward

A key principle of cybernetics is to start by identifying a target (or desired) outcome and then work to reduce the gap between the *present state* and that *target state*. Former Amazon executives Colin Bryar and Bill Carr credit the practice of "working backward" as a key element of the organization's dramatic achievement. Working backward involves beginning with a clear definition of a desired target state (outcome) and using that target to guide decisions and actions.[4] The same approach has been employed in effective collaborative efforts in many fields. The underdog 2002 Oakland A's captured in the book and movie *Moneyball* reverse engineered wins to on-base percentage.[5] The Natural Step uses a working backward approach called "backcasting" that paints a vision for the future to drive sustainable urban development.[6] Accordingly, the five stages of Outcome Mapping aim to draw out different aspects of the value being sought by beginning with the end in mind.

Outcome Discovery

The first stage, outcome discovery, answers the question, "What is our target?" The discovery stage is an initial, pre-mapping exercise that provides an opportunity for stakeholders to surface and share all the relevant context and concerns. This is particularly valuable if you're an outside facilitator coming in to guide the practices of Flow Engineering, but it can also be surprisingly revealing to even the most seasoned members of a group.

Typically, a group will come together to conduct the discovery phase of an Outcome Map whenever there is a feeling of confusion, dissatisfaction, misalignment, frustration, competing priorities, etc. Table 5.1 outlines some common vague conditions that could become actionable if transformed into a target outcome.

TABLE 5.1: Common Situations That Can Be Transformed into Actionable Outcomes via Outcome Discovery

Issues Inside an Organization	Competitive/External Challenges
Do not have clear OKRs and KPIs.	Financial constraints.
Low organizational performance.	Lacking strategic direction.
eNPS stagnant or dropping.	Lack of clarity around the customer.
Cross-organizational misalignment.	Cannot convince stakeholders to act.
Acting like a "feature factory."	NPS stagnant or dropping.
Tech debt accumulation.	Customers are leaving or complaining.
Too much WIP.	Customer journey is suboptimal.
Rework or delays.	No data on customer experience.
Improvement initiatives stalled.	Few insights into product usage.
Difficult to prioritize new activities.	Sales are down.

It's quite common to have leadership objectives or even objectives and key results (OKRs) but to lack clear goals at the team or value stream level. Maybe there's been a recent change, and it's unclear where to focus or how to proceed. A team might not know or agree on what their desired outcome (future state) is. In this case, the discovery phase helps surface the raw information that can be refined into a clear, collective target outcome. Without this, everyone could be moving in opposite directions.

In many cases, teams have already been tasked to achieve a particular outcome and simply need to strategize on how to accomplish that goal. If everyone feels clear and aligned, you could skip the discovery stage and move straight to building the Outcome Map as detailed later in this chapter. But if you're an outside facilitator or if the group is struggling with many competing ideas, this discovery process is essential.

The discovery stage of Outcome Mapping includes five steps (or prompts). Participants are asked to list out the following categories:

- context
- goals
- pains
- questions
- ideas

Each of these steps act as a prompt. Participants can share anything that comes to mind, and there will likely be overlap between the categories. What one person sees as *context*, another person thinks of as a *question*. *Pains* and *goals* are often two sides of the same coin. The purpose here is not to get the correct answer into the correct category but to provide the space for all factors to surface. It's better to have things surfaced and placed in multiple categories than not surfaced at all.

By making space for context, ideas, questions, pains, and goals, discovery provides a venue that encourages participation, warms up the group with a familiar activity, and demonstrates the value placed on sharing perspectives. You'll find step-by-step guidance on conducting outcome discovery and all of the other mapping activities at the end of this chapter.

Defining the Target Outcome

Stage two, defining the target outcome, answers the question, "What outcome do we want to achieve?" It is the first step in crafting the actual Outcome Map. In many cases, the desired outcome will become clear in the outcome discovery stage that came previously. In others, the outcome has been handed to a team from leadership or another source, in which case they can skip outcome discovery and start here by clearly defining the target outcome.

The importance of clarifying the desired outcome—defining value—before embarking on any kind of flow improvement can't be overstated. Sometimes it's clear where to focus—one fire may be raging while others are merely smoldering. But if there's no emergency, or if there are multiple influential stakeholders each with distinct priorities, it becomes much more challenging to identify the most valuable investment. Importantly, making the desired outcome explicit defines what done looks like. This helps oppose the destructive tendency to work on many things but not finish any.

Defining Benefits

Stage three, defining benefits, answers the question, "Why does this outcome matter?" Typically, not all stakeholders fully understand and appreciate the benefits of achieving the desired outcome. The outcome may be tied to corporate strategic goals, which may be too far outside the daily considerations for many team members to appreciate. For this reason, involving the group in explicitly thinking through and stating all the benefits of achieving the target outcome helps ensure that teams build the necessary associations to be motivated by it.

This stage captures the value of the desired outcome. In other words, why should the team ignore everything else that they could be doing in service of this one, focused outcome? The value (benefit) should be considered from three distinct perspectives:

1. Value for customers.
2. Value for the organization.
3. Value for individual contributors.

These benefits may be obvious to some people, but they're often not obvious to everyone involved. It's always helpful to make the overarching context clear and explicit. What benefit will arise if this outcome is achieved? The benefits define the value delivered by achieving the outcome. If you struggle to define the benefits, that's either an indication that you should not be working on this or that you haven't fully understood the broader context in which you're working. Putting energy into clarifying this purpose can help enormously, especially if the benefits of the project are ever called into question at a later time. A truly powerful target outcome creates a win-win-win scenario across all three groups (customers, the organization, and contributors). This drives alignment and fuels motivation.

This stage also provides a chance to connect the target outcome to critical goals like OKRs; external factors such as market trends, guiding principles, and values; or other goals, such as faster feedback. This anchors the target outcome in the team and makes it tangible and powerful as a motivation moving forward. Most importantly, it's an initial validation that the outcome really matters and is worth pursuing.

Defining Obstacles

Stage four, defining obstacles, answers the question, "What could get in the way?" If there were no obstacles to achieving our desired goal, we would already be there. Obstacles range from not having the skills necessary to achieve an outcome, to facing unknown technical challenges, to dealing with competitive threats—they are the things actually or potentially impeding us from reaching our desired future (target outcome).

Looking at obstacles helps identify pain points and get all of the team's fears and challenges out into the open so that the team can form a strategy to avoid them. It is very important to make these obstacles explicit early in the process so they can be dealt with consciously by participants. Some people may hesitate to give voice to doubts and concerns, but this reduces the group's ability to anticipate and avert them. Inviting people to name potential risks provides a safe venue for the cautious, wary, or pessimistic perspectives to provide value and be heard up front.

After all, a failed initiative is extremely expensive. We can't afford an environment in which people don't have the courage or opportunity to speak up. Allowing doubts to be expressed ensures that the whole group is able to think consciously about these concerns. If those concerns do become a reality, the group has already been primed to acknowledge them and can address the concern more quickly and comfortably.

Some people may have a positive motivation but have a strong tendency toward doubt and dissent and are more likely to be skeptical of any initiative.

It's important to make their concerns explicit so they can be considered and we can seek mitigations. Psychologist Adam Grant calls such people "disagreeable givers" and praises their potential contribution to an organization.[7]

Defining Next Steps

The final stage, defining next steps, answers the question, "How are we going to proceed?" Since Flow Engineering centers around flow improvement, a typical next step from Outcome Mapping is to schedule a Current State Value Stream Mapping workshop (see Chapter 6) to dig into the current flow and identify areas for improvement. Next steps may, however, include setting up investigations, interviews, assessments, and other actions that help the team answer questions and test ideas to move forward in their work.

Chapter 9 goes into detail on the Flow Roadmap and the importance of accountability and single-threaded ownership, but suffice it to say, unless there's a clear commitment from someone to tackle a next step within a particular time frame, work is not likely to get done.

| CASE STUDY | **Getting Safety Wrong at a Rocket Ship Startup** |

The CEO of a fast-moving startup was eager to improve using Value Stream Mapping. After a brief exchange of context with a facilitator, they dove right into mapping the value stream. The goal was to identify waste, accelerate delivery, and improve quality. Perfect use of Value Stream Mapping, right? Not so fast.

First, having three target outcomes without a clear priority is a recipe for distraction and scope creep. Second, without a session to engage and gather context from the working group, the facilitator and CEO failed to share the expectations for the initiative with the whole group, resulting in a lack of psychological safety. Third, without the added context of benefits and obstacles provided by an Outcome Map, the purpose of and possible impediments to the improvements were unclear to the participants.

It wasn't until the CEO left the room that the other participants revealed an untold story and had a real conversation about the current state. The contributor perspective? "Our CEO drives us nuts with late changes and unspoken quality standards, resulting in tons of rework and anxiety." The CEO perspective? "Without my nudges and guidance, things drag on forever and end up wrong."

The facilitator then pivoted toward mediating a conversation between leadership and contributors that surfaced challenging but ultimately ground-breaking dialogue across the company. They'd neglected to do the groundwork of establishing the necessary ingredients for effective collaboration. To reset and realign, the group stepped back to walk through outcome discovery and define the outcome, benefits, obstacles, and next steps critical to making the mapping (and actions to follow) most effective. Externalizing this discussion onto a shared workspace gave everyone a representation to point at rather than each other, making it possible to create a future state flow that worked for every-one. Downstream interventions and interruptions were replaced with upstream definition and guiding principles.

Part of the work was helping teams find those flow solutions. But before you can get to solutions, you need to help everyone see the same picture. Flow Engineering can sometimes look a lot like therapy.

Jumping into Value Stream Mapping won't work unless you've first clarified the outcome you're seeking to accomplish—for the customer, the team, and the business. Outcome Mapping helps everyone get clarity on the most valuable shared target, but it also surfaces important contexts and conflicts. Facilitators need to be attuned to these competing goals.

How to Conduct an Outcome Mapping Session

As we stated at the beginning of this chapter, the first challenge to tackle in the process of Flow Engineering is to clearly define a desired outcome and important context impacting it. We do this by building an Outcome Map, inviting team members to dig into a desired outcome and begin charting the path to achieving it with open eyes. This section details the steps to conduct-ing your Outcome Mapping session.

Identify Key Stakeholders

First, it's important to understand that Flow Engineering mapping exercises are structured conversations with defined outputs. The basic foundation is for teams to meet. If teams have the opportunity to meet in person, that can greatly aid in effective communication, engagement, and trust-building. But many of our sessions are done remotely with the aid of digital collaboration tools.

So, who should be involved? It's critical that the people involved in executing the workflow are involved in clarifying the vision for how their own process might be improved. Autonomy is one of the most important intrinsic motivations according to many studies,[8] so the team needs autonomy in deciding how to evolve their practices. The contributing team should also include the people who have the situational awareness to accurately determine where changes can be made. When the map is their own creation, they understand that they have the power to adjust it as necessary. At the same time, not everyone on the team needs to be involved. In any meeting, we should aim to involve the minimum number of people required to make decisions that will be trusted and accepted by the rest of the team.

In general, you can maximize context and clarity by involving the same group in all of these mapping exercises, starting with Outcome Mapping. Being involved in Outcome Mapping maximizes clarity and engagement for participants; therefore, it's beneficial to get as many people as possible to participate. But practically, it can be difficult to manage an interactive workshop for more than twelve people (facilitation complexity multiplies as more participants are involved).

If you have fewer than ten people responsible for the initiative, we recommend you invite everyone to participate. If you have more than ten people responsible for the initiative, we recommend you choose representatives from each team and from each functional specialty across these teams. For example, a lead architect, product manager, department head, and the head of the testing team may all be good proxies for their team's concerns. Excluding any key function or stakeholder could cause the team to overlook key concerns or risk a lack of engagement from part of the team.

Time Allocation

The entire mapping session should take about sixty minutes at a brisk pace. Allocate two hours if this is your first time.

Materials Needed

To complete the Outcome Map (and all the other Flow Engineering maps), you will need a digital collaboration tool if you are remote or hybrid, or a physical dry-erase board, paper, sticky notes, and markers if you are all located in person. We like to use at least five varieties of color-coded sticky notes, but you can use a combination of colored markers and notes to categorize items.

How Participation Is Distributed

Everyone should be actively encouraged to participate equally. Ideally, the facilitator doesn't contribute directly and instead focuses on fostering safety and inclusion and encouraging the flow of activity.

How Groups Are Configured

One main notetaker builds the Outcome Map on the shared board (either in a digital collaboration tool or on a physical dry-erase board or piece of paper). Other contributors discuss to add, remove, or amend aspects of the shared map.

How the Mapping Board Is Arranged

Start by creating an area on a digital or physical board for the first stage of Outcome Mapping: *outcome discovery*. In this area, delineate space for the five categories mentioned earlier: context, goals, pains, questions, ideas. (See Figure 5.4 for reference.) If your team has already identified their target outcome (e.g., it has been handed to you from leadership), you can abbreviate this stage. Clarifying outcomes is almost always necessary.

FIGURE 5.4: Five Categories for Outcome Mapping

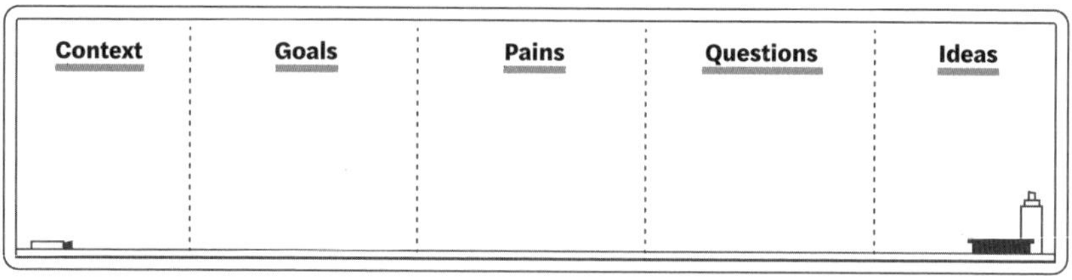

| Context | Goals | Pains | Questions | Ideas |

The five categories or prompts are context, goals, pains, questions, and ideas.

Next, create a second area on your board for the Outcome Map. This map consists of four columns: outcome, benefits, obstacles, and next steps.

FIGURE 5.5: Stages of Outcome Mapping

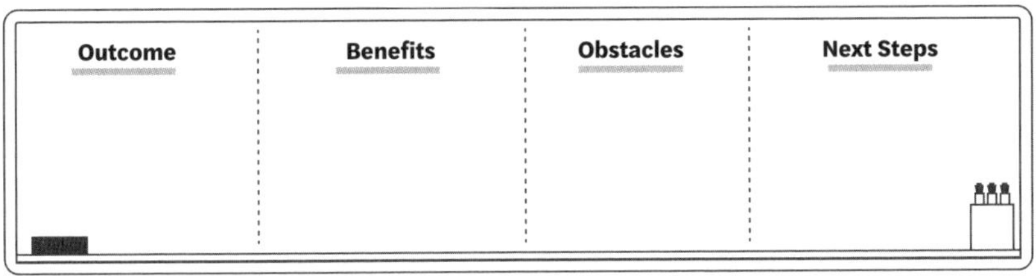

Be sure to leave plenty of blank space on the board. There will be several opportunities to use the blank spaces throughout the exercises.

The Outcome Mapping Process (Step by Step)

1. OUTCOME DISCOVERY

As a reminder, the first stage, outcome discovery, answers the question, "What is our target?" In this pre-mapping stage, the team surfaces a variety of possible target outcomes. As we outlined earlier, this could be anything that is causing dissatisfaction or misalignment on a team. This stage can be helpful when there are competing or unclear priorities. However, if the team already has a clearly understood outcome, they can skip this stage.

To conduct the discovery stage, first place blank sticky notes in the designated discovery area of the board. There should be a selection of colors (at least five), with each color assigned to a column category (e.g., context = yellow, goals = green, etc.). Start by having participants work independently, filling the blank sticky notes with their context, goals, pains, questions, and ideas. Remember, each of these five categories is meant to act like a prompt. Participants should include anything that comes to mind, and there may be overlap between the categories. Unlike in a board game, the rules here don't penalize. The purpose is simply to provide space to surface everyone's thoughts. (5 mins.)

Next, place each of these sticky notes in the appropriate category column in the discovery stage on the board. (See Figure 5.6.)

FIGURE 5.6: Example of the Discovery Stage of Outcome Mapping

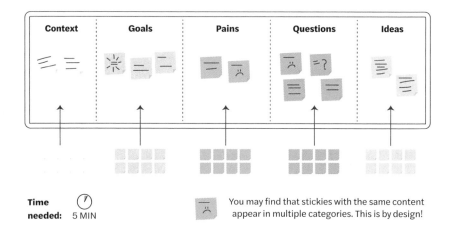

Time needed: 5 MIN

You may find that stickies with the same content appear in multiple categories. This is by design!

Discovery stage acts to surface the wide variety of active concerns for a group.

As a team, review the sticky notes. You will notice that many are related to the same few themes. For instance, you may find a sticky for "How do we prioritize?" in both *pains* and *goals*. This is fine. Often pains and goals are two sides of the same coin. You may also see there are multiple stickies in different categories that deal with past work or tech debt. Don't worry. This is by design. Some participants will think more in terms of questions, some in ideas, and some in pains. The discovery stage of the Outcome Map allows everyone to realize organically that they may in fact be on the same page (or, as we mentioned in Part 1, looking at the same challenge from different perspectives).

Encourage the team to identify perspectives and then present their understanding of the topics and themes that are appearing. The more they're driving the process, the more the result will reflect their collective understanding. (5 mins.)

Next, on a blank area of the board, group the notes into the themes or topics that start to surface. These groupings of themes may contain a mix of goals, pains, etc. (3 mins.) (See Figure 5.7.)

FIGURE 5.7 Notes Organized into Themes

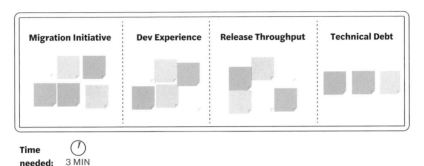

Time needed: 3 MIN

Color coding allows us to group themes while retaining the original item type.

Now, the team should vote on which group of topics (or theme) they think is the most important to work on right now. The team should decide how they would like to define "most important." Digital collaboration tools usually offer voting as a built-in capability to assist with this.

As shown in Figure 5.8, if you're working on a physical board or paper, you can vote by putting dots on the corner of the sticky notes with a marker. (TIP: When multiple items have been clustered together, the team votes can be collected on the upper-rightmost sticky note or the group title as a representative of that cluster.)

FIGURE 5.8: Example of Voting Using Dots

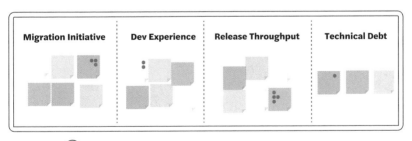

Time needed: 2 MIN

Voting allows the group to narrow the focus and align on a single theme to pursue.

Based on the grouping or theme that receives the most votes, work with the team to craft a target outcome that captures the information from the sticky notes and represents a valuable target. Remember to craft your outcome with the following in mind:

1. Value for customers.
2. Value for the organization.
3. Value for individual contributors.

For example, if the team selected the group in Figure 5.8 titled "Migration Initiative" and incorporated all the notes within that group, they may come up with a target outcome like this: "Eighty percent of critical legacy apps migrated to next-generation cloud by Q3." It's also fine to have a primary and secondary outcome—for example, "Increase throughput by 30%" balanced against "Maintain NPS." This can prevent overinvestment in the target outcome to the detriment of a critical metric.

Outcomes can be simple and concise, such as "Reduce production defects by 50%," or specific and exhaustive. In one workshop with a large engineering organization, the outcome started as, "We deliver a self-service internal development experience that makes it easy to learn and succeed, enjoyable to work, hard to do the wrong thing," which seemed broad and lacked measurability. After a brief discussion, we distilled it down to "eNPS (employee Net Promoter Score) up by twenty points and production defects down 20%." Less aspirational but more measurable.

The guidance for SMART goals can also be helpful in thinking about crafting a bulletproof target outcome. A SMART goal is Specific, Measurable, Attainable, Relevant, and Time-Bound.

For our purposes, you can think of outcomes and goals as nearly interchangeable, so don't worry about the nuance between them. In short, goals tend to be aspirational, and an outcome is the result or consequence of actions taken. We define effective action as action leading to a desired outcome.

Now that the team has selected the target outcome to focus on, it's time to build the Outcome Map to chart a path to achieving that outcome.

2. THE OUTCOME MAP: DEFINING THE TARGET OUTCOME

Once the team has identified the target outcome (either by starting with a defined outcome or crafting it together in the outcome discovery stage), they will build the Outcome Map around that target. The team should start by placing this target outcome on a sticky and putting it in the column labeled "Outcome."

3. DEFINING BENEFITS, OBSTACLES, AND NEXT STEPS

Next, the team will work through each of the remaining three columns one by one.

For each column, follow these steps:

- Step 1: Participants should reflect silently on the column prompt (e.g., benefits, obstacles, or next steps) to generate ideas. For instance, if they are working on the "Benefits" column, participants would start reflecting on what benefits the target outcome will bring to the team and organization. (1 min.)
- Step 2: Break the group into pairs. Each person in the pair should share their ideas on the column prompt generated during self-reflection. (2 mins.)
- Step 3: Each pair joins another pair to form groups of four. Each foursome shares and consolidates their ideas for the specific column. (TIP: Look for similarities and differences.) (4 mins.)
- Step 4: Next, the entire group votes on which items are highest priority and moves those ideas to the top of the column. (2 mins.)

The group repeats this sequence for all three columns, defining the benefits of achieving the target outcome, identifying the obstacles, and, finally, listing the next steps to achieving the outcome. (In total, working through all three columns should take around thirty minutes.) The reason for the iteration, collaboration, and consolidation here is to include and unleash everyone while avoiding simple issues like having a misspelled or vague item miss out on votes. A completed Outcome Map is shown in Figure 5.9.

FIGURE 5.9: A Completed Outcome Map

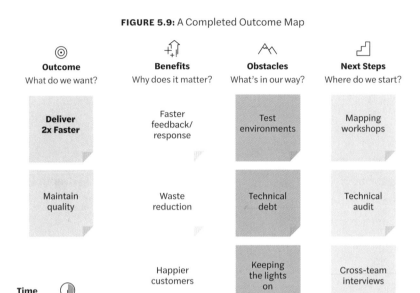

By the end of the mapping exercise, ask the group if any of the following questions are unanswered or unclear:

- What is our target outcome?
- What are the benefits of achieving the outcome?
- What obstacles stand between us and the outcome?
- What are our next steps toward achieving the outcome?

If there's still uncertainty, work through it before moving on!

Tips and Traps

- Avoid allowing a few people to dominate the session.
- If the facilitator is not responsible for delivering the outcome, they should not contribute ideas to the board.
- If mapping remotely, perform the exercise with participants' video turned on to improve engagement.
- Limit the scope of the session to goals and actions within this group's ability to influence.
- Share guidance on creating high-quality target outcomes, such as SMART (Specific, Measurable, Achievable, Relevant, and Time-Bound).

- If the outcome relates to flow improvement, Value Stream Mapping will help participants target specific parts of their workflow to improve.
- Implicit in the three-to-six-month time horizon for the target outcome is the idea that this effort be repeated as the target is achieved or the landscape and priorities change.
- If your outcome includes performance improvement, make sure one of your next steps includes establishing a baseline for measurement so that comparison can be made.

Riffs and Variations

- Expanded Outcome Maps could include additional columns like *measures*, *ownership*, and *methods*, depending on the time available and the desire for expanded scope and clarity. Where more detail and definition is necessary or desired, Outcome Mapping can accommodate it.
- In complex scenarios, it may be impossible to predict specific outcomes and may be more beneficial to frame outcomes as increased learning, reduced risk, or more options (e.g., place three bets to reduce financial exposure to unpredictable market and regulatory conditions). Next steps in complex scenarios may be running experiments, holding further discussions, or soliciting feedback from a broader population.
- Outcome Mapping can be performed repeatedly over the life of an initiative to periodically reestablish clarity.
- Impact mapping is similar to Outcome Mapping but focuses on external personas and a separate outcome for each. Outcome Mapping substitutes personas for benefits across multiple stakeholders without naming them specifically up front. If you have more time, you can craft your Outcome Map to branch and interconnect the same way an impact map breaks out each stage into direct contributions.

BOLT GLOBAL | **Software Delivery Team**

To illustrate how the Outcome Mapping process works, we'll look at the example of Bolt Global's software delivery team that we first looked at in the Introduction. Like many teams, Bolt Global is seeking to improve their software delivery performance. Knowing that the team needed to clarify their challenges and main goal,

Sharon gathered key stakeholders to meet and share thoughts, ideas, concerns, and questions so they could act quickly, collaboratively, and effectively. Figure 5.10 summarizes the challenges that Sharon and her team are facing.

FIGURE 5.10: The Challenge Landscape within Sharon's Area of Responsibility

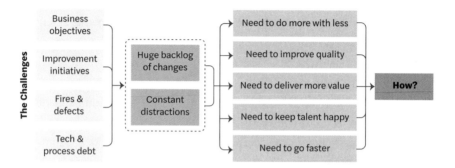

Sharon organized an Outcome Mapping workshop for her team to clarify their context and narrow their focus. Initially, the relationship between the diverse challenges they were facing was unclear. Issues would arise from time to time but were not made explicit to the whole group. Outcome Mapping gave the team a chance to make these concerns visible for consideration by the whole group. Figure 5.11 shows that the discovery stage of this session resulted in the team working through their known context and challenges to focus their efforts on releasing twice as often.

The Bolt Global team agreed with the need to increase delivery speed. But discussion surfaced a critical doubt for participants: that speeding up would compromise quality. Improving quality received the second-highest number of votes. It was clear to the team that they needed to focus on faster delivery but keep quality in mind at every step to ensure it was increased and not compromised.

The other concerns raised in the discussion were significant. Empowering members of the group to make their concerns explicit allowed them to feel their voices were heard. The anonymous voting on ideas also allowed the team to express or withhold support for ideas without risk. Seeing the results of voting together allowed the team to understand what otherwise would have been hidden: the views and motivations of others on the team.

FIGURE 5.11: The Bolt Global Outcome Mapping Process

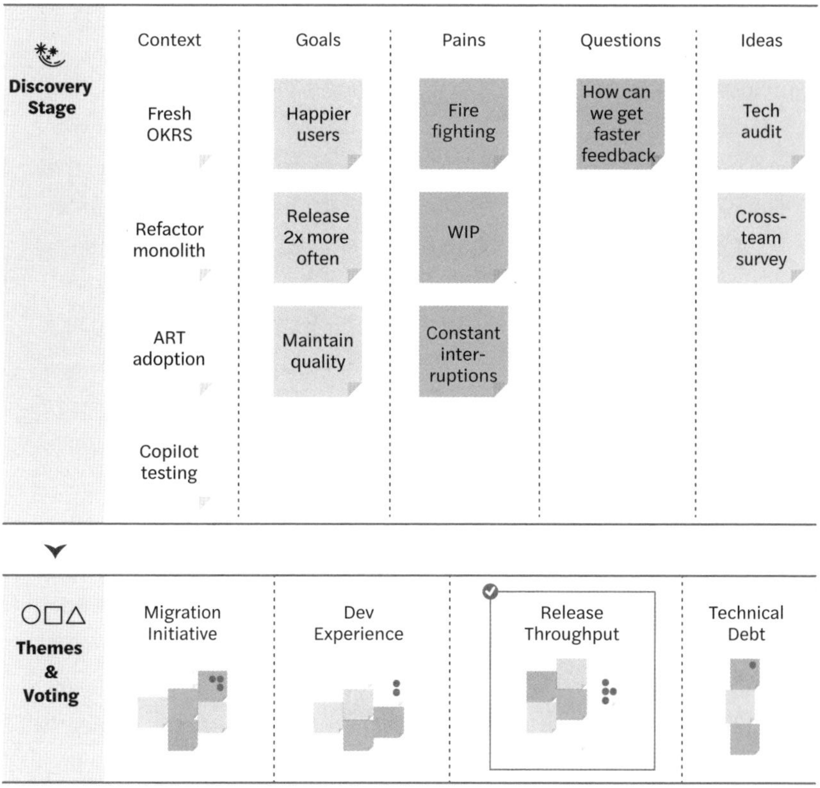

In short, this exercise made visible what was invisible and enabled individuals to align on value as a group. Social interactions involve risk, and some people are more sensitive to that than others. Teams need the best ideas to be surfaced, and they need confidence that others on the team will not be hostile or belittling to any ideas that are surfaced. Serious risks to a project sometimes appear as small doubts. And the most brilliant and innovative ideas can sometimes appear far-fetched at first. Teams need to be able to amplify these weak signals if they want to capture the biggest innovations and avert the most serious risks. Moreover, activities such as these engage the whole team in the creative process, which can be deeply fulfilling and enjoyable for those involved. This builds a bond between members of the team and typically also with the broader enterprise.

The Bolt Global team now turns to Outcome Mapping to dig into the desired outcome of doubling delivery speed.

Engaging with a Mandated Outcome

Target initiatives for a team are sometimes the result of thought or discussion at higher levels of the organization. The team tasked with responsibility for those outcomes may lack information or perspective on why those outcomes were chosen. So it's important to be humble and respectful of these organizational initiatives and give leaders the benefit of the doubt that the initiative is important and beneficial.

But it's normal that leaders higher in the organization may lack detailed understanding of what's necessary to achieve an outcome and may not have imagined other side effects of the initiative. The first stage of Outcome Mapping is to critically assess the intended outcome and to surface fundamental doubts and questions from the beginning.

Teams often don't feel they have autonomy to define or redefine the outcomes they've been tasked to achieve. The default operating model for most organizations is still a command-and-control model where people higher in the organization dictate both the outcomes they want their teams to achieve and the methods they should follow. In simple situations, that approach is adequate. But that approach deprives teams of a sense of autonomy, which undermines their instinctive motivation and creative capacity, as explained in Chapter 1. In complex environments, motivation and creativity are essential for success. When teams take ownership of the outcome, they can navigate any trade-offs while staying within the bounds defined by leadership.

In most cases, teams can subtly reframe an outcome in their own words while still keeping within the parameters set by leaders. Defining and reframing the benefits of the outcome can ensure that an outcome that seemed to only serve one group resonates with everyone. The process of Outcome Mapping is a powerful way of bringing the mission of a team to life because it encourages the team to think about and clarify the motivations and implications behind a target outcome.

It can happen that even after this process and discussion, the outcome doesn't make sense to the team, or they anticipate so many obstacles or side effects that the initiative doesn't seem likely to bring benefit. Such skepticism or even cynicism about organizational initiatives is common in larger organizations, and teams often find themselves trudging onward with little genuine motivation. Outcome Mapping can give teams the clarity to express their concerns in a more compelling way to leadership or to propose alternative ways to achieve a goal. This can save significant money, time, and morale by addressing in the short term what could be disastrous in the long term. Doubts and frustrations that are not articulated cannot be dealt with consciously but may manifest as resistance to change.

Leaders in some organizations may be particularly resistant to feedback from their teams. To maximize chances of success, proposed adjustments to a plan should be framed in a way that better enables the target outcome, rather than in a way that implies serious flaws in their thinking. Supported by an Outcome Map, the discussion becomes an invitation to clarify the map rather than present a flaw in logic or strategy. Diplomacy is pragmatic, but it's also respectful.

If the team can't envision a way to tactfully deliver feedback to leadership, the normal response is to grudgingly proceed with the activities. But when the team anticipates that an initiative will fail or bring no benefit, motivation and effort evaporate. If the plan fails, in their minds they can say, "I knew it would fail," and gripe privately to coworkers. Such a situation, while common, reflects a failure to engage the creativity, intelligence, and resilience of the team. We should do everything in our power to ensure everyone is clear and engaged on the mission and to figure out how to skillfully inform management of any concerns before beginning.

Conclusion

Outcome Mapping provides a fast framework for helping teams identify value, build initial clarity, and internalize the benefits of an initiative. The process is creative and iterative to allow the team to build and share insights together and to surface doubts and limitations that might derail the team if not acknowledged.

Outcome Mapping focuses on unifying around a valuable purpose from the beginning and is an important prerequisite for later mapping exercises. It should be repeated periodically to allow teams to adjust to changed circumstances and target new opportunities.

Key Takeaways

- Beginning with the end in mind provides clarity that helps teams highlight where and how to make improvements.
- The mapping is more important than the map because it provides a framework for productive and creative discussion that allows ideas to evolve.
- Doing each step collaboratively exposes and allows for resolution of hidden doubts and confusion.
- By cocreating a clear, visual asset that maps the path, Outcome Mapping helps to bridge the gap between teams, individuals, and areas of concern.

CHAPTER 6

Current State Value Stream Mapping

"The reason Value Stream Mapping is so effective is that it focuses attention on products and their value to customers rather than on organizations, assets, technologies, processes, and career paths."

MARY & TOM POPPENDIECK

FLOW ENGINEERING IS A LIGHTWEIGHT method for teams to improve flow throughout their ways of working. At the heart of this method is understanding the team's real goals, looking at how they currently work together, and then ideating on possible flow improvements. Our second type of mapping, Current State Value Stream Mapping, helps teams find this clarity (see Figure 6.1).

FIGURE 6.1: Value Stream Mapping Primarily Serves to Build Clarity

After decades of use in traditional manufacturing and knowledge work, Value Stream Mapping is more popular than ever as a way to visualize and gather actionable metrics on a team's workflow.

In the previous chapter, we learned how to use Outcome Mapping to discern value and answer important questions that build clarity and help focus our work. This chapter begins with a quick overview of what Value Stream Mapping is. We then take a look at the power of Value Stream Mapping to improve a team's understanding of how they work today and how their work could be reimagined. We discuss how to prepare for a Value Stream Mapping session, including who to involve, how often to do the exercise, and what you need in advance. We then explain how to actually conduct a Value Stream Mapping session, visualizing and measuring the current state of a team's workflow.

Where's the Stream?

John Shook and Mike Rother captured a key definition of value streams in the book *Learning to See*: "Value shall be specified from the standpoint of the customer. A value stream shall be identified for each product or service family—from concept to launch and from order to delivery."[1] In other words, everywhere you have a product or service, you have a value stream to create and deliver it.

It can seem impossible to map a value stream if you're unclear on where it is and what it looks like before starting, but that's what mapping helps us do. The key points to keep in mind is that the stream already exists and the flow is already present. Knowing that, we can recall past actions to see the sequence of activities leading to a customer outcome. This will reveal the stream along with its performance. It helps to have a few guiding principles to "see" value streams as a model before you step into mapping. Here are a few important ones:[2]

- A value stream is just a pattern. Where this pattern appears, you can apply a consistent set of practices.

- Where there is a customer, there is a value stream. The customer can be either internal to the business (as a stakeholder) or external.
- Every organization contains a network of value streams serving customers. No stream is independent. You have streams connecting directly to external customer outcomes and streams supporting those with internal stakeholder outcomes.
- Working backward is easier than forward. From a given customer outcome, you can discover the stream by asking, "What happened to deliver that?" until you get to the inception.
- Work backward from a specific customer outcome. Customers can be customers for many reasons and get value in many ways. To find the right stream, identify a specific outcome (e.g., an enterprise user using our latest feature or an internal developer deploying their own infrastructure). That way you can focus on the one stream of work that made it happen.
- Value streams can exist inside a mess. One person may have many responsibilities, each of which contributes to different value streams. There may be enormous variation and long delays between stages, which can confound attempts to identify value streams precisely. Part of Flow Engineering's goal is to address this mess and work to create more standard and simplified work.

What Is Value Stream Mapping?

The practice of mapping the flow of work originated more than a century ago and owes much to Frank Gilbreth's work on process charts published in 1921.[3] The practice of Value Stream Mapping was explicitly defined in the book *Learning to See* by John Shook and Mike Rother as a "tool that helps you to see and understand the flow of material and information as a product makes its way through the value stream."[4] Value Stream Mapping identifies the processes involved in the work, as well as metrics on speed, quality, waste, and load at each step of the value stream and for the entire flow.

Paula Thrasher laid out a useful framework in her 2020 DevOps Enterprise Summit talk "Interactive Virtual Value Stream Mapping - Visualizing Flow in a Virtual World." She laid out 5 Rs to identify value streams, starting from a delivered feature or change: choose something recent, real, reach, representative, and road tested.[5]

- Recent: Something in the recent past that you can remember.
- Real: Something that actually has business impact and not merely a software upgrade.
- Reach: Something that traversed the full value stream.
- Representative: Something typical of how you do work and not an emergency request.
- Road tested: Something that is in production, ideally with telemetry and customer feedback.

As we stated earlier, a value stream is just a pattern. Where this pattern appears, you can apply a consistent set of practices. Your organization is a collection of value streams; they're just not visible without mapping. Everything from hiring, customer onboarding, and support to roadmap definition, mergers and acquisitions, and quarterly planning can be treated as a value stream with either an internal or external customer. That means we can map, measure, and improve flow in all of these areas and more.

We identify a value stream by identifying the customer and working backward by asking, "What do we do that allows a customer to receive value?" Then we ask, "What do we do before that?" and so on, until we reach the inception of the workflow. Identifying and getting clarity on the value streams that make up your company reveals the invisible network of relationships and activities that actually drive your business.

Value Stream Mapping is the second of five principles of Lean introduced by James P. Womack and Daniel T. Jones in *Lean Thinking*. The first of these five principles states, "precisely specify value by product."[6]

As Don Reinertsen says in *Principles of Product Development Flow*, "The value added by an activity is the difference in the price that an economically rational buyer would pay for a work product before, and after, the activity is performed."[7] With Value Stream Mapping, we can collectively build clarity on how value is created in a process so that information can be used to reduce waste.

As shown in Figure 6.2, there are five stages to Value Stream Mapping:

1. Stream selection
2. Add activities
3. Add timing
4. Add dimensions
5. Highlight constraint

FIGURE 6.2: The Five Stages of Value Stream Mapping

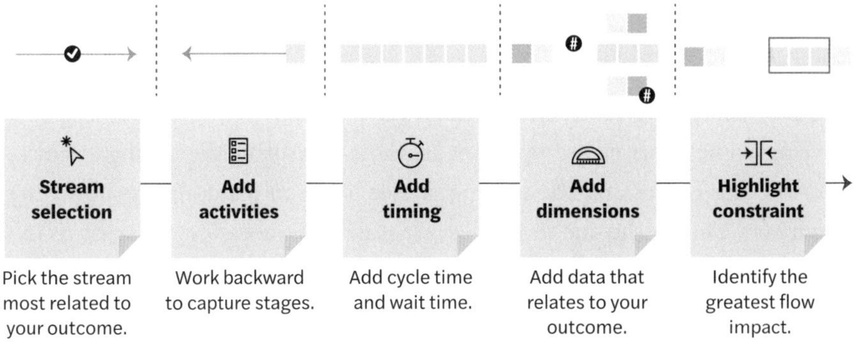

Stream selection	**Add activities**	**Add timing**	**Add dimensions**	**Highlight constraint**
Pick the stream most related to your outcome.	Work backward to capture stages.	Add cycle time and wait time.	Add data that relates to your outcome.	Identify the greatest flow impact.

Through these stages, we gain a clear understanding of the workflow most relevant to the target outcome and where to focus for the greatest improvement.

Teams and individuals often operate within a narrow segment of a value stream. This makes it hard for those contributors to grasp how their work enables or constrains other groups that depend on them. This leads to narrow attempts at improvement that fail to improve the whole system. Any value stream will have a single, rate-limiting step that constrains the overall flow of value delivered, but there are often several low-effort/high-impact opportunities to discover upon mapping.

Value Stream Mapping is a collaborative visualization exercise that reveals this constraint along with other impactful improvement opportunities. This exercise pairs visualization with performance measurement using qualitative and quantitative data. The resulting Value Stream Map serves as a shared visual representation of the work process that is a focal point for team discussions around performance improvement. This rapid version of Value Stream Mapping serves as a quick and easy on-ramp for more detailed and comprehensive maps as buy-in increases. Map quickly; show promise; go further.

For Value Stream Mapping to be effective, the team needs to be aligned on their objectives and aspirations. The purpose of Outcome Mapping (see the previous chapter) is to get a sense of where we are headed, whether we are all in agreement, the challenges and obstacles that could get in our way, what we still need to learn, and what success will look like. The goal with Value Stream Mapping is to create a visualization, supported by data, that reveals very specific improvement opportunities.

Combined with information gained from Dependency Mapping (see Chapter 7), Value Stream Mapping allows us to make accurate investment hypotheses based on data. This may be framed as cost savings, revenue increases, employee satisfaction, or customer satisfaction, among other positive outcomes. The most important aspect is measuring the timing of both the working phases and the waiting phases between handoffs, as shown in Figure 6.3. Time is the one thing we can't scale and the easiest thing for us to waste. It's also quite factual. Looking backward at a flow of work, we see the clock was ticking the entire time. Everything else is far more subjective, so if we can't capture at least the timing, it will likely be too difficult to agree on anything else we could measure.

FIGURE 6.3: Simplified Value Stream Map

Measurements

⚙ Cycle Time	1 hour	6 days	6 days	3 days
	[Start] ⟩	[Stage] ⟩	[Stage] ⟩	[Done]
⧖ Wait Time	12 weeks	2 weeks	3 days	

The format of a simplified Value Stream Map, highlighting the
key measurements of cycle time and wait time.

Value Stream Mapping balances qualitative information about the complete business workflow with a layer of quantitative information about performance and effectiveness. A Value Stream Map frames data from the point of view of contributors in the context of their customers and layers this data over an illustration of flow to make it easy for people inside or outside of an organization to understand a process.

Value Streams vs. Customer Journey

Customer Journey Maps depict a customer's journey from the moment that they identify a need through the moment they take interest in, purchase, use, and recommend a product or service. The Customer Journey Map is framed from the customer's point of view and represents their internal experience.[8]

Mapping the customer journey is a way for marketing, sales, product management, user experience, and business strategists to visualize and reason about the customer's experience at each stage of their interaction. Developing a sense of the customers' journey allows organizations to ease the path to providing what customers need.

Value Stream Maps also focus on the customer's experience of value. But unlike Customer Journey Maps, Value Stream Maps provide a behind-the-scenes look at the work that goes into delivering any valuable aspect of that journey. While the Customer Journey Map traces the customer's external experience with a product, Value Stream Maps depict the internal flow that makes the product possible. Table 6.1 (see page 84) highlights the differences between these two kinds of maps.

Many organizations are familiar with describing and working to improve the customer journey. But organizations (especially knowledge work organizations) are typically less familiar with the principles of designing workflows that are central to value stream performance.

As detailed in Figure 6.4 (see page 85), the customer journey is enabled by the value streams supporting it. The value streams of the organization provide the value that motivates and fulfills the customer journey. This interconnection of streams with each other and the customer journey forms the network of value streams we'll discuss further in Part 3.

Customer journeys are *the reason* your business is in business, and value streams are *how* your business is in business. By looking at the customer journey, we can work backward from customer outcomes to the stream of work that enables those outcomes. Every value stream either directly enables a customer journey or supports another value stream that is. If you're familiar with your customer's journey, you're well on your way to understanding your organization in terms of flow and mapping your path to better customer outcomes.

TABLE 6.1: Differences between Customer Journey Maps and Value Stream Maps

Aspect	Customer Journey Map	Value Stream Map
Perspective	External (from the customer's viewpoint).	Internal (from the organization's and stakeholder's viewpoints).
Definition	The series of interactions or steps a customer goes through when interacting with a product or service.	The sequence of activities required to design, produce, and deliver a product or service to a customer, capturing both work and information flows.
Primary Focus	Understanding and improving the customer's experience and relationship with a brand.	Identifying and eliminating waste in processes to improve overall efficiency.
Goal	Enhance customer satisfaction, loyalty, and overall experience.	Increase process efficiency, reduce waste, and improve delivery or production flow.
Components	Touch points, emotions, channels, pain points, and stages like awareness, consideration, purchase, retention, and advocacy.	Processes, flow of work and information, cycle times, queues, value-adding and non–value-adding activities.
Key Metrics	Customer satisfaction, Net Promoter Score (NPS), churn rate, Customer Effort Score (CES).	Lead time, cycle time, work-in-process, throughput, quality, value-added ratio. (See appendix for details.)

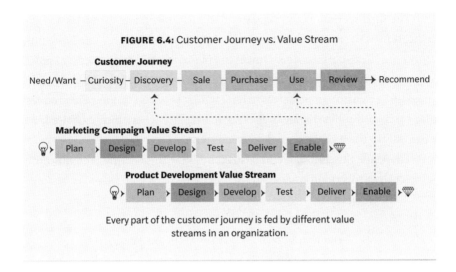

FIGURE 6.4: Customer Journey vs. Value Stream

Every part of the customer journey is fed by different value streams in an organization.

The traditional way of representing a Value Stream Map is shown in Figure 6.5 (see page 86). It is divided into three sections:

1. Information flows
2. Material flows
3. Lead time ladder

This diagram originated from the material and information flow diagrams used in the Toyota Production System. The information flow section may include detailed depictions of all the databases that track a production system, but it often simply depicts the most basic piece of information in a production process: a customer placing an order with a supplier.

The material flow aspect of the Value Stream Map depicts the production process. Knowledge work doesn't primarily deal with material objects, so the designation "material flow" is absent from most diagrams. Nevertheless, this is the heart of the diagram—the representation of the sequence of processes that move from raw materials (which in software development is typically just an idea) to a finished product (working software). Each process in this section can be annotated with relevant metrics, especially about load (items currently being processed in this step), time (cycle time + wait time), and quality (often the percentage of work completed successfully at this step).

The final section of the diagram, the lead time ladder, provides a visual indication of the most important metric in the process: time. Time is the only truly nonrenewable resource. Time is the main resource consumed by knowledge workers as they contemplate, discuss, write, and so on. And time is the main thing a customer perceives to be standing between making their request and having it fulfilled. Time is also the main place where inefficiencies hide, especially in the waiting period between steps.

The Value Stream Map emphasized in Flow Engineering is significantly simpler than this traditional diagram (Figure 6.5) but still gives special deference to tracking time.

FIGURE 6.5: The Traditional Form of Representing a Value Stream Map for Manufacturing

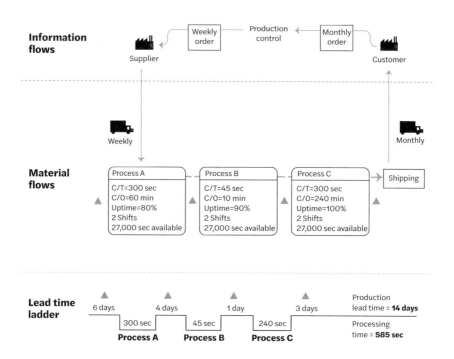

Source: Image adapted from Daniel Penfield, "Value Stream Map Parts," Wikimedia Commons, accessed November 2023, under Creative Commons Attribution-Share Alike 3.0 Unported license.

There have been many excellent books written about applying traditional Value Stream Mapping to digital work, beginning with Mary and Tom Poppendieck's *Lean Software Development* and continuing with Karen Martin and Mike Osterling's *Value Stream Mapping* and quite recently with Gary Rupp's encyclopedic *Driving DevOps with Value Stream Management*. Our goal with Flow Engineering is to build on the traditional practice by incorporating the simplest possible version of Value Stream Mapping to help teams get started and address the on-ramp gap (as explained earlier).

In our experience, Value Stream Mapping is widely espoused but not frequently practiced. There are many highly disciplined software engineering teams relying on sophisticated performance improvement processes. But for every sophisticated team, there are ten more teams that are floundering and struggling even to clearly understand their corporate goals, let alone to optimize their process.

With Flow Engineering we rely on a very simple version of a Value Stream Map that anyone can easily understand and create, as shown in Figure 6.6. For teams that are not yet familiar with Value Stream Maps, it's important to start with such a simple and lightweight approach. This is faster, and thus less expensive, to create, and it is also simpler to understand for the uninitiated. As you build familiarity, the other texts mentioned above can help you layer on more advanced techniques.

FIGURE 6.6: A Simple Flow Engineering Value Stream Map

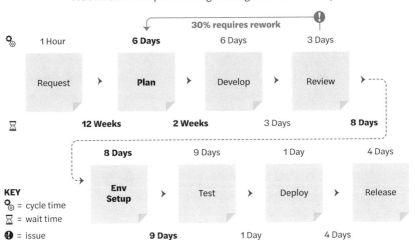

The most basic representation of a value stream begins with visualizing the sequence of activities involved in producing and delivering value to a customer. We then add metrics of cycle time (process time) and wait time to the visualization to complete the Value Stream Map, as seen in Figure 6.6. Often just that level of detail is sufficient to inform improvement efforts, but we can go well beyond the basics as needs or opportunities arise.

As the team discusses and investigates the Value Stream Map, it's natural to start annotating it with additional information as relevant. If there's a large backlog at one step, we may note the number of items in the backlog. If items are typically sent back from one step to a previous step, we may annotate this also. (See again Figure 6.6.) But those metrics are added in a just-in-time fashion as investigations indicate the need. This allows for an initial version of the map to be completed quickly and for the team to prioritize gathering data on the areas of most pressing need rather than aiming for complete data on every step.

One of the most valuable parts of this minimal Value Stream Map is that it doesn't take a massive investment of time from the team involved (especially if it's facilitated professionally). It's hard to convince a team that you're focused on eliminating waste and improving flow when the team has to stop what they're doing for a week!

CASE STUDY | **Sprint-Level Current State Value Stream Mapping**

A client was struggling to keep up with the demand for small updates from their users. They did an Outcome Mapping exercise that helped them settle on the goal of moving from monthly releases to biweekly releases. They then undertook a Value Stream Mapping exercise to clarify how their process could be improved to support this goal.

They began by reiterating the desired outcome in the top left corner of the map (see Figure 6.7): "Get to two-week releases." Stating the goal up front and keeping it visual focuses the team's efforts, making sure they don't get distracted trying to chase things that won't serve the goal. Similar to stating the agenda for a meeting, this saves time and effort and keeps people on the same page.

Since the team was working in four-week sprints, doubling the release frequency implied condensing all of the sprint activities into a two-week period. They started by enumerating the processes that happen in these sprints to determine how the process might be condensed. The goal in making this explicit is to identify activities that might be wasting time, duplicating efforts, or incurring penalties. For example, if sprint planning currently takes 1.5 hours every four weeks, will it be efficient for the team to do that twice as often?

FIGURE 6.7: Example of a Completed Value Stream Map

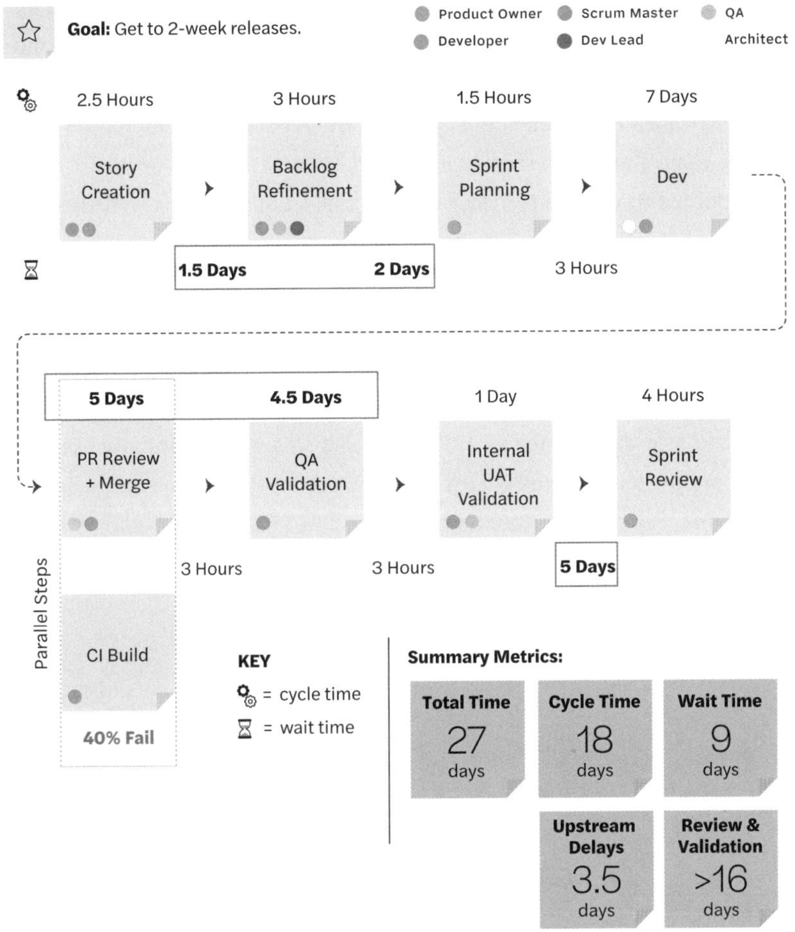

The value stream map is typically laid out in one horizontal flow. We have broken it here to better fit the page. Parallel steps are represented inside the dotted line box.

The team listed all the serial and parallel processes, the time these processes took, and the wait time between each step. They then added up the total time as well as subsets of the process that looked concerning so they could identify a constraint. The bottom right-hand corner of Figure 6.7 shows those summary metrics in pink.

The total process currently takes twenty-seven days (the lead time). That clearly won't fit into a two-week sprint. Of that, eighteen days is cycle time, while nine days is wait time. (Note that the pull request [PR] process is listed as taking five days, which presumably implies additional hidden wait time.)

Reducing wait time (one-third of the total time) is a big opportunity. The team was also concerned about how long it took to begin initial work and how much time was required to review and test completed work. It takes 3.5 days just to get started on work after an important improvement has been identified (which slows the team's ability to start building) and a total of sixteen days for testing (almost double the amount of time spent actually building). It's not uncommon in many organizations to spend more time testing and validating than building. Within this test and validation time, there are typically many hidden delays.

This big picture analysis helped the team identify three main hot spots, outlined in red in Figure 6.7. The first concern was the initial delay from the time a work item is identified to when the team actually starts development. The second concern was the peer review (PR) and quality assurance (QA) process, which together are the longest steps in the process. The third concern was the five-day waiting period after user acceptance testing (UAT) and before deployment to production and sprint review.

Why It Works: Gaining Perspective to Build Clarity

Committing to something where you may not directly feel or even witness the benefit is a stretch. It's a hard ask from people because it's often intangible and something people haven't done before. It's hard to trust that it's going to pay off. Value Stream Mapping certainly doesn't sell itself from that perspective. But the power of a collaborative mapping exercise is that everyone can be engaged. Contrast this with deadly boring meetings with zero engagement.

There are many reasons Value Stream Mapping is so powerful, but here are a few key points.

Perspective

Stepping back allows us to see the perspectives of others. Collaborating to create a Value Stream Map fosters a sense of empathy with unfamiliar roles and domains. It instills a sense that the team workflow is a system that can be developed. This invites creativity and optimization ideas to come from multiple people within the team. And this allows the team to build shared vision and goals and inspire creativity by designing a future state.

Systems Thinking and Visibility

Systems thinking and visibility help us see the whole picture so we can understand what to change. Value Stream Mapping promotes systems thinking because it provides a comprehensive view of the entire process or system rather than focusing on isolated parts. This holistic approach allows organizations to identify and understand the interconnections and dependencies within their workflows, enabling them to pinpoint inefficiencies and bottlenecks more effectively.

By mapping the entire value stream, from initial input to final output, organizations can see how individual components interact and impact the overall system. This insight facilitates more informed decision-making, aligns efforts with organizational goals, and promotes a deeper understanding of how changes in one area can affect others, leading to more effective and sustainable improvements. This exercise is often the first time that teams have visualized or measured the end-to-end process for delivering software. Typically one or more parts of the value stream consume a disproportionate amount of the total lead time.

Performance Measurement

As is often said, "What gets measured gets managed." Value Stream Mapping is a powerful tool for enabling data-driven decision-making about workflow improvements. A Value Stream Map can convert the vague and unknown into concrete, quantifiable insights into a team's processes, allowing them to base decisions on solid evidence rather than assumptions or intuition.

This data-centric approach also facilitates identifying specific areas for improvement, understanding the impact of potential changes, and tracking the effectiveness of implemented solutions. Measurement is crucial to separate facts from opinions and to bring everyone to the same quantifiable understanding.

Identification of Constraints

As the famous saying goes, "The constraint is the way." Eliyahu M. Goldratt's Theory of Constraints aims to prevent a common mistake seen in collaborative work and especially in knowledge work. It's easy to invest substantial time, money, and effort on improvement efforts that have little actual impact on customers. We can even have a negative impact if we work without the entire system flow in mind.

DevOps rose to prominence as a remedy to the problem caused in downstream operations due to the increased pace of Agile Software Development. Removing the constraint in operations was the key to unlocking the throughput of Agile development efforts upstream. Value Stream Mapping allows us to see that dynamic and reveal the flow constraint, which is where our efforts will have maximum impact.

Revealing Hidden Opportunities

Opportunities often lie hidden by daily work. Understanding how context of individual work affects customer satisfaction enhances employee engagement and motivation, as it makes the impact of their efforts more visible. This perspective is especially crucial as the toil of daily tasks tends to crowd out the overarching objectives and the next steps toward these goals.

Our consistent experience is that simply cocreating a Current State Value Stream Map reveals issues that allow teams to get at least 20% of their time back immediately. Common insights include seeing that there are two processes that can be done in parallel or that a meeting that isn't delivering much value could be replaced by an email. These low-hanging fruits ensure that Value Stream Mapping exercises more than pay for themselves. Twenty percent time reduction is equivalent to one day a week. How much is that worth to an organization?

Optimizing productivity by minimizing wasted time and effort increases the value gained from the talent and energy we have available. A Value Stream Map can capture information about wasted effort, cognitive load, collaboration issues, quality gaps, or anything else you want to layer onto the basic structure of steps and timing. Let's take a moment to explore what Value Stream Mapping often looks like in a real-world situation.

BOLT GLOBAL | **Continued**

To understand how to improve the throughput of their product development life cycle, Sharon gathered her team as well as key contributors upstream and downstream to map their current workflow.

They started by pasting the target outcome, "Release twice as often," from their Outcome Mapping session onto the top right corner of their canvas. Sharon wanted to make sure this outcome remained the focus of their mapping efforts and make it easy to refer back to.

Next, Sharon and the group laid out all the activities involved in contributing to their delivery of value, working backward from the delivery of their last release. After laying out each activity step, they layered on measurement of each activity's cycle time and the wait time between.

The team discovered a number of clear opportunities just from reviewing the timing measurement. Given this was her first time with Value Stream Mapping, Sharon decided against layering on additional information like quality, roles, value-added time, etc. until she'd been able to show some results and gain further buy-in.

As shown in Figure 6.8 (see page 94), in a simplified example of their value stream, they noticed that the environment setup step takes 45% of the total time in the value stream. If they tackle this constraint, they could be most of the way toward their target outcome and then be able to look for other bottlenecks and constraints. They could also pursue multiple issues simultaneously if they have the capacity.

Having narrowed down the constraint, Sharon and the team begin to dig deeper to find out how to address it.

FIGURE 6.8: Identifying a Constraint in the Value Stream

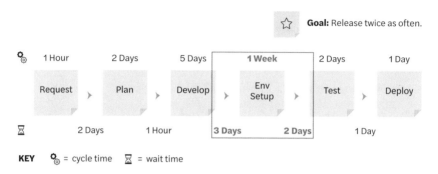

How to Conduct Value Stream Mapping

Structuring Invitation

Invite representative stakeholders involved in a common value stream to come together to clarify the current work process so improvements can be identified. The group maps a path to addressing key questions:

- What sequence of activities constitutes the complete workflow?
- What is the measured performance of the complete workflow?
- What is our highest-impact improvement opportunity?

Aim to take about ninety minutes at a brisk pace. Allocate at least two hours if this is your first time.

How Space Is Arranged and Materials Needed

- Use a digital collaboration tool or a physical dry-erase board or paper and sticky notes.
- Allow for space to lay out eight to twenty distinct steps horizontally.

How Participation Is Distributed

- The group should include up to ten representatives of the key contributors to the value stream.
- Everyone participates according to their knowledge of the step in question and the value stream overall.

How Groups Are Configured

- One main notetaker builds the Value Stream Map on a shared board.
- Other contributors discuss to add, remove, or amend aspects of that shared map.

Sequence of Steps and Time Allocation

1. STREAM SELECTION

Start by identifying the particular value stream you seek to improve. Follow the principles from the "Where's the Stream?" section presented earlier in this chapter to help you. (We've provided a simplified list here to help.)

- Work backward from a specific customer outcome (e.g., a new feature delivered).
- Recent: Something in the recent past that you can remember.
- Real: Something that actually has business impact and not merely a software upgrade.
- Reach: Something that traversed the full value stream.
- Representative: Something typical to how you do work and not an emergency request.
- Road-tested: Something that is in production, ideally with telemetry and customer feedback.

2. ADD ACTIVITIES

The whole group works backward from the stage where value is delivered (see Figure 6.9), plotting each distinct step (as a note or item) in sequence back to the start of the value stream (the request that triggered the work). The simplest systems are just a linear sequence of steps. You may also have parts of the process that run in parallel, in which case you can denote that by showing one step above the other. (10 mins.)

FIGURE 6.9: Example Value Stream Map for Software Development

3. ADD TIMING

Next, estimate the typical cycle time spent on each step and write this *above* that step (10 mins.). Then, estimate the typical delay between each step and write this *underneath* the gap between steps. (10 mins.) Then, highlight the cycle or wait times with the longest durations as possible improvement candidates (2 mins.), as shown in Figure 6.10.

FIGURE 6.10: Sample Value Stream Map Showing Cycle Timing and Wait Timing

4. ADD DIMENSIONS AND TOTAL METRICS

Sum the total cycle time from all steps and the total wait time between steps. Then, sum these to determine the end-to-end process (lead time) duration. Add the totals to the bottom corner of the space. (2 mins.) Add any extra dimensions that seem relevant to your target outcome, such as percent complete and accurate (%C&A), and total them if they're quantifiable (Figure 6.11).

FIGURE 6.11: Annotated Value Stream Map

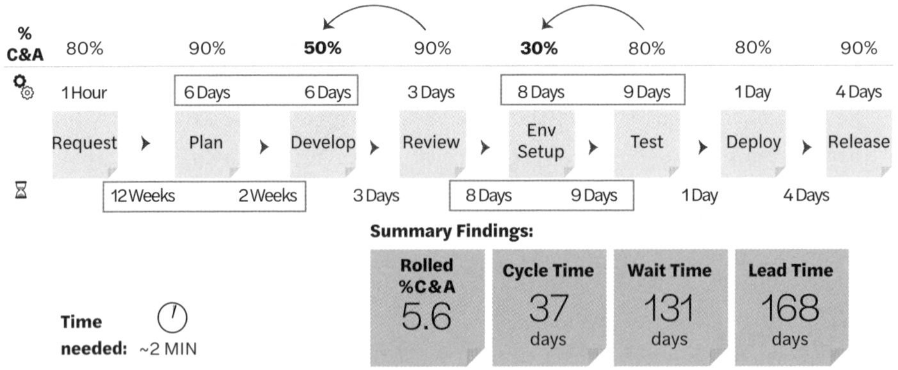

| % C&A | 80% | 90% | **50%** | 90% | **30%** | 80% | 80% | 90% |

| | 1 Hour | 6 Days | 6 Days | 3 Days | 8 Days | 9 Days | 1 Day | 4 Days |

| Request | Plan | Develop | Review | Env Setup | Test | Deploy | Release |

| | 12 Weeks | 2 Weeks | 3 Days | 8 Days | 9 Days | 1 Day | 4 Days |

Summary Findings:

	Rolled %C&A	Cycle Time	Wait Time	Lead Time
	5.6	37 days	131 days	168 days

Time needed: ~2 MIN

This annotated version of the map depicts percent complete and accurate (%C&A) for each stage, bold text for particular areas of concern, rework (curved arrows) for stages where errors are detected, and totals for cumulative measures.

Most metrics across the Value Stream Map are summarized by simply totaling them up. One exception is the %C&A, which is summarized as the "Rolled %C&A". This is the product of all the %C&A values in sequence (i.e., 60% × 50% = 30%). This reflects how quality issues at any stage limit the flow of complete and accurate work at all later stages.

Other information, such as roles owning each stage, can be placed as colored dots with a corresponding legend, or tools used in each stage can be depicted in small notes below each stage. (See Figure 6.12.)

FIGURE 6.12: Example Small-Scale Value Stream Map

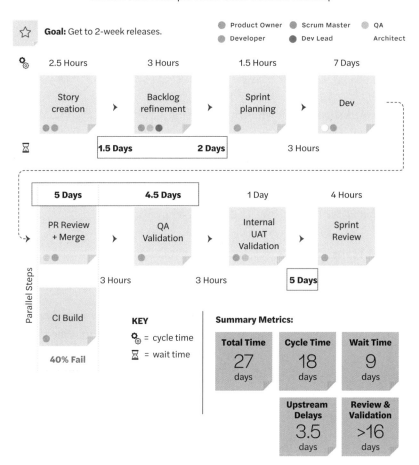

A small-scale Value Stream Map depicting the target outcome, roles, totals, hot spots, and parallel activities.

5. HIGHLIGHT CONSTRAINT

As a group, identify the improvement candidate (constraint) that would make the single biggest improvement to the end-to-end duration. This becomes the target for future work and is the constraint used in Dependency Mapping, as explored in the next chapter. (5 mins.) (See Figure 6.13.)

FIGURE 6.13: Identifying a Constraint on a Value Stream Map

KEY   = cycle time   = wait time

The workshop is complete when the group can answer the initial questions with shared confidence:

- What sequence of activities constitutes the complete workflow?
- What is the measured performance of the complete workflow?
- What is our highest-impact improvement opportunity?

Tips and Traps

- Use an Outcome Mapping session to help the group clarify their goals before starting a Value Stream Mapping session.
- Mapping can be accelerated by providing a scaffold representing a typical value stream map for that activity, which is then modified by the group. This can be as simple as the structure shown in Figure 6.10, starting with the steps Request, Plan, Develop, Review, Test, Deploy, and Release. This not only saves time but provides participants unfamiliar with Value Stream Mapping a clear reference point to orient themselves.
- Communicate to the team that the current workflow has evolved in this way for countless reasons, and we can't change the past. What's important is seeing the current reality, accepting it, and working to improve

it. We must start from where we are. There's no sense imagining where else we could have been.

- Likewise, avoid referring to the value stream as it is intended to operate or will operate after improvement. Focus on the most recent iteration or a representation of several recent iterations. We'll get to the future state in Chapter 8.

- The team must remain focused on what happens currently, not how the process was designed, how it ideally works, or how it will work in the future. Consider the last time the stream was traversed—and ideally the last few times to get a more representative sample for measurement.

- Focus on what's happening most often. This involves repeatedly asking the team, "How long does it usually take?" and reminding them that "it depends" isn't an acceptable excuse for deliberation. Recency bias and a number of other cognitive biases hinder our ability to make these judgments without facilitation.

- If you're looking for accurate information, it's helpful to work from right to left (from customer outcome backward to initiation) because working backward disrupts the normal process of reconstructing memories based on expectations and general knowledge, as Fiona Gabbert, Lorraine Hope, and Ronald P. Fisher explain in "Protecting Eyewitness Evidence."[9]

- Strive to represent a typical, recent flow of the value stream. If the last iteration wasn't anomalous, refer back to it specifically. If it was, you can still use it with clear notation of the anomaly.

- Including a sponsoring stakeholder can deepen their understanding of the process as well as demonstrate a serious commitment to the improvement effort. Just make sure a high-powered individual doesn't motivate contributors to share overly rosy accounts.

- Avoid allowing a few people to dominate the session; check in with those who have fallen silent to provide input, offer feedback, or ask questions.

- Don't try to thoroughly accommodate edge cases. If the flow seems to branch based on variations in process, capture it in a note but focus on what happens most often.

- Don't settle on "it depends" to describe a variable flow of work; have an expert make a guess and offer it up for a second opinion.
- Don't aim for precise measurements. For our purposes, rough estimates are sufficient.
- If you struggle to get input for estimation or any detail, it can help to make a guess as the facilitator and allow the group to correct you if they can.
- If there's disagreement among the participants on how long an activity takes, unless you can get consensus quickly, simply take the worst-case time.
- To add an extra dimension of clarity to highly variable timing, you can capture best-case time and worst-case time. This can reveal the extent of volatility that causes unpredictable delivery.
- Focus the scope of the Value Stream Map on steps that are within this group's ability to influence. It can be demotivating to agonize over what can't be changed.
- Information flow is one of the most important additional dimensions to add to a map, as it can have a serious impact on quality, throughput, and value. Use Dependency Mapping (see Chapter 7) to better understand how information flow may be relevant to the constraint (or candidate constraints).
- It can be very helpful for both a facilitator and the mapping participants to start from a Customer Journey Map (as depicted in Figure 6.4) if that map is available and known by most of the participants. Leveraging a familiar frame of reference can be a great starting point to introduce the value stream to folks who haven't seen a Value Stream Map before.
- One of the key gaps that sabotages efforts to effectively map value streams is constraining the scope before you start. John Cutler outlines it in a list of traps for visualizing work: "There might be a high PIP—planning in progress—or lots of work marked as Done, but not in the hands of customers. There's a fear that tracking stuff 'too early' will 'muddy up the system.' There's a fear that tracking stuff 'after finishing' will make it seem like the team is too slow."[10] If the full scope of work is not acknowledged, it can't be addressed.

Riffs and Variations

It pays to have skilled, outside facilitation for this process for a few reasons:

- A perspective from outside the organization is far less likely to bring an agenda, bias, or political influence to the process, which will drive superior results.
- Collaborative mapping can be painful if the group loses an effective focus, such as drifting into focusing on past decisions rather than improving the current system of work.
- A skilled facilitator can maintain a positive and constructive environment for mapping.
- A skilled facilitator knows when digging may turn up gold and when to move on. They will know what questions to ask and what seems like a strange measurement based on experience with other teams.

All of this saves valuable time and maximizes value. Gathering a team can be expensive if you're not getting value from the session, and it can impact morale and trust if the team feels they're wasting time. A skilled facilitator can likely complete a session in half the time while keeping the team engaged. You may already have Agile coaches, Scrum facilitators, dojo trainers, community of practice leads, or teachers in your group. They may have a head start in building their facilitation skills. It's all right to pilot the process with a facilitator and team willing to try and learn!

Expanded maps can add additional dimensions, including the following:

- Quality: Percentage of work done completely and accurately to expectation at each step (referred to as %C&A, percent complete and accurate).
- Efficiency: Time in each step spent on value-adding work as a percentage of total time.
- Work in progress: How much work is typically in progress at each step.
- Queues: Where work items accumulate before being acted on.
- Roles: Which roles are involved in each step.
- Tools: Systems involved in each activity.
- Artifacts and deliverables: What each step produces.

Figure 6.14 depicts how additional dimensions can be added atop a simple Value Stream Map to add context depending on the target outcome.

FIGURE 6.14: Value Stream Map with VAT and %C&A

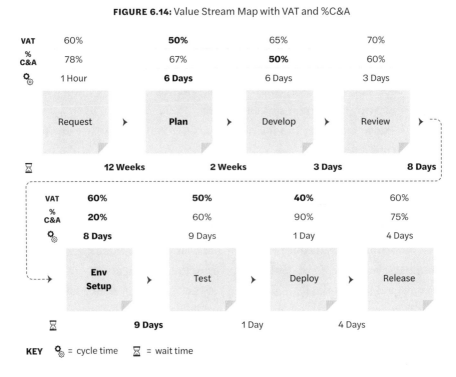

A simple Value Stream Map showing added dimensions of value-added time (VAT) and percent complete and accurate (%C&A) for each stage.

These added dimensions are optional only because, depending on the target outcome, they may be more or less relevant. It's valuable to start simple and layer on detail rather than aim for too much and exceed the appetite and patience of the group.

Tracking the quality of work at each step typically requires intensive data-gathering and analysis. It can also be a bit of a sensitive topic when teams have not previously given each other clear and kind feedback on work quality. The way of approaching this taught in Karen Martin and Mike Osterling's *Value Stream Mapping* is to record this as the percent complete and accurate

(%C&A) at each step.[11] This metric means what percentage of work leaving this step is both complete and accurate and thus doesn't need to be sent back to a previous step for rework and clarification.

Value Stream Mapping should be performed repeatedly to periodically reestablish clarity within a team. Once mapping is performed and improvements are implemented, the constraint will emerge elsewhere, and mapping can reveal a new constraint candidate to continue progress. This is often achieved by mapping every three to six months depending on the scope of improvement.

It's possible to parallelize the exercise by having each participant create their own representation of the value stream (and associated data). These representations can then be presented and discussed with the team before reconciling them into a unified representation. This challenges and engages each contributor to refine and build their understanding. Merging the maps reveals the difference between each individual perspective, providing clear feedback for each contributor to learn from. This also provides the most complete "raw data."

It's also possible to map asynchronously in environments where buy-in and time are scarce. Jim Benson, cocreator of Lean Coffee, shared a story of working with procurement in a large construction firm. He allowed a big group to build out a map as individual contributors over five days. Over time, more and more people gathered to build and discuss the map. In the end, the map lived on the same wall and evolved over the next six months of value stream improvements.[12]

There are similar approaches that may be more compatible with your current practices, such as event storming or swimlane diagrams, but if there isn't any form of measurement applied to the flow, it can be challenging to identify and align on a constraint.

If next steps seem unclear or blocked, you can use 15% Solutions[13] to define a first safe step. This is an exercise from Liberating Structures that helps people overcome a feeling of overwhelm or powerlessness in the face of large challenges. It prompts participants to answer the question, "What can you do without more resources or authority that would get you 15% of the way to a solution?"

It's possible to map extremely complicated workflows with Value Stream Mapping, but with added detail comes the trade-off of time and readability. Aim for the "Goldilocks zone" of just enough detail to take confident next steps. It may be necessary to craft a map with many notes or comments to capture the insights and observations of the team, as shown in pink comment boxes above and below the value stream in Figure 6.15.

FIGURE 6.15: Sample Value Stream Map with Many Notes

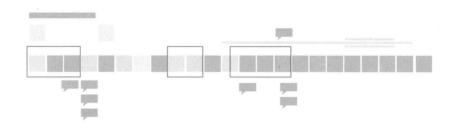

Value Stream Maps can include whatever information is
necessary to drive progress and improvement.

Within a Value Stream Map, you can use visual indicators to draw out other information. For example, Figure 6.15 shows a variety of colors representing the following:

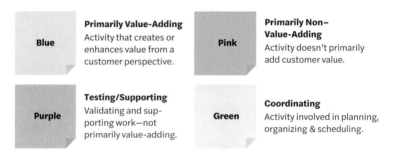

This allows you to do a quick pass with participants to allow them to vote on which of the four they think best applies to each stage. This can help draw attention to critical stages, as opposed to those that may constitute waste.

Ensure the context is made clear: The analysis is focused on activities, not roles. People get understandably very concerned when it may be implied that their role is not adding value.

Data-Gathering Requirements

It can be tempting to believe that you need to gather all of the relevant data before starting on a mapping exercise. That temptation leads directly to the overwhelming reality that data from the development process is typically spread across many systems, not formatted in the way we need, and potentially inaccurate due to data not being adequately maintained. Data also ages quickly, and a few inaccurate data points can distract the group.

But don't worry! You don't need high-precision data. Approximate information is usually the best way to get started. We want to move in small and incremental steps based on a reasonably accurate image of the whole system we're managing. Striving for quality data is a waste of time if you don't need it to expose a constraint.

Since a typical end-to-end process takes days, weeks, or months, uncertainty on the order of hours or even days on a single step may be insignificant. The purpose of Value Stream Mapping is to identify likely bottlenecks in the process so they can be investigated further with Dependency Mapping (see Chapter 7.) Most teams find that 20% of their existing workflow is waste they can get rid of right away.

Each time you run these mapping exercises for a team, you can supplement your initial assessments with more accurate and precise data. Chapter 13 goes into detail about the tools and practices of Value Stream Management as a way to capture and distill the data needed on an ongoing basis.

Yes, we may miss something by trusting the group's estimates. But if the alternative is a mapping process that is long and overwhelming, we suggest aiming for good enough instead.

CASE STUDY | **The Devil is in the Details**

When presenting the methods of Flow Engineering at an Agile conference, Steve was approached by an Agile coach working in a bank. He shared a horror story that had shaken his faith in Value Stream Mapping and made leadership in the bank skeptical of Value Stream Mapping in the future. Why? Their mapping efforts took a room full of victims four full days, where they mapped out an exhaustive two-thousand-step release process. In the end, nobody was happy with the process or the outcome.

They were able to make a second pass and simplify the stream to fifteen steps, but by that point, they were running on empty and severely demotivated. This is an example of the value of starting simple with careful facilitation.

One of the most important jobs for the facilitator is driving the process forward, keeping things simple, and helping the whole group be satisfied with approximations. In Value Stream Mapping, perfect is definitely the enemy of good. Not only is simplicity an enabling constraint, it saves costs, morale, and energy.

Conclusion

Effective action depends on clarity. And clarity begins with orienting our work in its larger context. Value Stream Mapping allows a group to collectively establish a shared mental model of both the goal of their work and the method for carrying it out. This seemingly simple exercise provides individuals with the mental context needed to work effectively as a team.

Our approach to Value Stream Mapping is distilled from more complicated traditional techniques to make it approachable and something teams can engage in regularly. This not only helps improve performance, but it also helps create a unified understanding of what's going on and where we should be focusing our energy.

Stepping back allows us to see the perspectives of others and gain distance from our daily work. Making work visible and, especially, visualizing the end-to-end system of work helps us avoid the trap of local optimization. And measurement provides a qualitative overlay on the work that allows teams to identify trends and set specific goals.

The result of Value Stream Mapping is identifying likely constraints that deserve a deeper inspection through Dependency Mapping (as we explore next). Value Stream Mapping is broad but not deep; Dependency Mapping is deep but not broad. The goal of the next chapter is to uncover the primary factors contributing to constraints by digging deeper.

Key Takeaways

- Value Stream Mapping can be quick and effective for sensemaking, alignment, and setting focus (i.e., building clarity).
- A modest amount of thoughtful measurement can highlight constraints that are impacting flow.
- Despite the measurement present in the map, simple Value Stream Mapping is more qualitative than quantitative. Detail and accuracy aren't necessary to get valuable insights.

CHAPTER 7

Dependency Mapping

"Everything is connected to everything else, but not equally strongly."

DONELLA MEADOWS, *Thinking in Systems*

THE PURPOSE OF DEPENDENCY MAPPING is to dig deeper into areas of the value stream that appear to be constraints in order to build clarity on the process and metrics of that part of the stream. (See Figure 7.1.)

FIGURE 7.1: Dependency Mapping Primarily Serves to Enhance the Clarity Built by Value Stream Mapping

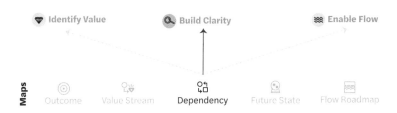

Nothing exists in isolation. Value Stream Mapping shows how each role or part in a process fits into a broader whole. Importantly, Value Stream Mapping can also reveal the impediments to flow for a team. An exhaustive Value Stream Mapping process would include fine-grained process mapping and detailed metrics gathering at every step in the process. But the rapid Value Stream Mapping done in Flow Engineering does not require detailed metrics on each step of the value stream. We intentionally sacrifice precision for speed and ease. We aim to gather just enough information to identify a critical constraint.

Dependency Mapping is specifically designed to improve the resolution on this critical constraint so we can identify precise remedies. Dependency Mapping also gives us a chance to investigate the chain of dependencies that contribute to the critical constraint.

The technical equivalent to this practice is a "trace," such as a stack trace of a running application or tracing the route of a packet through a network, allowing you to discover and then debug a problem by isolating a general area and then digging deep. With Dependency Mapping, we also aim to gather just enough information to uncover viable opportunities for improvement. We're not aiming to map every dependency across every stage of the Value Stream Map. Instead, we're aiming simply to run a trace on a problematic section of the flow (as shown in Figure 7.2) so the return on invested time and effort is extremely high.

FIGURE 7.2: Dependency Mapping Targets Only Dependencies That Impact the Constraint

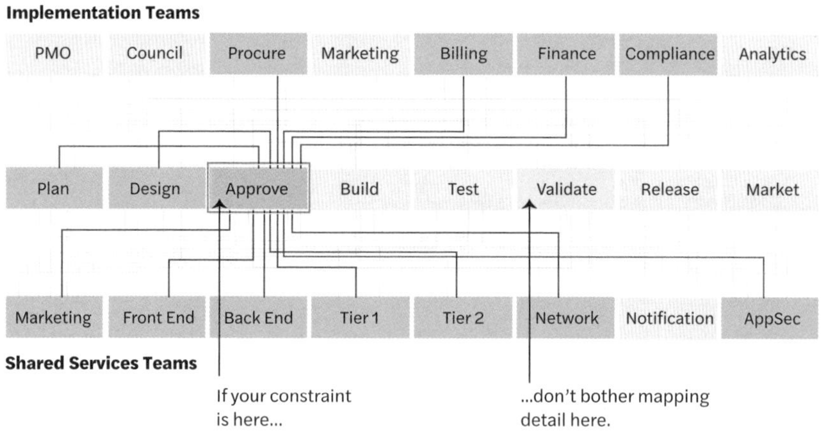

One of the biggest risks in any improvement initiative is improving the wrong thing. Extra processing is one of the seven types of waste identified in Lean (see Chapter 8.) It's wasteful to improve part of the process that doesn't have a significant impact on the whole. It's also wasteful to gather more data than necessary to determine where improvements can be found. The purpose of Dependency Mapping is to challenge our assumptions about where problems lie by digging deeper into likely hot spots.

There are countless optimizations that a team could make, but all but a few of them are useless in improving throughput and quality. Figure 7.3 shows some of the many dependencies a team might have, but it doesn't provide any clear indications of which might need to be addressed to improve performance. The combination of Value Stream Mapping (for comprehensiveness at a low resolution) and Dependency Mapping (to improve resolution and identify indirect causes of problems) provides a way to identify improvements that can have a material effect on team performance.

FIGURE 7.3: Example of the Extent of Dependencies

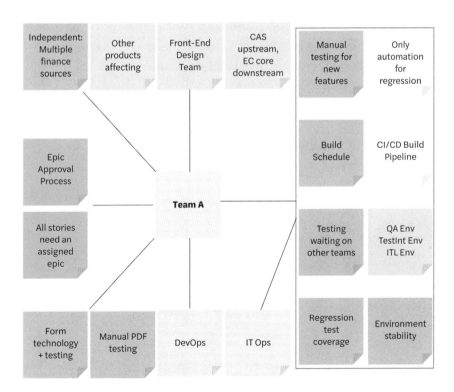

Visualizing all of a team's dependencies can be useful but doesn't identify what might need to improve.

There are several types of diagrams that show cross-team or cross-system dependencies, but they're rarely able to show the impact of those dependencies on the flow of work. And they're rarely linked to a constraint, which means they take longer to produce and can be distracting. Our focus is primarily on finding the constraint holding back a single value stream. However, it's common that addressing that constraint will also aid many other streams. The goal is a Pareto Effect (or Pareto Principle)—that is, achieving 80% of the impact with 20% of the effort.

What Is Dependency Mapping?

Dependency mapping is a lightweight collaborative process for building clarity on a value stream's key dependencies. The constraint in the value stream is analyzed to identify any external teams, information, tools, or processes required for that piece of work. This is often the starting point for a cross-team investigation to address the limitation. Similar to technical Dependency Mapping, where you reveal all the libraries, APIs, databases, etc. that an application requires to operate, we do the same here—but for workflow.

As shown in Figure 7.4, there are five stages to Dependency Mapping:

1. Start with constraints.
2. Zoom in on a constraint by creating a sub-Value Stream Map.
3. Identify hot spots.
4. Identify direct causes for hot spots.
5. Dig deeper into the constraint.

FIGURE 7.4: The Five Stages of Dependency Mapping

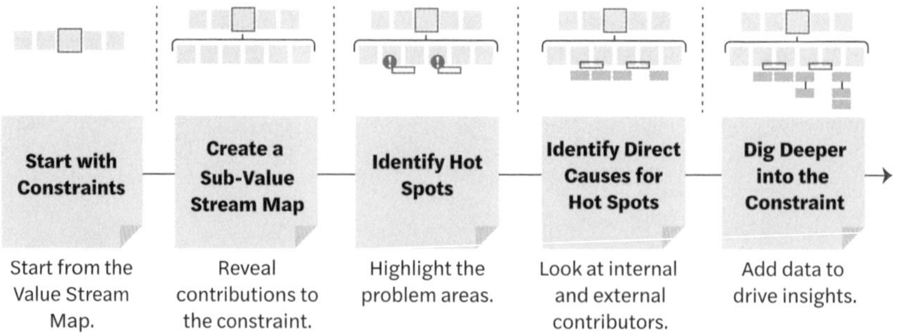

Start with Constraints	Create a Sub-Value Stream Map	Identify Hot Spots	Identify Direct Causes for Hot Spots	Dig Deeper into the Constraint
Start from the Value Stream Map.	Reveal contributions to the constraint.	Highlight the problem areas.	Look at internal and external contributors.	Add data to drive insights.

With these stages, we gain a clear understanding of the dependencies most impacting the constraint and which focal point within the dependencies will enable the most effective improvement.

What Do We Mean by Dependencies?

As with the other maps, Dependency Mapping begins with visibility: we need to become aware of and be able to communicate direct and indirect dependencies and their impact on the team before we can hope to address them. In Dependency Mapping, we identify the immediate dependencies that cause a constraint and which team is responsible for them. We then dig into understanding what processes underlie that dependency and whether those processes depend on other groups. Often, we don't have the knowledge needed to define these additional levels, which means that even mapping dependencies requires us to collaborate with leaders in other departments. Since addressing those dependencies will almost certainly require collaboration from other departments, beginning by building shared clarity alongside other teams is a powerful foundation for making improvements.

Factors that can cause a constraint are endless, so open discussion is important so that everyone can share insights and compare perspectives. Remember, assumptions on how to improve are just hypotheses at this point. Only by carrying out the change and demonstrating improvement can we be sure that we correctly identified the constraint and the appropriate remedy. Such is life.

This experimental approach can be found in Lean, Agile, and DevOps management approaches and requires an intellectual honesty that is rare but priceless in the business world. Factors that can cause constraints include other shared services departments, excessive meetings, approval processes, challenging work, too much work in progress, etc.

There can be internal constraints (e.g., there is only a single individual capable of performing a complicated activity or there are tools that we can't use effectively) or external constraints (e.g., a team we hand work off to or a mandatory approval process).

One team we worked with revealed that a process they depended on in each development sprint required them to submit a request to a shared services group. There was a three-business-day service level agreement (SLA) on that request that caused the team to delay parts of their work almost twice a month.

A common example of an external dependency that can affect the team's ability to deliver value is reliance on a Program Management Office (PMO). It's common for PMOs to evaluate requests using a committee composed of part-time participants from other groups. To limit the time required for these members, they often meet only once a month to review the product planning process. In this situation, some decisions may have to wait until the next PMO meeting (or longer) before they can be reviewed and approved. So teams seeking to experiment with an architectural change may first need to get approval from the PMO. Such delays can impact the team's velocity in very serious ways.

Even more commonly, Change Advisory Boards (CABs) sometimes require evaluation of any production change. A change review process that involves architects from outside the team doing the development is often more "change theater" than an actual protective layer. It is rarely possible for a part-time member of a CAB to invest the time and possess the knowledge required to thoroughly evaluate the possible impacts of a change. Decisions are often made on more superficial grounds, such as trusting the track record of the team requesting the change.

Another example is when we need the operations team to customize an environment to support a new feature by installing or upgrading a software package or changing configuration. That process might consistently take four days each time because a four-day SLA has been set. Teams tend to treat the SLA like a deadline and prioritize other work in progress until the SLA is coming to an end. Such a cross-team dependency can impact work in almost every sprint and can account for much of the lead time in delivering a new feature.

Visualizing these dependencies allows the team to think together about the basis of beliefs and observations that have been made explicit. Any member on the team or outside the team is free to review or question the observations because they've been made visible instead of being buried in an email or lost in a distant conversation. It rarely makes sense for a team to do everything themselves. We need to rely on other teams, and nothing is ever truly autonomous. Making structural changes to these team dependencies

can often be the most powerful improvements we can make to a process to improve flow.

What Dependency Mapping Enables

It's incredibly easy to foster misunderstanding in a large, siloed environment. Each group often has its own goals, agenda, and workload, combined with a unique perspective. If one team is being impacted by another, it can be extremely challenging to get on the same page with a ticket, a document, or even a meeting. Having visual resources allows you to point to specific pain points and show the larger context of what you're working with and aiming to achieve. This can work wonders to bridge the gaps created by silos. Beyond that, maps can provide a tool to build mutual respect, empathy, and even relationships.

Why Dependency Mapping Works: Finding Clogs and Leaks to Enable Flow

There are three main benefits of this approach to Dependency Mapping:

- **Only dig where there's gold.** There's no need to analyze or understand every dependency in the value stream. Your value stream also doesn't exist in a vacuum. Often, the biggest roadblocks are caused by connections to other areas of the organization or lack of internal skills, tools, or resources. By focusing on the most impactful constraint, you can most efficiently and effectively use your time and effort to diagnose the constraint without trying to boil the ocean.
- **Maps can be a Rosetta Stone.** Maps facilitate constructive conversations with peers who don't necessarily speak your language. Addressing dependencies often requires us to cross organizational boundaries, build alliances, and understand others' points of view and priorities. While that might be unfamiliar territory for some, making such changes can

bring enormous benefits to the organization and to the teams involved. With a Dependency Map, you can share a visual representation of your constraint with groups that may be unfamiliar with your value stream and provide them just enough context to help or point you in the right direction.

- **Get a deeper understanding of what people actually do.** Shared services and complicated subsystem teams like databases or infrastructure can seem like a black box from the outside. A Dependency Map provides a visual resource to enable a productive conversation with groups outside your own. With the map, you can highlight unknowns and make it easier for others to fill in gaps in your understanding. While you're at it, you can develop and demonstrate an understanding of what external parties are contributing to the value stream. This helps you cultivate a mutual understanding, trust, and a productive relationship.

BOLT GLOBAL | **Continued**

By mapping their value stream, Sharon's team identified a constraint and a catch. The most impactful constraint in their release flow—the environment setup process—was not actually handled by Sharon's team. They depend on an infrastructure team to provision new environments and data, a process that could take up to twelve days. This step had to be done for every release to ensure they had clean development and testing environments for each of Sharon's three teams. (See Figure 7.5.)

The infrastructure team is run by Karl. His team looks after all the development, testing, and production environments for a dozen product teams. His team is always swamped with work, including constant interruptions from production issues and notifications. They also have long-running projects that they've been working on, for years in some cases. Karl has to essentially ignore any external requests or risk drowning entirely. He's at or above capacity at all times. There's no room for his team to even think about Sharon and her concerns. Even if they were aware of Sharon's target, how could they justify helping out?

Karl's team is very cohesive. They deal with very similar situations every day, so they have very similar perceptions, goals, and activities. This creates a strong team identity. But they regard other teams outside of theirs as entirely separate, somewhat antagonistic groups—even though they work within the same organization. They're *others*. This self-other dichotomy affects the way the team perceives and values others, as well as their views, intentions, and activities.

FIGURE 7.5: Dependency Map of the Constraint: Environment Setup

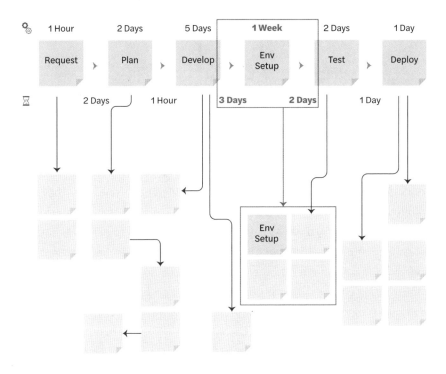

KEY ⚙ = cycle time   ⧖ = wait time

Sharon's team has many dependencies. But the ones she needs to focus on are those that impact her constraint.

Creating cohesion and a unification of effort across an entire organization requires aligning those views, intentions, activities, and identities. This focus can dramatically increase the power of peoples' efforts, much as a weak light can be amplified like a laser if the wavelengths become coherent. As shown in Figure 7.6 (see page 118), shared value facilitates shared clarity. Shared clarity facilitates shared activity. Shared activity facilitates collective identity.

FIGURE 7.6: Gap between Sharon's Team and Karl's Team

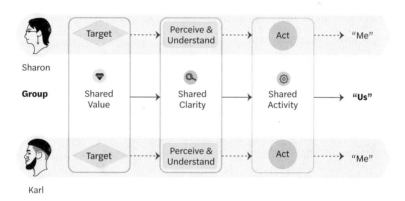

Sharon

Group   Shared   Shared   Shared
              Value   Clarity   Activity

Karl

Bridging the gap between Sharon and Karl requires sharing value, clarity, and activity.

Issues of value, clarity, and flow become harder as you scale the size of a team. For example, Karl and Sharon possess two very different perspectives. They deal with totally different systems, totally different people, and totally different concerns on a day-to-day basis. As a result, they've also got different goals, so their values are not naturally aligned. The classic tension between development and operations in software development arises because developers are tasked with implementing change, whereas operations is tasked with maintaining stability. Individual subgroups within an organization might want to maximize something or minimize something, but as we become more influential in an organization, the challenge increasingly becomes how to appreciate competing points of view and balance competing priorities.

Based on her limited perspective, Sharon might place the blame on Karl, complain about his team, or simply feel powerless and stuck. Such feelings are natural, even if they don't contribute toward a solution. Instead, they tend to make everyone feel unpleasant and pessimistic. One enemy of collaboration is blaming others and feeling entitled that our problems should be everyone else's top priorities. We can't solve every problem, and we won't always succeed in solving even our main problems, but by focusing on specific issues and taking a skillful and strategic approach to addressing them, we maximize our chances of improvement.

As shown in Figure 7.7, Sharon has three assets that she can use to make a case for collaboration. By sharing the Outcome Map, she can help Karl understand how her target outcome is serving shared organizational and customer goals. The Value Stream Map provides a visualization to discuss how she's isolated environment provisioning as a key bottleneck in her team's end-to-end process. And the Dependency Map provides details on how the bottleneck she identified is tied to Karl's team.

This gives Sharon and Karl a chance to jointly discuss the overarching context, to raise doubts and challenges, to identify unknowns, and to specify measures of success. The key in this process is that Sharon and Karl (and any other relevant members of their teams) are jointly involved in the problem-solving process. The power of working together toward a solution in this thinking process can't be overstated.

FIGURE 7.7: Three Assets for Collaboration

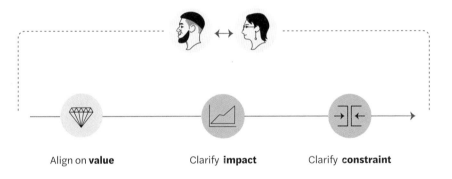

Align on **value**   Clarify **impact**   Clarify **constraint**

When you're addressing cross-team dependencies, it's helpful to
take another pass at the Outcome, Value Stream, and Dependency Maps
together with leaders from those teams to align perspectives.

This is a chance for Sharon to become aware of Karl's doubts and concerns and for them both to acknowledge the additional learning that they may need to do to find a solution. Their next step is to jointly create a Dependency Map for the environment creation part of the process. In this context, Sharon's team (and other teams within the organization) is a customer of Karl's team. This new diagram is shown in Figure 7.8 (see page 120).

FIGURE 7.8: The Dependency Map Jointly Created by Karl and Sharon

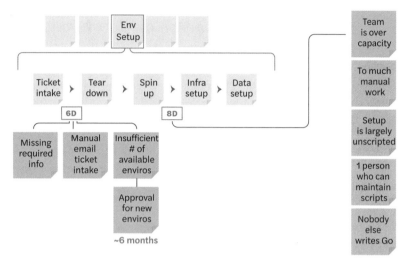

Creating the Dependency Map for environment setup was a useful exercise for Karl. His team was very familiar with that process but had never taken the time to visualize it or measure the associated times. Many of his team's planned and desired improvement initiatives would impact this process, but he had not previously thought about how those improvements would impact other departments' workflows. Some of these points seem obvious when stated but can be easily overlooked in the busyness of daily work.

Together they investigated the environment setup process to gain a shared understanding of how they could each contribute to a better state of flow. Often in hand-off situations, there is information or a communication mechanism that could be easily improved to makes everyone's work more efficient and effective.

Digging deeper into the dependencies revealed that Karl's team is short on capacity and could benefit immensely from some of the engineering capabilities inside Sharon's team. His team relies on scripts written in the Go programming language, but they have only one Go specialist on their team. Karl and Sharon agreed on some shared efforts that leverage Sharon's team's skills to automate some of Karl's most challenging responsibilities. In this way, they identified areas they can trade efforts for each other's mutual benefit.

In this scenario, successfully connecting and collaborating across organizational boundaries lifted a constraint in a way that benefits both groups.

How to Map Dependencies

Structuring Invitation

Invite stakeholders from inside and outside the team who have a deep understanding of the constrained step and its dependencies to come together to further clarify the current state. Summarize the value of the target outcome identified previously and the constraint that was clarified. The group maps a path to addressing the following key questions:

- What is the precise process through which this step is enabled?
- What are typical timings of the sub-steps in that process?
- What other challenges are we aware of in this process?

How Space Is Arranged and Materials Needed
- Use a digital collaboration tool or an actual dry-erase board/paper and sticky notes.
- Allow both vertical and horizontal space to map out direct and indirect dependencies and capabilities.

How Participation Is Distributed
- Include up to ten representatives with deep knowledge of the constraint and its dependencies.
- Everyone participates according to their knowledge of the dependencies in question.

How Groups Are Configured
- One main notetaker builds the Dependency Map on a shared board.
- Other contributors discuss to add, remove, or amend aspects of that shared map.

Sequence of Steps and Time Allocation
1. START WITH CONSTRAINTS
Make a copy of your Value Stream Map if you can easily do so. To simplify the visualization, you can remove all the data that doesn't relate to the constraint you identified at the end of your Value Stream Mapping session. For example,

in the Bolt Global illustration, their focus constraint was "Environment Setup." (See also Figure 7.9.)

FIGURE 7.9: Suspected Constraint Identified in Value Stream Mapping

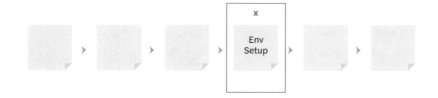

2. ZOOM IN ON A CONSTRAINT

With this joint team, zoom in on the constraint by creating a quick sub–Value Stream Map. This map should analyze the sub-steps that make up the constraint, as shown in Figure 7.10.

FIGURE 7.10: Example Sub–Value Stream Map

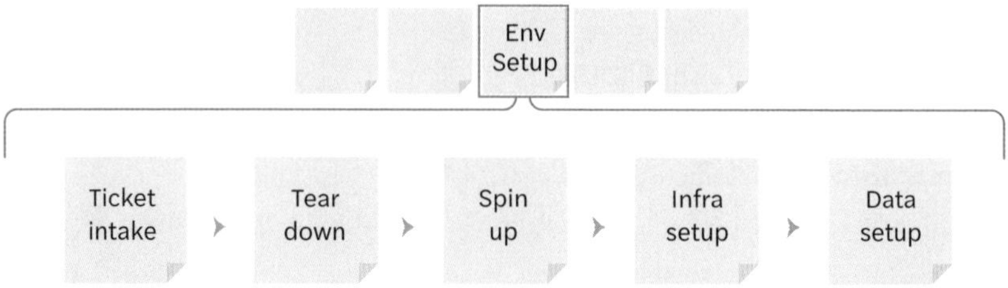

Illustrate the activities that make up the dependency.

3. IDENTIFY HOT SPOTS

Work with the joint team to identify where work is most constrained and the impact of those constraints (wait times). Rough estimates should be enough to highlight areas of concern. Figure 7.11 shows two extended waiting periods after "ticket intake" and after "spin up." These are areas to dig into for further analysis.

FIGURE 7.11: A Sub–Value Stream Map to Illustrate the Dependent Workflow

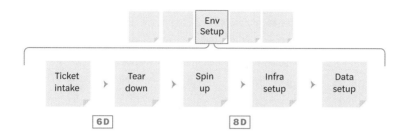

4. IDENTIFY DIRECT CAUSES FOR HOT SPOTS

From the hot spots, add any internal or external dependencies that affect the performance of the step(s) involved. (See Figure 7.12.) Examples include:

- limited staff/capacity
- budget constraints
- equipment availability
- technology limitations
- skill set of team members
- approval processes by other departments
- interdepartmental coordination and communication
- dependency on support from other teams (e.g., IT, HR)

FIGURE 7.12: Direct Causes of Hot Spots

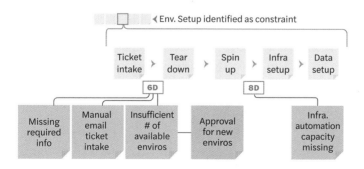

Identify causes of hot spots and areas beyond the group's control. Approval to increase environment capacity is noted in orange as beyond the group's immediate ability to influence.

5. DIG DEEPER INTO THE CONSTRAINT

The Five Whys is a simple approach made famous by the Lean movement. For the most impactful constraint, we simply ask why that constraint exists. We continue digging deeper into each answer, uncovering more and more whys behind the main constraint. Figure 7.13 illustrates how this digging can reveal an opportunity for improvement.

FIGURE 7.13: Practice the Five Whys to Dig Deeper into the Suspected Constraint

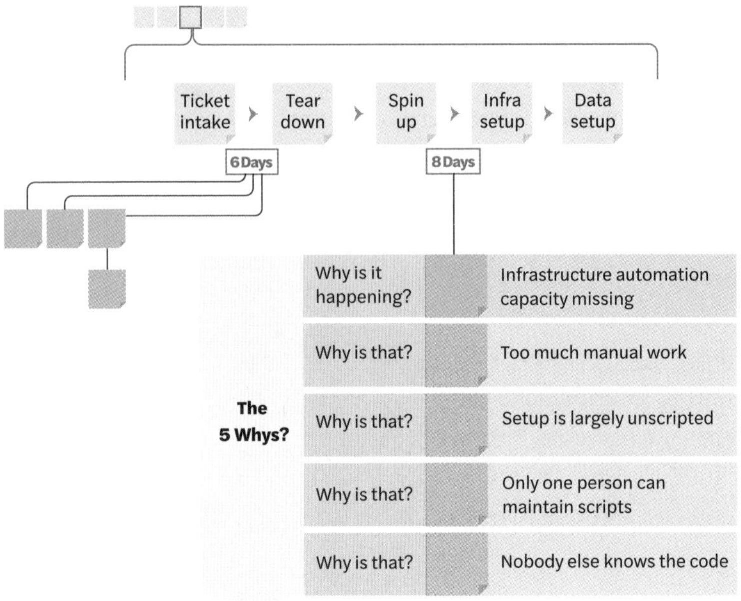

Tips and Traps

- Always remember that you're on the same team as those you depend on!
- Consider conflicting incentives. If the group you depend on is incentivized to do nothing, then don't expect them to jump at the chance to help you out. For example, if your focus is innovation and change and the team you depend on is rewarded for stability and consistency, you'll have to carefully present the common ground that appeals to you both.
- Be ready with your Outcome Map and Value Stream Map to share context on what you're trying to accomplish and what you've done so far. By presenting a compelling target outcome (which you can ideally

link to your dependencies' goals and incentives), you may be able to win favor across the aisle. Likewise, by demonstrating that you've considered other options and you've identified a clear constraint, you can show that you've done your homework and you're not needlessly demanding assistance.

- Service level agreements (SLAs)—either explicit or implicit—can eat up a significant portion of lead time if there's little incentive to act as quickly as possible. Like any time window, it's subject to Parkinson's Law (i.e., "Work expands so as to fill the time available for its completion."). That means it can be safe to assume that any dependency with an SLA will consume the maximum time the SLA allows.
- Approach Dependency Mapping with curiosity, not accusation or demand. As Stephen Covey advises in *The 7 Habits of Highly Effective People*, "Seek first to understand, then to be understood."[2]
- Leverage the same IKEA-effect principle you've benefited from elsewhere. By collaborating, you're more likely to gain alignment and buy-in.

Riffs and Variations

- Dependency Mapping can be a powerful way to plan for disaster recovery scenarios, assess security vulnerabilities, or reimagine how to reduce costs from a more holistic perspective than a single stream.
- A dependency matrix allows you to comprehensively map dependencies from team to team across large sections of your organization. If you're looking for a more comprehensive representation, a dependency matrix can cover a large number of teams and interactions.
- Wardley mapping can be useful to explore the strategic impact of interdependent capabilities. If you have the time, energy, buy-in, and expected value to look beyond your constraint, it can be a useful investment in a systems-level view.
- A SIPOC Diagram (Suppliers, Inputs, Process, Outputs, Customers) can be used to describe process dependencies in further detail.
- A RACI Matrix (Responsible, Accountable, Consulted, Informed) can be used to describe human dependencies (approvals, meetings, consultations) in further detail.

CASE STUDY | **Revisiting the Checkbox Project**

The Checkbox Project mentioned in Chapter 1 and similar org-spanning initiatives often suffer from extremes of under analysis or over analysis. On one hand, if a team spends too much time analyzing and plotting out every possible dependency for every initiative, they'll never get started with the actual work, and a lot of that effort will be wasted with dependencies of little or no consequence. On the other hand, charging into the work without any analysis is like running barefoot through a room full of LEGOs with the lights off.

The secret, untold story of the Checkbox Project is that not only do similar efforts happen often, but the Checkbox Project depicted in the case represented the third attempt to implement the checkbox. Not only that, but these types of cross-cutting projects are not uncommon and typically involve all the same dependencies, as shown in Figure 7.14. That means the organization could have looked at prior and similar attempts and mapped a representative value stream and dependencies to understand how to proceed more effectively.

FIGURE 7.14: A Visualization of Dependencies across the
Flow of the Checkbox Project

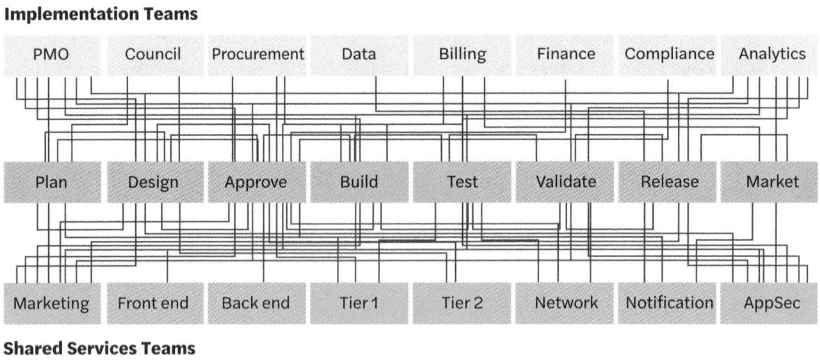

The complexity of the Checkbox Project is not unusual, but it often goes unaddressed because of the common model of project ways of working in organizations. Because initiatives like the Checkbox Project were treated as one-off efforts (despite a long history of similar attempts), they never had a chance to design a high-performing, sustainable flow.

Another often overlooked consideration about dependent teams and shared services is that they all have preexisting workloads and priorities that get interrupted by every project that falls in their lap. In the case of the Checkbox Project, they faced issues like these:

- The middleware team was in the middle of upgrading their architecture to support future volume.
- The front-end team had externally facing botnet attacks and was firefighting WAF protection.
- The BI team was just put into a new org with different priorities.

Every other group had a similar story. As a result of disrupting all of these teams by "bringing the work to them," they suffered the disengagement, disorientation, and distraction of large-scale interdependent work without having the opportunity to improve flow through continuous improvement of a value stream.

Without a way to engineer a solution, dependencies will continue to be a problem for the next project

Conclusion

Most teams are under substantial internal and external pressure to improve performance. It's common for teams to be hard on themselves if they can't perform as well as they want. It's also common for those higher in the organization to ask for or demand higher performance. These internal pressures are often proxies for competitive pressures outside the organization.

Psychological pressure without psychological clarity just creates stress and fear. Being able to see and understand dependencies allows teams to become more conscious of the environment in which they're working: the external or internal dependencies that impact their ability to sustainably deliver a high level of performance.

Mapping dependencies can guide a team to clarity by surfacing the factors that need to be increased, changed, or reduced to unlock greater throughput. Insourcing, collaboration, workarounds, and renegotiating expectations can help address the limits of external dependencies. Targeted training, redistribution of work, and targeted investments of time, work, or money can all augment internal capabilities.

Nothing exists independently. Seeing our outer and inner dependencies gives us the insight we need to rise to new challenges and make effective changes. Increasing a team's autonomy to engage with customers, define their product direction, supply solutions to their own needs, and rapidly deliver to customers enables both effectiveness and joy in work.

Key Takeaways

- Delivering work through a value stream relies on external dependencies and internal capabilities.
- To address bottlenecks in a value stream, begin by identifying key dependencies and capabilities that support that part of the process.
- Dependencies that inhibit the team may require working across departments to limit the dependency, increase those capabilities, or enable the team to self-service.
- Dependency or capability improvements that are focused on improving the value stream allow teams to build a clear business case for the improvements.

CHAPTER 8

Future State Value Stream Mapping

> "When we start thinking about ways to line up all of the essential steps needed to get a job done into a steady, continuous flow, it changes everything."
>
> JAMES P. WOMACK AND DANIEL T. JONES, *Lean Thinking: Banish Waste and Create Wealth in Your Corporation*

THERE ARE THREE KINDS OF VALUE STREAM MAPS: Current State Maps, Ideal State Maps, and Future State Maps. Current State Maps are a view of what's happening right now. We introduced these in Chapter 6.

FIGURE 8.1: Future State Mapping Opens the Door to Enabling Flow

Ideal State Maps depict what the value stream would look like in an ideal world if we had all the necessary capabilities and resources and could remove

all wait time between steps. The purpose of the Ideal State Map is to determine the upper limit of possible improvements and to elicit creative ideas from the team about how processes might be restructured.

By definition, teams will never reach an ideal state. But this map acts as a constant beacon for improvements and a place to park our most creative vision of how the team might perform. The Ideal State Map serves to inspire people and is a worthwhile exercise when you have time and buy-in.

But, for the purposes of Flow Engineering, when we are looking at fast mapping to get us to our targets, we're going to concentrate on the Future State Map, which serves as the near-term achievable target.

Future State Maps are pragmatic estimates of what an improved value stream might look like in six months. The Future State Map becomes the basis for determining actions to take with the Flow Roadmap described in Chapter 9 and forms the foundation for enabling improved flow.

FIGURE 8.2: Current, Ideal, and Future State Maps

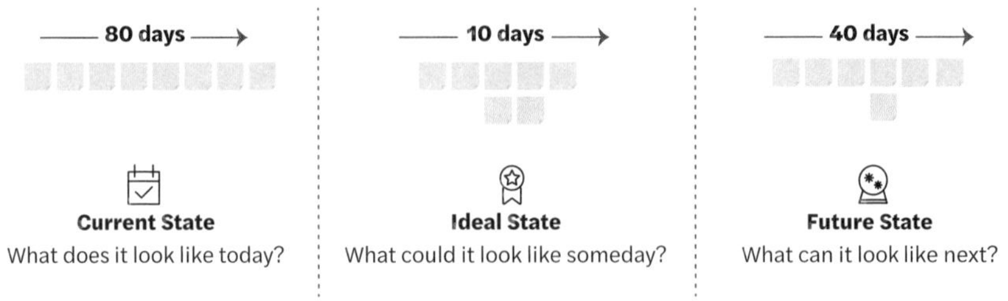

──── 80 days ──→   ──── 10 days ──→   ──── 40 days ──→

Current State
What does it look like today?

Ideal State
What could it look like someday?

Future State
What can it look like next?

Each of these variations of a Value Stream Map represents different potential states for the same workflow.

Mapping the Ideal State Value Stream

With any significant undertaking, it's helpful to begin with a clear vision of what's possible. Such a vision is important not because it reflects a reality we may ever inhabit, but because it liberates energy for the project and aligns the team around a common goal. The biggest challenge in large organizational initiatives is getting the team aligned around a common vision; lack of shared and sustained vision is the most frequent reason such initiatives fail. Thus, investing in building such a clear vision is critically important at the outset.

The Ideal State Map has the same structure as the Current State Map (see Chapter 6) but represents the smoothest version of the workflow that we can imagine. What is the theoretical maximum sustainable speed and ease with which this work could be completed?

Lean practitioners famously strive for single-piece flow. If there was only one piece of work to be completed at a time, how quickly could it be planned, built, tested, documented, and deployed? Imagining single-piece flow helps teams identify the maximum achievable speed, the speed without wait time due to batching or multitasking. Most wait time arises because teams have large amounts of work already in progress, preventing them from immediately taking action on a new piece of work as soon as it's ready. Instead, work piles up and waits around.

Reducing or eliminating wait time can often reduce lead time by 80% or more. But the team can still look more deeply at processes that currently take a long time. Is there a practical way that we could imagine it getting done more quickly? What if the subcomponents required for a step were pre-created and readily available? What if there were two or more people who could work on one step in parallel? Is a process simple enough that it could be delegated to other workers who are less busy?

If your Current State Map has identified other areas of concern, such as process quality at a particular step, this is an opportunity to imagine how quality could be built into the process at each step. Quality cannot be added to a work item later in a flow, it must be ensured from the beginning. Can or should we enable particular aspects of quality at an earlier step? Instead of doing a code review later in a process, could we use pair programming to ensure quality during development? Should our user stories be validated in detail with a customer at the outset? Could working prototypes provide a faster way to get feedback rather than going all the way through the development process?

This creative reimagining of the work process opens the door to dramatic performance improvements. Think of the impact of replacing a three-day server provisioning process with spinning up a Docker container in less than a minute. Imagine replacing a manual compliance process with an automated attestation process. Such transformations may require work to implement, but crafting an Ideal State Map establishes the business case for such improvements from the outset.

In this way, the Ideal State Map defines a theoretical maximum speed, ease, and quality that we could achieve as a team. Not every proposed improvement can or should be carried out, but this sets a high goal for us to strive for. But which of these improvements should we actually prioritize? That analysis is the purpose of defining a Future State Map.

What Is Future State Mapping?

Future State Mapping is a way of enabling better flow by visualizing a desired target state and identifying gaps between it and your current state. A Future State Map adopts the same format as a Value Stream Map with two differences:

1. It depicts an intended future state for the value stream rather than the current state.
2. It is annotated with the improvement opportunities required to get to that future state.

Future State Mapping supports the practice of the Improvement Kata. As mentioned in Chapter 2, the Improvement Kata is a practice of continuous improvement (kaizen) through iteratively identifying a future target state (planning), working to achieve that state (doing), analyzing the new current state (studying), and adjusting the process based on observations (acting). This Plan-Do-Study-Act (PDSA) cycle is also known as the Deming or Shewhart cycle. The goal is to establish improvement as a habit.

In this case, the Future State Map establishes the future target state we are seeking (Plan). The Flow Roadmap introduced in the next chapter offers guidance on how to move toward that future state (Do). After a predetermined period (typically three months), we reassess the current state through Value Stream Mapping to determine the effectiveness of our interventions

(Study) and improve or adapt (Act). We then proceed to define a new target state, and the PDSA cycle resumes. As the team builds familiarity with the process, they can accomplish these activities more quickly. You may also recognize this iterative process as a cybernetic loop, as introduced in Chapter 2.

Three months is typically long enough to allow for dramatic change but short enough to be able to predict a possible future and follow up in a timely way. This Improvement Kata cycle is depicted in Figure 8.3. The Outcome Map defines the target (1), the Current State Map and Dependency Map (2) inform the improvements to define a Future State Map (3), which informs the Flow Roadmap crafted in the next chapter to define the path to the future state (4).

FIGURE 8.3: Flow Engineering Cycle of Mapping as an Improvement Kata

Future State Mapping happens in four stages, shown in Figure 8.4:

1. Review the target outcome and findings from previous maps.
2. Identify targets for improvement.
3. Redesign the stream.
4. Measure the future state.

FIGURE 8.4: The Four Stages of Future State Mapping

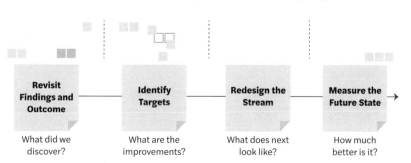

Why Future State Mapping Works

Future State Mapping brings several specific benefits:

- Envisioning a future "how." It's too easy to get caught up in daily work and lose sight of our target outcome, but a target outcome alone doesn't demonstrate how we might reach that outcome. A Future State Map creates a vision of flow that embodies or enables our target outcome.
- Providing a cybernetic target. Establishes the clearest target state that we want to achieve. This refines the target set in Outcome Mapping and continues to leverage our cybernetic approach: establishing a target condition and navigating in that direction.
- Enabling continuous and discontinuous improvement. Allows us to define not only improvements to flow but also complete reinventions of it. The map can show improvements like elimination of waste, better information flow, changes to role ownership of steps, etc. The map can also show dramatic reinvention, such as reorganization, elimination, parallelization, etc.
- Enabling system interventions beyond the team. The constraints in our workflow are often due to dependencies outside the team. We need to be able to "work across the aisle" with colleagues in other departments to envision flow improvements that will benefit the whole organization. The Future State Map provides a clear, shared artifact to define "where we're headed" and facilitate conversations with others.
- Eliminating waste. Continuous elimination of waste is the essence of Lean. Physical work can easily waste physical materials. In knowledge work, waste primarily takes the form of wasted time, energy, money, and human potential.

What Do We Mean by Waste?

In the dynamic landscape of knowledge work, efficiency is critical, but it can be hard to find. Looking for waste can be one of the easiest ways to boost both productivity and morale. Some waste is obvious when pointed out, but we just haven't noticed it—and it can be difficult to see without a map to call it out.

Value Stream Mapping has traditionally targeted various types of waste in the physical world. In knowledge work, the eight wastes of Lean can be summarized by the acrostic DOWNTIME:

Defects: e.g., bugs, test and automation failures, rework, unplanned revisions, inadequate knowledge transfer, missing documentation/information. Quality controls such as code reviews, automated tests, architectural reviews, and so forth are ways of ensuring that work meets quality thresholds at each step of the value stream. Such controls have a variety of impacts and can also add delay or cost to our work. It's important to see these kinds of quality controls in the broader context of optimizing delivery and not just assume they should always be in place for every kind of work. Optimizing delivery is a fine balancing act, and teams can benefit as much from limiting controls as they can from expanding controls.

Overproduction: e.g., features never/rarely used, abandoned tasks, data duplication.

Waiting: e.g., delays, slow handoffs, queuing, waiting for approvals, unnecessary/inefficient meetings. Parallelizing processes where possible can be a way to reduce waiting. Wait time often emerges because people later in a value stream are not available to begin working as soon as work arrives. This leads to accumulated work in progress. This accumulation is a drain on contributors who consider waiting and queued items still active, while others consider it "out of sight and out of mind."

Non-utilized talent: e.g., missing capabilities, insufficient tooling, inadequate training, underutilized staff, bad/missing incentives, lost morale. The waste of human potential is the most tragic waste.

Transport: e.g., moving data between different teams/systems/databases/tools, manual handoffs, unnecessary business travel. Removing handoffs and middlemen from a flow is a way of reducing transport. Working to provide self-service tooling for other teams is also a way to lower transport costs.

Inventory: e.g., queues, backlogs, work in development/staging environments, work in progress/process (WIP), code/design branches. Work in progress is the silent killer of productivity. It brings no benefit to customers and burdens workers with increased context switching and confusion. Knowledge work accumulates easily and invisibly, with no theoretical limit to how much half-finished work a person or team may accumulate. In *Making Work Visible*, Dominica DeGrandis amplifies David Anderson's maxim "stop starting and start finishing." By focusing on shipping work before taking on any new work, you reduce the amount of work in progress. This step is critical to prevent the silent cost of task switching (humans can't multitask activities that require conscious thought) and to reduce wait time.

Motion: e.g., unnecessary handoffs, context switching, data transfer/duplication, moving work to development/staging environments. Reducing detrimental cognitive load can help reduce motion waste. When tasks (or distractions) exceed our cognitive capacity, the information that is germane to our work fades from our working memory. We compensate by repeatedly switching between tasks, checking references, and so forth, all of which creates inefficiency in our process.

Extra processing: e.g., unnecessary gates/approvals, excess requirement details, unnecessary approvals, unnecessary reviews/validation, gold-plating, excess internal user acceptance testing (UAT), excess external UAT, doing thorough analysis when rough data will suffice, creating polished docs when rough docs will suffice. Simplifying and modularizing architecture can reduce the waste of extra processing by allowing us to solve simpler and more constrained problems.

Dominica DeGrandis also laid out a simple list that summarizes waste in the context of time (the five time thieves) and the impact on individual contributors:[1]

- **Too much work in progress:** Work started but not yet finished.
- **Unknown dependencies:** Something unexpected that needs to happen in order to finish work.
- **Unplanned work:** Interruptions that prevent you from finishing.
- **Conflicting priorities:** Projects and tasks that compete with each other for attention.
- **Neglected work:** Partially completed work that sits idle.

In almost every case, these types of waste can't be perfectly eliminated, but they should be known and managed intentionally. Key to Value Stream Mapping's "value-added time" are two factors to consider when thinking about waste: *Would our customer happily pay for this activity?* Balanced against: *Would removing this undermine the value to customers, stakeholders, or contributors?*

BOLT GLOBAL | **Future State Mapping**

Initially, it didn't occur to Sharon that she might have to reach out to other teams to address the issues her own team was facing. By digging into the constraint, she discovered the need to work with Karl to address dependencies out of her control. By understanding the contributing factors from Karl's perspective, she could see which countermeasures were likely to deliver performance improvement.

Sharon and Karl collaboratively pinpointed areas for improvement, such as improving information flow and automating handoffs, but a breakthrough happened when Sharon shared the Dependency Map with her team and they discovered that the capacity issue delaying environment changes could be addressed by a member of her team. This person could write code and issue pull requests for Karl's team and train a backup person to prevent a single person from being a bottleneck. They have also been toying with the idea of forming a guild to train others on how to do the same across multiple teams.

The team emerged with a streamlined vision for the software development life cycle. The vision involved a significant reduction in the number of steps from idea inception to product release. Now, handoffs between roles are smoother, and there's a newfound focus on automation and collaboration. Both Sharon's and Karl's teams feel more engaged, aligned, empowered, and focused on what will really move them forward.

This mapping lays the groundwork for a more agile and responsive flow of work. It sets the stage for the team to work toward doubling their release frequency, aligning with the organizational goal of accelerated software delivery.

How Future State Mapping Works

Structuring Invitation

Armed with new insights from the Dependency Mapping session, reconvene the team involved in the original Value Stream Mapping exercise, along with any other key people from the Dependency Mapping session, to strategize on proposed changes.

The purpose of this session is to point out the precise constraints identified in the Dependency Mapping session, strategize on alternative workflows that would address the constraint in question, and set a vision for the target future state workflow.

How Space Is Arranged and Materials Needed
- Use a digital collaboration tool or an actual dry-erase board/paper and sticky notes.
- The workspace is designed similarly to the Value Stream Mapping session.

How Participation Is Distributed
- Everyone participates equally.
- It's particularly important to get involvement from those who are most affected by or responsible for the constraints.

How Groups Are Configured

- One main notetaker builds the Future State Map on a shared board.
- Other contributors discuss to add, remove, or amend aspects of that shared map.

Sequence of Steps and Time Allocation (60 Mins.)

1. REVIEW TARGET OUTCOME AND FINDINGS FROM PREVIOUS MAPS

Begin by reviewing the previous maps, especially the Current State and Dependency Map, noting in particular the overall goal of the initiative and the primary bottleneck in your current process. (5 mins.) Make a copy of the Current State Map to use as the new Future State Map. (See Figure 8.5.)

FIGURE 8.5: Current State Map with Bottleneck Highlighted

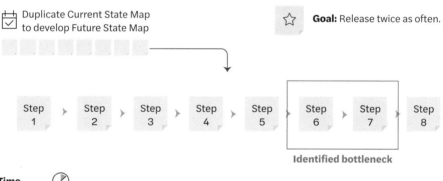

2. IDENTIFY TARGETS FOR IMPROVEMENT

Review the eight wastes of Lean (DOWNTIME) for a reminder of the many forms that waste can take. We've repeated a simplified form of that list here for ease of reference:

1. Defects	5. Transport
2. Overproduction	6. Inventory
3. Waiting	7. Motion
4. Non-utilized talent	8. Extra processing

Review your dependency map and incorporate findings into your future state design. Make note of any other areas on the map that seem to be "low-hanging fruit" (i.e., areas where you could readily make improvements). Mark these as areas for improvement (kaizen bursts), small continuous improvement efforts that could reduce delays, improve quality, etc. (20 mins.) (See Figure 8.6.)

FIGURE 8.6 Future State Map with Improvement Areas Noted in Green

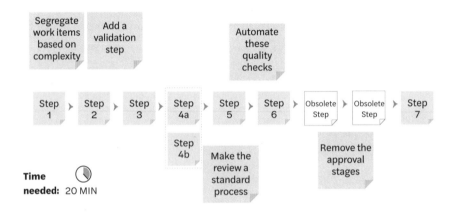

3. REDESIGN THE STREAM

Modify the parts of the map that constitute the bottleneck, removing wait time where it seems possible to do so, replacing serial steps with parallel steps where possible, preprocessing work to make a step faster, and so forth. (20 mins.) (See Figure 8.7.)

FIGURE 8.7: Future State Map Reduced to Seven Serial Steps and One Parallel Step

4. MEASURE THE FUTURE STATE

Estimate the waiting and cycle times for the (improved) future state value stream. This sets the target timing the team aspires to. Focus on what can be achieved in the next three to six months. (15 mins.) (See Figure 8.8.)

FIGURE 8.8: Future State Map with Cycle Timings

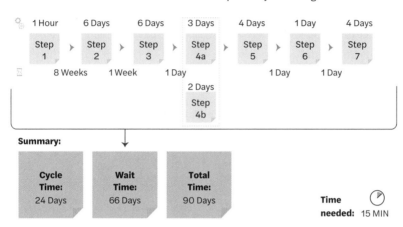

Summary:

Cycle Time:	Wait Time:	Total Time:
24 Days	66 Days	90 Days

Time needed: 15 MIN

Tips and Traps

- Before ending the mapping session, schedule a follow-up session to review progress and map the next set of incremental improvements.
- Don't get bogged down in detailed discussions of improvements. The goal here is to set a target. Details can get worked out once the Flow Roadmap (Chapter 9) has established a timeline for the future state.
- Don't identify too many improvements (kaizen bursts). Three is probably a good number for your first mapping initiative. The team can take on more as they gain confidence.
- Consider a shorter improvement horizon, such as four to six weeks, for your first Future State Map to ensure you follow up and check in on progress.
- Wait time is a key target for flow improvement. Depending on the type of work, it may be difficult to greatly improve cycle time. But wait time can almost always be reduced by improving handoffs between teams and reducing the amount of work in progress.

- To reduce wait time in one step, you can consider adding more people or resources to help, preprocessing the work to simplify the effort required or simply increasing the team's awareness of the backlog. Sometimes just making a team more aware of the work backlog at a particular point can ensure that work items get processed more expeditiously.
- A common reason for a team being overloaded is excessive work in progress (WIP). The only way to reduce the overall WIP is by setting strict limits on when new work items can be accepted into the stream. WIP limits hurt. No one wants to say "no" explicitly. But the consequence of not setting such limits is that we say "no" implicitly to all tasks by dragging them out.
- A key motto for limiting WIP is David Anderson's "Stop starting and start finishing,"[2] highlighting the importance of completing tasks over initiating new ones.
- The Future State Map allows you the opportunity to set near-term goals. This ties in well to objectives and key results (OKRs) or other company goal-setting strategies. You should expect to iterate on this Future State Map every few months, using it as a target for planned value stream improvements.

Riffs and Variations

- Precede this mapping session with an Ideal State Mapping session. The Ideal State Map depicts the theoretical smoothest and fastest path to delivering value and represents the goal that each Future State Mapping exercise moves toward. Ideal State Mapping gives a team the chance to really use their imagination and aim to revolutionize the value stream.
- Ideal and Future State Mapping can also enable discontinuous improvement, as mentioned earlier. There's an opportunity to not only incrementally improve but to reimagine, revolutionize, and redesign the value stream if conditions like buy-in, support, and capability allow. Team Topologies and Wardley mapping can all facilitate this larger-scale reinvention. We'll explain more about making bigger organizational changes in Part 3.

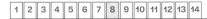

CASE STUDY | **Aligning Value Stream Stakeholders in Travel Tech**

A global travel tech provider received a huge "aha" moment and a key learning from collaborative Value Stream Mapping. This client was mapping a partner integration workflow to improve throughput. They aimed to build integrations with every major travel platform. But it's hard to work through that list when your lead time is eight months and the queue is fifty partners deep!

The mapping effort included participants from across the value stream. The mapping revealed that 50% of the value stream was spent waiting because of poor information flow and handoffs. We created a Future State Map that reduced the lead time to an expected three months with minimal improvement efforts. But the immediate achievement appeared at the very end of the first workshop: An individual from marketing, downstream of everything else in the stream and often surprised by work dropped in their lap, remarked, "This is the first time we've ever been in the same room together!"

TABLE 8.1: Results of Mapping at a Travel Tech Company

Baseline Flow	Optimized Flow
23 steps	6 steps (including parallel steps)
12 stakeholders	2 stakeholders
12 contributors	4 contributors
8 months	3 months
11 meeting stages	Meetings replaced with decision automation, ownership, collaboration, and coworking
9 call/email steps	Automated weekly customer touch points; relationship calls vs. status calls
9 embedded subprocesses	3 embedded subprocesses

Beyond that alignment boost, the performance boost was even more surprising. Within an afternoon of mapping, we uncovered a massive opportunity to improve flow across partner integration. Fully loaded cost savings was $150,000 per year over three years. Opportunity cost saved: three additional partner integrations a year over three years, representing a $720,000 opportunity

Conclusion

Future State Mapping sets the target for improvement, particularly for enabling flow. From a cybernetic perspective, we use it as a navigational aid to direct us from the current state of a stream to a desired future state, using this Future State Map as the target condition. As with navigation, the bigger challenge is the incremental adjustment that is required along the way. The next chapter introduces the Flow Roadmap, a way to systematically sequence and prioritize desired improvements that will bring the future state to life.

Key Takeaways

- Future State Mapping builds on the previous maps to envision an achievable future state target.
- This target is the first step in a high-level, cybernetic Improvement Kata.
- Future State Maps target the main hot spot or bottleneck in the Current State Map and highlight multiple improvement opportunities (kaizen bursts).

CHAPTER 9

The Flow
Roadmap

> "The ultimate purpose of taking
> data is to provide a basis for
> action or a recommendation
> for action."
>
> W. EDWARDS DEMING

NOW THAT WE'VE EXPLORED the four main types of maps—Outcome, Value Stream, Dependency, and Future State—we can take a closer look at the Flow Roadmap. It's common for organizations to create roadmaps to help people inside and outside the organization get a sense of how they intend to progress. Product companies will frequently maintain both a Product Roadmap (depicting intended improvements to the product) and a Technical Roadmap (depicting intended improvements to their technology infrastructure).

FIGURE 9.1: The Flow Roadmap Primarily Serves to Enable Flow

The Flow Roadmap focuses on improvements to enable flow across the value stream. The Flow Roadmap does not describe *what* you will create; it's

a plan for improving *how* you will create. Creativity and innovation are as important to workflow as they are to products. The Flow Roadmap is a plan for how to improve workflow.

What Is the Flow Roadmap?

Traditional roadmaps are useful communication and alignment tools to help inform groups and individuals about what they can expect in the future, but they don't talk about how the future will happen. This "how" is the gap that Flow Roadmaps fill. Flow Roadmaps plot actions, experiments, and mechanisms to improve the way you deliver your initiatives, features, and traditional roadmap items.

There are three stages to Flow Roadmapping, illustrated in Figure 9.2:

1. Identify improvement opportunities.
2. Prioritize each activity.
3. Sequence activities into a roadmap.

FIGURE 9.2: The Three Stages of a Flow Roadmap

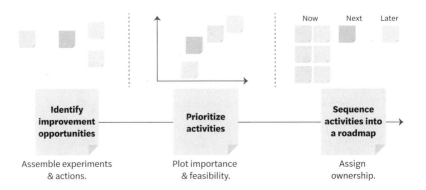

Why Flow Roadmapping Works

Flow Roadmapping allows you to navigate to your target destination based on the three elements of action—value, clarity, and flow. It brings four specific benefits:

- **Transforms insights into action.** The Flow Roadmap is the culmination of the previous maps. The prior mapping exercises clarify the value the team is seeking to achieve and offer clarity into the flow, the primary constraints, and what the future could look like. The Flow Roadmap grounds those insights into a practical sequence of next actions.
- **Prioritizes activities by importance and feasibility.** The fast, visual organization of possible actions into importance and feasibility allows us to identify what actions are the most promising next steps and which we can safely defer. Setting priorities enables us to deal with tasks sequentially rather than taking on parallel work in progress.
  - » **Importance:** Relative value considering the target outcome. Often substituted with impact.[1]
  - » **Feasibility:** How readily, easily, and capably the action could be performed.
- **Quantifies or qualifies progress.** Setting specific, measurable indications of progress ensures that we can validate that actions are moving forward and having the desired effect.
- **Assigns ownership.** Assigning ownership provides clarity of communication and accountability. This sets explicit expectations for every team member involved.

BOLT GLOBAL | **Navigation Needs A Compass and A Map**

Mapping is a great opportunity to identify value, build clarity, and visualize improved flow, but that's useless unless it's made actionable. As we discussed in Part 1, improvement and change is extremely difficult without an on-ramp. Sharon reflects on a caution she read in *Value Stream Mapping*: "All too often we see organizations with beautifully designed current state value stream maps but no future state value stream maps. Or beautifully designed future state maps, but no action plan for realizing the future state."[2] Without action, her return on time invested mapping and gathering insights would be compromised, and she may not get another chance to gather everyone.

To get started, Sharon needs to transform the insights discovered during mapping into actions. Reviewing the previous maps, Sharon collects the notes that highlighted the most promising countermeasures to address the constraints preventing the team from delivering twice as often. The team had determined environment setup and a dependency on the infrastructure team to be the constraint. Through Dependency Mapping, they identified several issues that could significantly improve the performance of the value stream if addressed. These issues were transformed into actions and experiments to improve performance:

TABLE 9.1: Issues Transformed into Actions/Experiments to
Improve Flow at Bolt Global

Issue		Action/Experiment to Improve Performance
Often missing required information.	→	Template for new requests (automate in the future).
Manual email ticket intake.	→	Submit requests via forms into the task management system.
Insufficient number of available environments.	→	Consider alternate options. [TBD]
Team over capacity and constrained.	→	Sharon's team has a contributor who can augment Karl's team capacity.

Since Sharon's team can't do everything at once, these actions needed to be prioritized. To keep that quick and minimal, Sharon focused on two dimensions: (1) importance (to capture relative value) and (2) feasibility (to capture how readily the action could be performed). This provided a natural distribution that created tiers of actions. The most feasible and important are natural starting points; other improvements could wait.

Based on the clarity from this exercise, the team was able to distribute these actions over time to minimize work in progress (WIP). They could also address dependencies across actions by ensuring that paired dependencies were addressed at the same time and sequential dependencies were addressed in sequence.

Most roadmaps stop there, but experience taught Sharon a few things that pushed her to clarify further. She'd been in too many retrospectives where ideas surfaced and were never acted on, there were plans for next steps with no clear targets, and efforts existed without an owner.

Adding measures of progress to actions made it clear how the team would evaluate the impact of the actions, and adding ownership to each action made it clear who would drive the action forward. Figure 9.3 shows the Bolt Global team's completed Flow Roadmap, incorporating the kaizen-driven actions and supporting detail.

FIGURE 9.3: Sharon's Completed Flow Roadmap

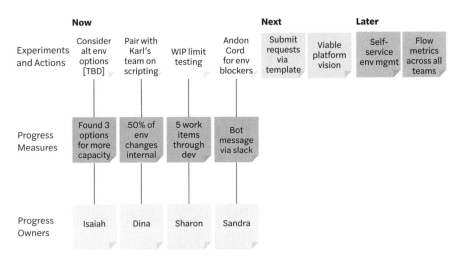

The completed Flow Roadmap shows actions across three time horizons, measures of progress, and ownership of next steps.

Sharon's team drew up the Flow Roadmap and shared it with Karl and other peers as well, as product leadership, to enable better communication and collaboration. Confidence, trust, alignment, and engagement went up, and lead time began to go down. The roadmap continued to be a living document that both teams referenced and built upon over the following months to stay clear, aligned, and moving forward effectively.

How to Create a Flow Roadmap

After mapping outcomes, value streams, dependencies, and future state, you have incredible insights into how to transform your workflow and improve performance. To move from insights to action, the Flow Roadmap is the key to unlocking your first steps.

Below is the step-by-step process. You can follow the instructions to the letter, pare it down to something faster and less detailed, or dig as deep as you like. Just like with the rest of Flow Engineering, you decide what level of detail and time is most appropriate. Just remember, you may miss something going too fast, and you may waste time going too deep—but the great thing is, you can adjust!

Structuring Invitation

Invite stakeholders likely to be involved in next steps. Revisit the target outcome and express the need to define actions for next steps. You've uncovered and clarified opportunities—now it's time to act on them. The group maps a path to addressing these key questions:

- What are the highest-priority actions to deliver our target outcome?
- How will we measure progress?
- Who will own the progress?

How Space Is Arranged and Materials Needed

Use a digital collaboration tool or an actual dry-erase board/paper and sticky notes. The finished map will look like Figure 9.4. It has three main sections. In the upper left, we include a copy of the Future State Map, the main source for improvement items gathered in Stage 1. In the lower left, we create space for the prioritization exercises done in Stage 2. And in the lower right, we build the actual Flow Roadmap, the linear list of next actions to be generated in Stage 3.

How Participation Is Distributed

- Bring up to ten representatives with deep knowledge of the insights uncovered by previous maps.

- Everyone participates according to their knowledge of opportunities and potential countermeasures.

How Groups Are Configured
- One main notetaker builds the Flow Roadmap on a shared board.
- Other contributors discuss to add, remove, or amend aspects of that shared map.

FIGURE 9.4: The Flow Roadmap Board

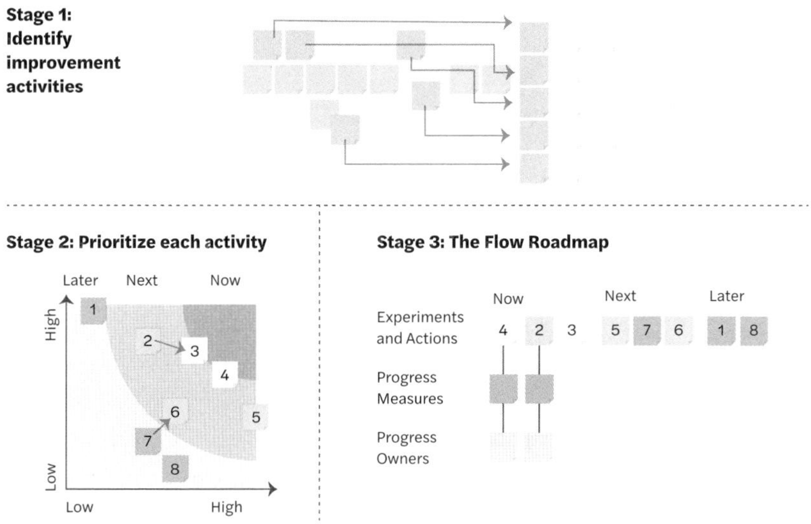

Stage 1: Identify improvement activities

Stage 2: Prioritize each activity

Stage 3: The Flow Roadmap

Sequence of Steps and Time Allocation

1. IDENTIFY IMPROVEMENT ACTIVITIES

The first stage is conducted in the upper section of the workspace. List the target improvement areas (kaizen bursts) identified while working on the Future State Map. Figure 9.5 on page 152 shows the diagram created in step three of Future State Mapping. (See Chapter 8.) To realize that intended future state, various changes are required, which are shown as green sticky notes. There may also have been other improvement areas identified in the Value Stream Mapping and Dependency Mapping exercises. All of these improvement areas are candidates for inclusion in the Flow Roadmap.

FIGURE 9.5: The Future State Map Showing Improvement Areas

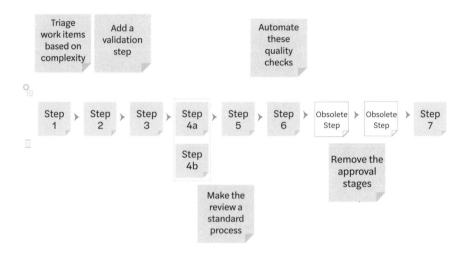

The Future State Map generated in Chapter 8 forms the basis for Flow Roadmapping. The blue sticky notes depict the intended future steps, while the green sticky notes represent areas where change is required to achieve that future state.

Next, separate the improvement suggestions to begin identifying next steps, as seen in Figure 9.6. If these improvement areas are not clear or small enough to act on, you can break them down further. For each improvement area, identify specific actions that would be required to implement the improvement. Place these actions below the corresponding improvement area.

FIGURE 9.6: Improvement Opportunities Broken Down into Actions

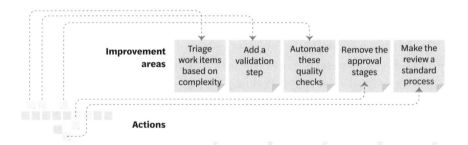

2. PRIORITIZE EACH ACTIVITY

Move to the second section of the board, as outlined in Figure 9.4. This is where you will conduct the prioritization of each activity. Work together as a group to plot the importance of each improvement by creating a ranking column to the right of the actions created in the prior step. (See Figure 9.7.) Each possible improvement is ranked on the vertical axis in order of importance by asking, "How critical is this to realizing our target outcome?"

FIGURE 9.7: Possible Improvements Ranked by Importance

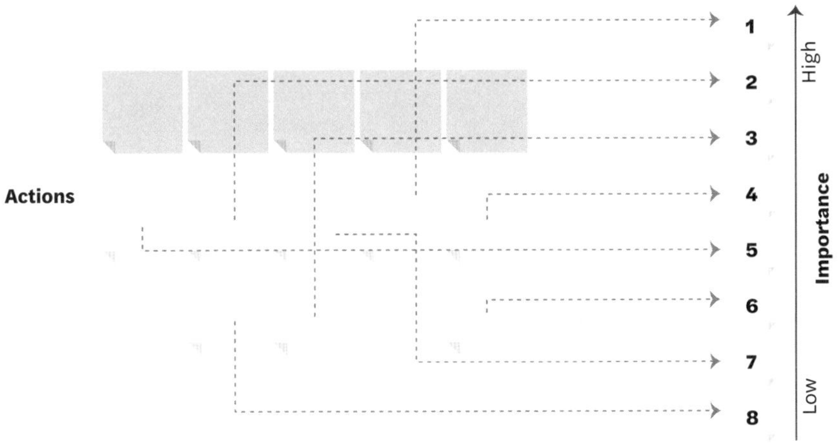

Now, plot the feasibility of each action by moving each improvement idea along the horizontal axis based on how feasible it is, as shown in Figure 9.8 (see page 154). For each item, ask, "How easily can we accomplish this?"

These four criteria can help you determine feasibility:

1. Activities that require multiple **contributors** are less feasible than those that require a single contributor.
2. Activities for which we currently lack a **capability** are less feasible than those for which we currently have the capability.
3. Activities with **dependencies** on other teams are less feasible than those that depend only on this team.
4. Activities with unknown **scope** are less feasible than those with known scope.

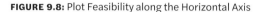

FIGURE 9.8: Plot Feasibility along the Horizontal Axis

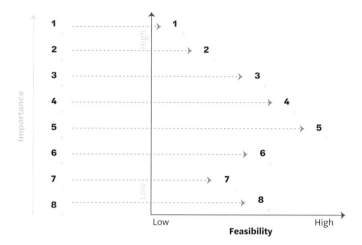

Next, indicate dependencies between items, as shown in Figure 9.9. When delivery of one item depends on delivery of another item, we depict that relationship on the diagram. For example, in Figure 9.9, Item 3 depends on Item 2 and Item 6 depends on Item 7.

FIGURE 9.9: Indicate Dependencies between Activities

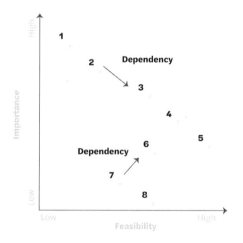

Now, divide the improvement suggestions (plotted by importance and feasibility) into now, next, and later based on their distance from the upper-right corner. (See Figure 9.10.) We have color-coded the items to show which ones fit into which category.

FIGURE 9.10: Improvement Activities Categorized by Time Horizon
(Now, Next, Later)

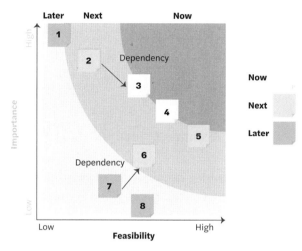

Now is in yellow, next is in blue, and later is in pink.

3. SEQUENCE ACTIVITIES INTO A ROADMAP

We now begin generating the actual Flow Roadmap. Move to the third section of the workspace, as illustrated in Figure 9.4.

Copy items from the previous step and arrange them in sequential order by now, next, and later, taking into consideration the dependencies between items, as seen in Figure 9.11.

For example, since Item 4 was high in both importance and feasibility but had no dependencies, you should do that first. Item 3 was also high in importance and feasibility but depended on Item 2. So the next priority items are Item 2 and then Item 3.

FIGURE 9.11: Items Arranged in Sequential Order: Now, Next, Later

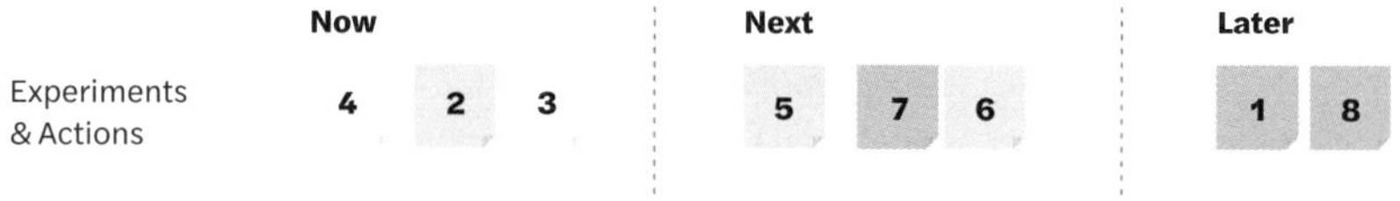

	Now			Next			Later	
Experiments & Actions	4	2	3	5	7	6	1	8

Next, identify measures of progress for the "Now" items. Below these items, add another sticky note to indicate one or more measures of progress, as shown in Figure 9.12 (see next page).

FIGURE 9.12: Identified Measure of Progress

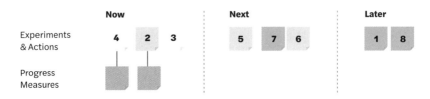

	Now	Next	Later
Experiments & Actions	4 2 3	5 7 6	1 8
Progress Measures			

Example Measures of Progress

It can be challenging to choose an appropriate measure to evaluate progress, but the simplest guideline can be summed up as, "How will you know you're making progress?" This is not only critical to ensure you're heading in the right direction at the rate you expect, but it's also vitally important to effective communication with peers, stakeholders, and contributors. A good reference of useful measurements has been collected by Gartner and represented in Table 9.2.

TABLE 9.2: Gartner's Flow Metrics Cover Technical, Product, and Business Concerns

Technical	Product	Business
Code change size	Lead time	Product cost
Code delivery speed	Cycle time	Product value
Code refactoring rate	Throughput	Return on investment
Code review churn	Work in progress	Product quality
Code quality	Flow efficiency*	Net Promoter Score
Technical debt	Work item profile**	Customer satisfaction

*The percentage of lead time an item is actively being worked on
(total cycle time/total lead time).

** Also referred to as Flow Distribution[3] and includes features, defects, debt, and risk but can also include experiments or specific subtypes like rework.

Source: Gartner, "Analyze Value Stream Metrics to Optimize DevOps Delivery," August 2020.

Other valuable metrics to consider in the context of value stream performance include the following:

- feature adoption and usage
- deployment/release frequency
- change failure rate/escaped defects
- mean time to recovery (MTTR)
- Andon pulls (calling out blockers and issues in flow)
- contributor/stakeholder satisfaction

Metrics are not the only measurements to consider. You can just as easily use milestones to establish a progress marker (for example, completing an experiment, completing a survey, establishing a liaison for a dependency, or implementing a change that facilitates a larger action).

Measurements are key aspects of a cybernetic control system. The choice of metrics is a strategic decision. Measuring too much can waste energy; measuring too little can leave you unable to see. Measures will affect behavior and can be gamed. Evaluate them in the light of your target outcome to protect against the risk of measurement myopia.

Next, below the measures of progress, assign owners for those actions based on the skills and capacity of your team. Add another row of sticky notes beneath the "progress measures" to identify the owners, as shown in Figure 9.13.

FIGURE 9.13: Example of Adding Assigned Owners

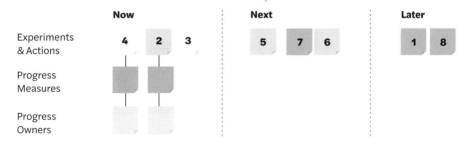

Tips and Traps

- In general, teams should focus mostly on items in the "Now" category, but if your team has the capacity, feel free to expand your efforts into the "Next" and "Later" time horizons. However, it is essential to recognize that the further into the future we plan, the less predictability we have.

- Earlier iterations of Flow Roadmaps included "methods of progress" rather than owners. This was intended to drive further clarity on the "how" for continuous improvement, informed by systems like V2MOM and conversations with thought leaders like Mike Burrows. Mike called out the idea of "Measure before Method,"[4] which informed the initial design of the map, but at this stage, method is less important than who might lead the effort. Have someone take the lead and let them figure out the details of how.

Riffs and Variations

- Feel free to use any alternative approach to roadmapping or planning out next steps. Identifying measures of progress and assigning ownership are valuable to make progress visible and accountability clear, but the important thing is taking action and not taking on too much. Other dimensions to consider include anticipated obstacles and chosen methods.

- Roadmap items can be themed and/or organized to align to objectives and key results (OKRs) or other large-scale initiatives. Color coding items to themes like "information and data visibility" or "improved capability" can help connect the dots from your efforts back to high level initiatives.

- At this stage, it can be valuable to perform a retrospective or follow up with a survey to capture learning and improve future efforts.

- John Cutler has collected and shared a large library of valuable roadmapping and prioritization guidance in his blog articles. He has also collected a library of practices like "The Magic Prioritization Trick,"[5] which provides an alternative step-by-step method for arriving at a "Now, Next, Later" roadmap.

CASE STUDY | **Moving from Insights to Action in a Large Procurement Organization**

A large Fortune 500 software organization ran a Flow Engineering program with the aim to increase flow and value output across their procurement defect resolution flow. Participants included the heads of delivery, engineering, program management, architecture, product management, and infrastructure. Their vision for the past several years had been to improve developer productivity.

Years before, they'd laid out a "what" roadmap to optimize performance and efficiency through technical changes and automation. But it hadn't paid off in lead time or customer or contributor satisfaction. Value Stream and Dependency Mapping revealed that while all the previous performance improvements had focused on the middle stages where automation was closest to developers, huge delays and friction lay both upstream and downstream beyond their automation efforts (upstream in support analysis, investigation, and reproduction and downstream in test environment verification and full release regression).

There were weeks of delay and weeks of activity with little value-added time. The percentage of active time across the two hot spots was only 5%. Visibility into the problem areas led to a clear deconstruction of the dependencies connected to the hot spots and identifying countermeasures across two major themes: (1) information and data visibility and (2) key capabilities. The group realized they lacked critical information to effectively act on defects and to manage the flow of those defects. They also lacked critical capabilities to act on insights they discovered. The actions and experiments to address these gaps included efforts to distinguish standard from nonstandard work, build interfaces with dependent teams, and implement passive monitoring of test environment state and usage.

Progress indicators don't have to be metrics. Because the team lacked visibility and clear ownership of these goals, their progress indicators were mostly the completion of milestones toward their goal:

- In-app support (self-service) is scoped as a roadmap item.
- App dependency liaison assigned.
- Customer extensions and customizations categorized and scoped.

- Top five most problematic customer use cases documented.
- List of "most customized" customers.
- Infrastructure state visibility scoped.

Each change above hit the sweet spot of important and feasible and lay the groundwork for real progress toward their target outcome. There were also clear actions for future time horizons to provide opportunities to pull improvements forward as the low-hanging fruit was picked. Figure 9.14 shows the progression from challenges and ideas through prioritization and plotting the final roadmap.

The team progressed from a state of disorientation and frustration over past efforts that didn't seem to improve key measures to a state of clarity and alignment on actions connected directly to their most critical hot spots.

FIGURE 9.14: Flow Roadmap Creation Progressing from Problem Areas and Concerns to Actions

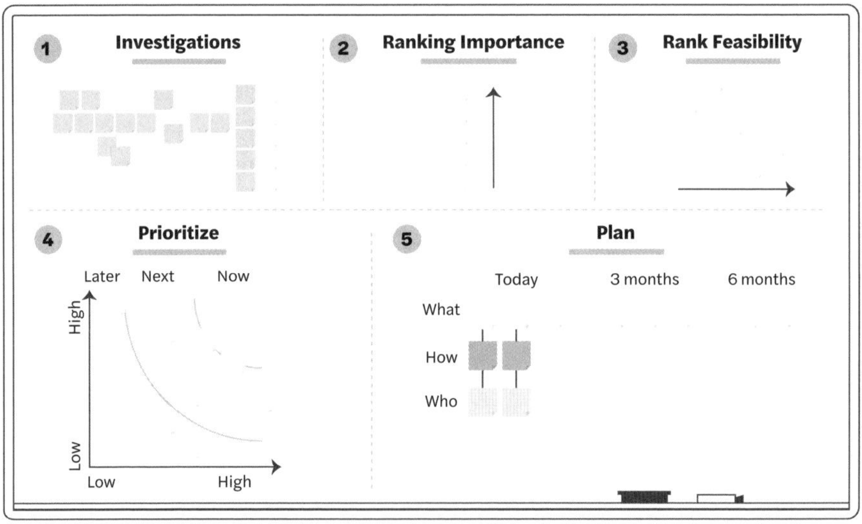

Conclusion

Creating a Flow Roadmap directly supports any other roadmaps you maintain, such as Product and Technical Roadmaps. The Flow Roadmap is a plan for a team to improve its capacity. By improving flow, we're improving delivery performance, allowing all of our work to be completed faster and at a higher quality.

This approach allows for relatively quick prioritization and estimation. As with the other maps, the goal is not to define a perfectly detailed plan. Instead, the goal is to provide just enough clarity to take your next action (and then the next and the next) with confidence and alignment.

With clear definition and priority of action, it's easier to create a roadmap you can feel confident in and that can impress even the most skeptical executive. The roadmap also provides a shared vision that every individual contributor can use to navigate in the right direction.

Flow Engineering is about finding the fastest path to effective action. From within all possible goals, Outcome Mapping establishes which will have the greatest value. From within parts of their workflow, Value Stream Mapping and Dependency Mapping provide clarity on the one constraint that has the most impact. And from within all possible activities, Future State Mapping and Flow Roadmapping focus the team on what changes will unlock flow. This is a powerful way to achieve target outcomes and also prevents disengagement, disorientation, and distraction.

Focus is important, but in large organizations, we also need to scale up, scale out, and sustain our improvement efforts. In Part 3, we'll look at ways you can use cybernetic principles to amplify the impact of Flow Engineering and leverage additional techniques to address enterprise scale and complexity.

Key Takeaways

- Insights from Flow Engineering workshops can be plotted and prioritized to create a clear and actionable roadmap, the Flow Roadmap.
- The Flow Roadmap complements other planning documents, such as Product and Technical Roadmaps, by focusing on improving flow—how work gets done.
- The Flow Roadmap captures actions, measurements, and ownership across increasing time horizons.
- The Flow Roadmap is a clear artifact that can be shared with leadership, peers, and individual contributors.

PART 3

Navigating the Landscape

CHAPTER 10

Principles of Flow Engineering

"As to methods, there may be a million and then some, but principles are few. Those who grasp principles can successfully select their own methods."

HARRINGTON EMERSON

HAVING CHARTED A COURSE from your current state to a target state, we'll now offer guidance on taking that journey and on enabling flow over larger scales and longer time frames.

We've spoken throughout this book of the need to move to effective action by targeting valuable outcomes, clarifying the path to progress, and steadily navigating toward improved flow. Taking the helm and guiding teams through this Flow Engineering process is not complicated, but it still requires courage and clarity.

We'll begin by sharing a set of principles that can guide and inform your efforts to engineer flow. Because instilling principles in an organization requires inspiration, discipline, and mindfulness, Chapter 11 offers advice on how to lead a team in these ongoing flow improvements. Chapter 12 shares common obstacles that often present headwinds to teams and what you can do to avoid them. Chapter 13 shows how the mapping exercises of Flow Engineering culminate in Value Stream Management, the ongoing practice of tuning performance based on these principles. Finally, Chapter 14 shows how to steadily increase your influence beyond your team to the broader organization.

Progressing from your current state to a target state requires effective action from the entire team. The most reliable way to scale performance improvement across a team or organization is to train consistently in a set of core principles.

The Power of Principles

Effective action depends on the ability of each individual to identify value, build clarity, and enable flow. As mentioned in Chapter 2, remedies to the challenge of scale fall on a continuum between prescriptive and generative, with Flow Engineering aiming to facilitate a balance between these two extremes.

These approaches emerge from two different ways of seeing an organization: the prescriptive approach is based on the view that an organization can be designed and engineered like a machine, while the generative approach is based on the view that an organization is composed of living workers whose behavior necessarily emerges from their own values and understanding.

Both approaches are needed, specifically because an organization has a dual nature: organizations are both a designed system and a living system, as expressed by Fritjof Capra and Pier Luigi Luisi in *The Systems View of Life*.[1] This dual nature leads to profoundly different interpretations of what explains an organization's difficulties and what we can do to enable its success. The purpose of Flow Engineering is to enable process transformation that is strategically oriented but also authentically motivated. One of the most powerful ways to scale and sustain this transformation is to teach simple and repeatable principles that can be applied in many contexts.

Principles are supremely valuable in the context of engineering flow because they provide guidance to all people at all times. Principles guide effective action not only for individuals but for large groups of people. They are far more adaptive than any prescriptive method or playbook. Principles are generalizations that can readily be applied to many patterns. Just like collaborative mapping is a superpower for effective collaboration, principles are a superpower for effective action.

In a cybernetic context, principles act as a decentralized, nonlinear, and inside-out control system. They're decentralized in that they can be held in each individual's mind and more easily recalled from passive memory than a detailed playbook. They're nonlinear in the sense that they can be applied in various contexts to varying degrees and simultaneously in different contexts by many individuals. And they're an inside-out control system in that they allow individuals to act autonomously by following the same guidance, the same navigation system.

Principles as Decision Filters

Decision filters are a tool used to streamline and improve the decision-making process in various methodologies, particularly business and project management. The core idea is to use a set of criteria or "filters" through which decisions must pass before being made. The structure of a decision filter is as follows: "Faced with a decision between X and Y, we choose X over Y." In this way, decision filters enshrine the values of an organization and make them practical for daily decision-making.

An example would be the following guidance from Satya Nadella, CEO of Microsoft: "If a developer ever has a choice between working on a feature or developer productivity, they should always choose developer productivity."[2] These filters help ensure that decisions align with strategic goals, resource constraints, and other important factors. Two specific examples are valuable in the context of Flow Engineering: Agile decision filters and Lean decision filters.

Agile Decision Filters: In Agile methodologies, decision filters focus on flexibility, customer satisfaction, and iterative progress. The Agile Manifesto laid out values as decision filters to serve as guideposts at the crossroads of any decision.[3] Decisions are evaluated based on how well they adhere to Agile principles like "responding to change over following a plan" and prioritizing "individuals and interactions over processes and tools." These filters help teams stay aligned with Agile values and ensure that decisions support an iterative, adaptive approach to project management.

Lean Decision Filters: In Lean management, decision filters are centered around principles like waste reduction, efficiency, and delivering value to the customer. Decisions are assessed on their ability to eliminate unnecessary steps, improve process efficiency, and enhance value creation for the end user. Examples include "Value trumps flow, flow trumps waste elimination," as stated by David Anderson.[4] These filters guide teams and organizations to make decisions that are in line with Lean thinking, focusing on streamlining operations and maximizing customer value.

In both cases, the decision filters serve as a guiding framework, helping teams and organizations make choices that are consistent with their overall approach and goals. They act as a checkpoint, ensuring that decisions contribute positively to the project or organization's objectives. Next, we'll introduce the five principles of Flow Engineering.

The Five Principles to Guide Flow Engineering

The principles shared here draw on multiple sources, but we've organized them into the five principles of Lean first introduced by James Womack and Daniel Jones in their book *Lean Thinking*.[5] Within these, we've cited some relevant points from other well-known contributors to the field, including Mary and Tom Poppendieck, W. Edwards Deming, Eli Goldratt, Steve Spear, and Peter Senge. Many of these thinkers evolved their ideas independently, but notwithstanding some nuanced distinctions in their views, we feel comfortable presenting their views in an integrated fashion here.

While there are many other principles that you might find valuable to adopt, the following constitute a minimum set of instructions that everyone in a team should become familiar with: specify value, map the value stream, create flow, pull don't push, and pursue perfection. (See Figure 10.1.)

FIGURE 10.1: The Five Principles of Lean

| Specify Value | Map the Value Stream | Create Flow | Pull Don't Push | Pursue Perfection |

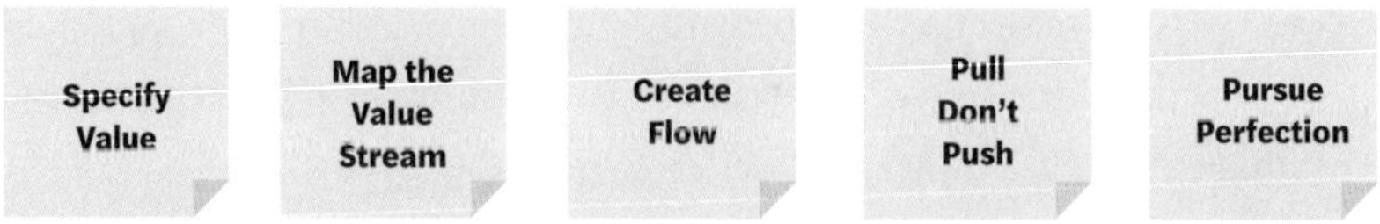

1. Specify Value

The central importance of value was introduced in Part i. Although the term *value* is commonplace, the paper "Measuring Value" describes its complexity:

> Value is subjective and volatile...Economists and accountants track and calculate value using the same mathematics that physicists and engineers use to calculate mass, distance, and energy. But value is fundamentally different from physical things. Value is subjective and transitory because it is a measure of how positively we feel about something, and whether it addresses a need.[6]

The subjectivity and volatility of value is why value must be specified. Value is always experienced by a particular being at a particular moment in time. It is a positive feeling of appreciation. What a valuable product brings is moments of enjoyment, relief, or effectiveness. In exchange, committed customers will pay money, a transaction that, again, reflects a momentary decision to part with something of value to receive something of greater value. Revenue figures are a summary of conditions and outcomes.

> Representing the value of something in terms of dollars is a way of combining every possible characteristic of a thing into a single dimension. This is similar to how a scale reduces an object to the single dimension of weight. It tells you nothing about the nuanced qualities, history, or potential of the object it's weighing. A scale cannot distinguish between a human being and several piled-up bags of rice. Since value is not an intrinsic quality of things, any measurement of value is necessarily subjective and subject to change.[7]

The subjectivity of value leads to an interesting challenge. Because there are multiple parties involved in creating and consuming a product, each of them exists in mutual dependence. Each party needs to experience a net positive value for the relationship to be sustainable long term. This is what mathematicians call "constrained optimization." Similar to game theory, this implies that the optimal solution is not an absolute maximum for any one party. Where any one party's interests are optimized to the detriment of other parties, the system becomes unbalanced, threatening the long-term relationship.

But it is precisely because value is subjective that this optimization problem is solvable. Delivering value is an act of cooperation, not a zero-sum game. The primary purpose of Outcome Mapping is to help all of the participants develop a clear sense of the value of a particular improvement opportunity. By enumerating the target outcome and benefits, the group has the opportunity to collectively understand the larger goal.

A simple Outcome Map, organized into columns for outcome, benefits, obstacles, and next steps, can still include a diverse set of concerns. Figure 10.2 shows a standard Outcome Map with an analysis of the purpose that each outcome and benefit serves.

Value is an emergent property. It is experienced by a particular person at a moment in time. Value is enabled by a flow of work and feedback. It's relatively easy to measure work, but since value is subjective, we can only measure value by getting feedback from those experiencing it. Value should inform every decision, action, and investment. Design for feedback to enable value.

FIGURE 10.2: A Simple Outcome Map Representing Diverse Concerns

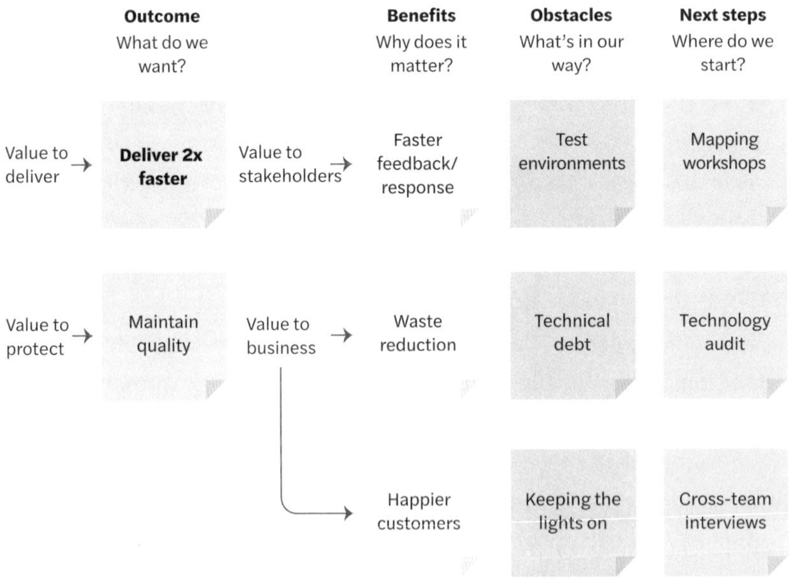

Outcome		Benefits	Obstacles	Next steps
What do we want?		Why does it matter?	What's in our way?	Where do we start?
Value to deliver →	**Deliver 2x faster**	Value to stakeholders →	Faster feedback/ response	Test environments	Mapping workshops
Value to protect →	Maintain quality	Value to business →	Waste reduction	Technical debt	Technology audit
			Happier customers	Keeping the lights on	Cross-team interviews

2. Map the Value Stream

The practice of Value Stream Mapping is central to Flow Engineering, but why? A value stream is a system for producing benefit through a sequential series of contributions. Since a value stream is an interdependent system, it is greater than the sum of its parts.

When we focus attention on a problem, our minds naturally narrow and fixate locally on that issue. This leads to a tendency to focus on the parts rather than the whole, as illustrated by Iain McGilchrist's *The Master and His Emissary*.[8] It's also much easier to quantify and address point improvements. We can find endless shortcomings in the particular parts of a system, but unless improvements are targeting the constraint in a system, they will not lead to a net improvement in throughput.

Every activity should align to a value stream. Our internal model of work needs to be continually realigned to focus on the value we are delivering. We experiment intentionally and unintentionally with many activities, but we need to constantly rein in those that are not bringing value. When every part of the value stream is aligned with this aim, the flow is naturally improved because it eliminates steps that do not add value.

W. Edwards Deming, Peter Senge, Mary Poppendieck, Stafford Beer, and countless other thinkers of the twentieth century emphasized the importance of understanding the organization as a system. Deming identified system thinking as one of four topics in his System of Profound Knowledge. Peter Senge identified systems thinking as the fifth discipline required to create a learning organization in his eponymous book *The Fifth Discipline*. The series of activities that make up a system work together to perform a function, such as achieving a business aim. Deming's theory of knowledge emphasized that managers must understand the systems they oversee to manage effectively.

We make assumptions and use particular ways of thinking to understand situations and resolve problems. Western rationalism has habituated most of us to very linear ways of thinking. Even the medium that we use to express information can skew our thinking. If you primarily use slides, this biases both the creator and the audience toward very simple concepts that can be explained graphically one idea at a time. If you principally use spreadsheets, you tend to assume that all knowledge can be organized into linear matrices, where everything adds up in a linear system. If you tend to use documents, you'll again tend to assume that a linear system expressed as text is enough to describe a situation.

Deming pointed out that internal barriers between departments can interrupt the flow of information and materials and thus disrupt systems.[9] His work suggests that organizations should foster collaboration across departments and teams to improve overall flow.

Mapping the value stream (as with any mapping exercise) is a method of communicating visually. (See Figure 10.3 for a simple example.) As mentioned in the introduction, 30% of the human brain is dedicated exclusively to visual processing.[10] Likewise, Principle 7 of the Toyota Way emphasizes the use of visual controls so that problems are not hidden.[11] Simple visual indicators and summaries that can be expressed on a single page are very powerful.

FIGURE 10.3: A Simple Flow Engineering Value Stream Map

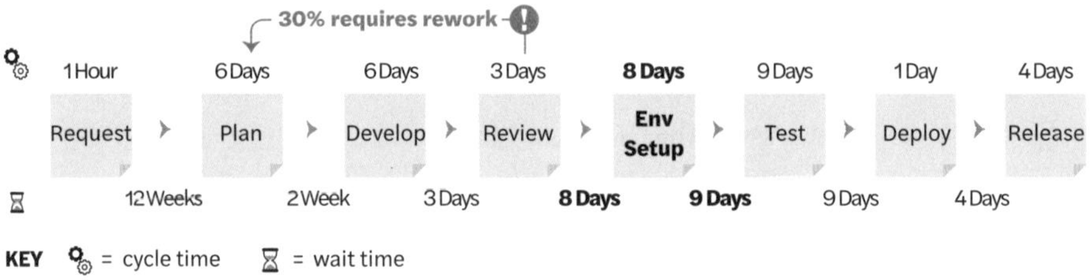

	Request	Plan	Develop	Review	Env Setup	Test	Deploy	Release
cycle time	1 Hour	6 Days	6 Days	3 Days	**8 Days**	9 Days	1 Day	4 Days
wait time		12 Weeks	2 Week	3 Days	**8 Days**	**9 Days**	9 Days	4 Days

30% requires rework

KEY = cycle time   = wait time

Visibility enables observability; observability enables clarity. Observability means to infer the internal state of something by measuring its external characteristics. This depends on visibility, as well as contextual information. The ability to infer something's internal state is the source for generating clarity, an adequate explanatory model.

Clarity is the most valuable resource we can influence. Our ability to respond correctly, and thus not waste time or energy, depends on clarity about the most useful response. Effort invested in gaining clarity allows us to avoid waste and risk.

3. Create Flow

Principles 2, 3, and 4 of the Toyota Way are to create flow, avoid overproduction, and level out the workload.[12] These three are closely related. Flow implies a quality of steadiness in motion; it implies that the outflow is equal to the inflow over time. Overproduction implies that valuable time, energy, and resources have been expended in producing things whose value is not being realized. This is the very definition of waste. Avoiding such waste requires leveling out the workload, also known as *heijunka*. A level workload creates consistency across time and across the stream, again implying that the rate of inflow remains roughly equal to the rate of outflow. This implies that overproduction is not happening, even temporarily or at substages of production.

Continuous process flow brings problems to the surface. The difficulty of achieving such steady flow reveals where there are parts of the process that are subject to stagnation, overproduction, or unevenness. To remedy this, organizations need to move materials and information fast and link processes and people together.

Figure 10.5 shows a Value Stream Map with wait times between each stage highlighted. In this case, the wait time represents ~80% of the total lead time (131 of 168 days). The long waiting periods between steps are the opposite of flow. The reason for the wait between stages is typically because the teams responsible for the next stage of work are not available to begin working immediately, usually because they are already busy with other work.

FIGURE 10.4: Value Stream Map Highlighting Wait Times

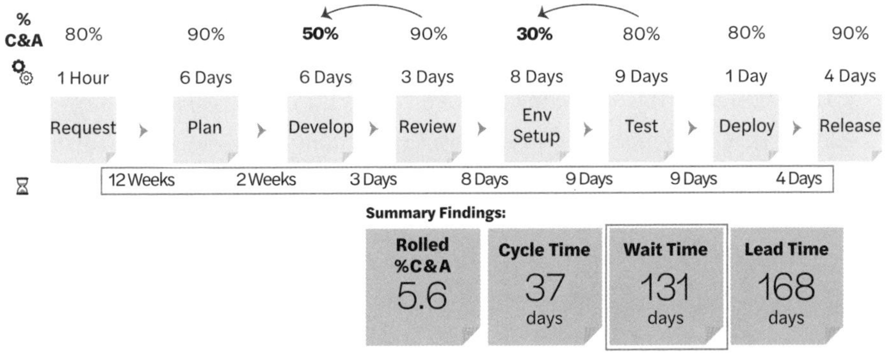

Optimizing for flow is contradictory to optimizing for resource utilization. The book *This is Lean* described this as "the efficiency paradox."[13] Keeping each machine, person, or process maximally utilized seems like it is more efficient; this is called "resource efficiency." But this is only true if you consider each of these resources as independent.

This takes us back to why systems thinking is fundamental to this process. Russell Ackoff summarized this dynamic of interdependence as, "A system is never the sum of its parts; it's the product of their interaction."[14] Every part of the system consumes value as it works, but the entire system needs to work in harmony to *produce* value. Thus, every system operates at a loss unless it is well-coordinated enough to produce more value than it consumes.

To maximize value, we must instead focus on "flow efficiency." Resource efficiency isolates each contributor to assess the percent of time it's working divided by the time it is available. By contrast, flow efficiency measures how quickly each work product *could* be produced (cycle time) divided by the actual lead time. Both approaches superficially seem to make the best use of resources, but optimizing for resource efficiency by staying busy all the time undermines the production of value by leading to a dramatic increase in lead time and work in progress. (The math behind this is based on the Kingsman's Approximation.)

We have deeply ingrained habits of assuming that we should maximize the use of all capacity. But a system is more than the sum of its parts. The root of the challenge lies in how variable the work is. If there is little or no variability in how long a work step takes (as would be the case with purely operational value streams like in manufacturing), each resource can move closer to 100% utilization. But if there is significant variation in how long work takes (as is the case with more developmental value streams like software development or design), resources need slack capacity to be able to accommodate this variation. If everyone is maximally busy, there's little extra time or energy to address new challenges, and overall wait time tends to go way up.[15] Utilizing a resource 100% appears to maximize its individual productivity but at the expense of making it impossible to deal with variation. *This is Lean* summarized this using the concept of an Efficiency Matrix, as shown in Figure 10.5.

Variation, thus, inhibits efficiency. It is for this reason that early attempts at replicating the success of the Toyota Production System emphasized reducing variation, as W. Edwards Deming illustrated in his book *Out of the Crisis*.[16] For example, Six Sigma aims to reduce variation and defects down to six standard deviations (σ - sigma) or 3.4 defects per million units.[17]

The linear relationship between resource efficiency and flow efficiency is also rarely linear. A linear relationship only holds true if every stage in the process experiences the same amount of variation and can process its work in the same period of time. In reality, there is significant variation not only in work products but in how long different *stages* of a process take to complete. Even in a manufacturing process, where variation can be systematically reduced, one stage of the process will always take longer than other stages.

FIGURE 10.5: The Efficiency Matrix

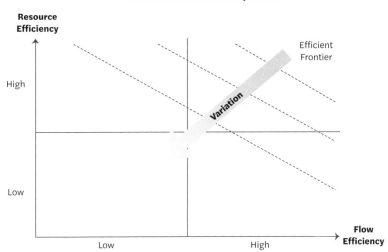

The trade-off between resource efficiency and flow efficiency leads to an Efficient Frontier: a range of possible utilization options, shown as the dotted line in the upper right. The greater the variation in the work, the more that Efficient Frontier is pushed down. *Source:* Modig and Åhlström, *This is Lean*, 105.

Eli Goldratt's primary contribution to the world of management is understanding that flow is always limited by one and only one constraint at any given time. This is known as the Theory of Constraints (TOC) and was the subject of his famous book *The Goal.*[18] The Theory of Constraints asserts that total system throughput can only be improved when the constraint is improved. This constraint can come from culture, process, environment, or technology. That factor is not necessarily visible without the right observation. To increase performance, you need to target the constraint.

According to Goldratt, addressing the constraint is done using five focusing steps. These steps are a distillation of the TOC process for improving flow and include:[19]

1. Identifying the constraint.
2. Exploiting the constraint.
3. Subordinating everything else to it.
4. Elevating the constraint.
5. Preventing inertia from setting in by repeating the process.

Value Stream Mapping lets us visualize workflow as a horizontal progression. By examining the full end-to-end workflow, we can discover a governing constraint that is limiting overall performance. The most impactful governing constraint will always be at one point along that workflow. (See Figure 10.6.) To address it, we can zoom in on what's happening within (or upstream of) the constrained activity by using Dependency Mapping. We may also need to zoom out to address external dependencies and capabilities contributing to the limitation. Addressing the vertical slice that is acting as a governing constraint to the overall horizontal flow is the key to improving performance.

FIGURE 10.6: Theory of Constraints Step 1: Identify the Constraint

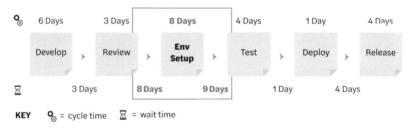

Next we exploit the constraint by extracting as much value from it as possible—for example, by improving the utilization of that *one* resource. (See Figure 10.7.)

FIGURE 10.7: Theory of Constraints Step 2: Exploit the Constraint

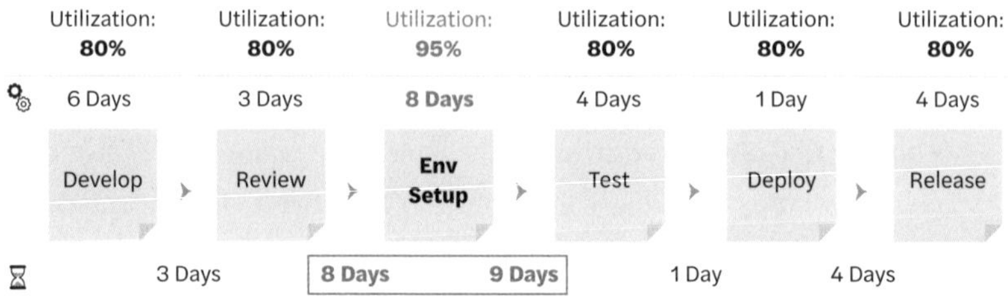

The third step is to subordinate everything else to the constraint. This can involve organizing to reduce wait times before or after that step to avoid pileups or involve ensuring upstream quality and reliability. The resource utilization can be tuned up or down to best support the constraint. (See Figure 10.8.)

FIGURE 10.8: Theory of Constraints Step 3: Subordinate Everything Else to the Constraint

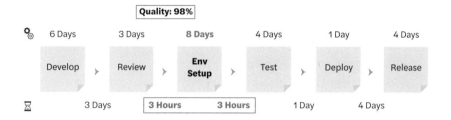

The fourth focusing step in the Theory of Constraints is to elevate the constraint. Having organized around the constraint, if more throughput is required, the remaining option is to increase the capacity of the constraint itself—e.g., by adding an additional parallel resource. (See Figure 10.9.)

FIGURE 10.9: Theory of Constraints Step 4: Elevate the Constraint

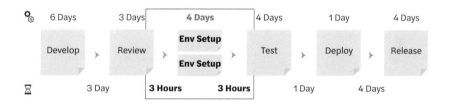

4. Pull Don't Push

The way to avoid overproduction is to use *pull* systems instead of *push* systems. This means to give customers what they want, when they want it, and in the amount they want. Not more.

A simple linear flow is sufficient to manage the simplest assembly line, one which produces consistently day after day. But even one variable is enough to destabilize this process. And customer demand is always variable. This is why a pull system is so powerful. It allows the whole production system to synchronize to the pace of customer demand and avoid overproduction.

Steve Spear's book *The High-Velocity Edge: How Market Leaders Leverage Operational Excellence to Beat the Competition* lays out a set of principles as "the ideal" that summarizes a great deal of the value of a pull-based system across a number of dimensions. As he stated,

> This ideal implied that production and delivery should be:
>
> - Defect-free—never compromising customer satisfaction.
> - On demand—only in response to real need.
> - One piece at a time—providing those who needed something exactly what they could put to use, not overburdening them with the obligation to hold things in anticipation of future need.
> - Immediate—providing those who needed something what they needed without imposing any wait time on them, but, if this was impossible, small batches of finished goods might be kept on hand to provide the illusion of immediacy.
> - Without waste—never spending time, effort, creativity, and other efforts in ways that wouldn't be valued by someone else.
> - Safe—so no one gets hurt physically or emotionally or is professionally threatened.
> - Secure—so that material, services, or information go only to those intended and not others.[20]

The ideal described above illustrates how pull has significant implications for value, clarity, and flow. Push is always a guess of what may be needed in the future; pull is only ever driven by established need (value). Pushing implies a lack of clarity on the need for our work, leading to the assumption that we should produce, even if there is no demand; pull creates a direct connection between what is needed and what is delivered. Creating a pull-based system of work is an extraordinary feat, but each step toward it brings improved value, clarity, and flow.

Pull manifests itself in different ways within an organization, but let's look at a few ways it can apply to individual contributors and dependent teams:

- As an individual contributor, if I can pull work, information, or capabilities (access on demand), I can do what I need when I need to and avoid delays or capacity overload (too little or too much work) at any given time. Rather than having a batch of committed work to complete (that could be accomplished by others or grow stale waiting for my attention), I can pull one task at a time, as I have the capacity to act on it. Rather than having a testing environment sitting idle and waiting for use, I can spin up or reserve capacity on an on-demand or shared pool of dynamic resources. If I can pull information and capabilities from other teams via self-service (by referencing shared documentation) or from an information radiator (like a dashboard), I don't have to interrupt that other team; I can simply pull without disruption or distraction.

- Meetings are often employed as a way to broadcast information that is valuable to the recipients, but meetings often consist of much low-value information (noise) and little high-value information (signal). The disengagement and distraction endemic to businesses operating at scale often implies that attendees are not mentally present, even if they attend. The signal is often worth the noise, so the waste of pushing out information is preferable to the risk of failing to convey the information. A pull-based equivalent implies that the information should be made available in a shared system and pulled by recipients as needed.

- For dependent teams, like shared services teams, every pull (every request for assistance) represents a disruption unless it gets buffered in a queue. The queue creates a delay, which impacts lead time. By implementing mechanisms like prioritization and triage (where different types of requests are routed differently and with varying urgency), we can more easily mitigate the costs of queuing (delay) and leverage the benefits (buffering). By implementing self-service capabilities, or even something as simple as a team API (a specification defining information about the team, its capabilities, and responsibilities—which we'll discuss later on in the chapter), we can allow those dependent on us to get what they need when they need it without interruption or delay.

By their nature of being minimal, engaged on-demand, and value-centric, pull-based systems are highly efficient and effective. They maximize value, clarity, and flow but also increase visibility and measurability. If we can measure the time between a need surfaced and a need fulfilled, we can understand and improve our speed of action, learning, and adaptation. The more we rely on push as a model for action, the more risk, waste, delay, assumption, and load we inject into the flow. Pull allows for just-in-time, just enough, and just the right people.

FIGURE 10.10: Excess Work in Progress Is a Sign of Lacking Pull Systems

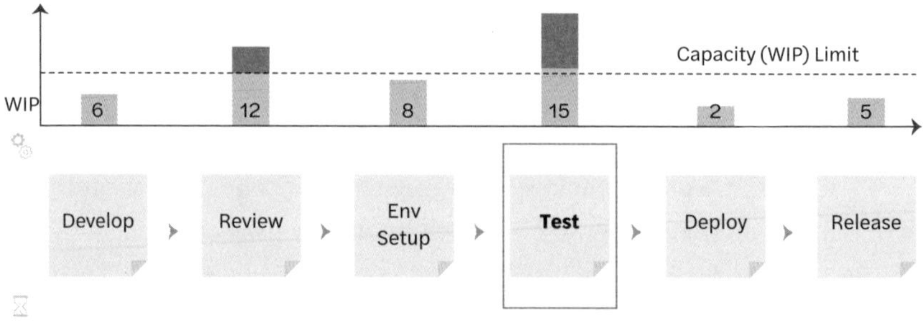

A pull-based system is a powerful way of reducing batch size, as shown in Figure 10.10. Reducing batch sizes reduces the amount of inventory (including work in progress, or WIP) in the system. It also allows the system to become more flexible and responsive, improving flow and decreasing the time products spend in process. In addition, reducing batch sizes lowers detrimental cognitive load. For example, if a production failure occurs due to a large batch of changes, it is difficult to discern which specific change caused the failure. Small batch deployments reduce the risk and pinpoint the source of failures.

We mentioned WIP limits in Chapter 8 under Tips and Traps for Future State Mapping. WIP limits are a classic example of a governing constraint. Counterintuitively, limiting WIP enables you to get more done. Here's why it works:

- Improved communication and collaboration: Limiting WIP means the team's attention is less fragmented across disparate work items, leading to more cohesive and collaborative work.
- Easier identification of bottlenecks: With fewer concurrent tasks, bottlenecks in the workflow become more visible and easier to address.

- **Easier prioritization:** WIP limits compel teams to focus on the most critical tasks first, aligning efforts with key project goals.
- **More effective planning:** Limiting WIP leads to more predictable work-flows, allowing for better planning and forecasting.
- **Increased team morale:** A more manageable workload from limited WIP helps prevent burnout and boosts team morale.
- **Enhanced flexibility and responsiveness:** Reduced WIP enables teams to quickly adapt to changes in requirements through reduced exposure to prior commitments.
- **Reduced context switching:** By focusing on fewer tasks at a time, contributors experience less context switching, leading to greater efficiency.
- **Faster completion times:** Limiting WIP results in quicker task completion, accelerating overall project progress.
- **Enhanced quality:** A focus on fewer tasks at a time leads to higher-quality outputs and fewer errors.
- **Improved focus and productivity:** Focusing on a limited number of tasks to lower detrimental cognitive load and the risk of distraction.

Single piece flow is the most extreme version of WIP limiting, where only one work item is under development at any given stage in the flow of work. It can be extremely challenging to implement and not often feasible, but it provides an unparalleled level of simplicity, clarity, and focus to work flowing through a value stream. When contributors aren't juggling work, they not only experience less detrimental cognitive load and distraction, but there's also less waste from context switching. In single piece flow streams or segments, contributors will often "mob" and work on the work item together simultaneously. This has the added benefit of maximizing information flow across the team in real time, but it can also help rapidly onboard new team members into unfamiliar work without overwhelming them. Single piece flow is also supremely measurable. If there's not a large batch of work flowing through the system at any given moment, each work item can be much more clearly measured, and flow constraints become far more obvious within daily work. It's easy to miss a constraint when you can simply switch to another task and forget about the blocker or delay.

5. Pursue Perfection

In Lean, perfection is pursued by continuously removing waste. Directly or indirectly, waste is a result of not understanding or being able to deliver value in a more efficient way. Therefore, learning is central to removing waste.

Implicit in enabling learning is a sense of psychological safety, as emphasized by Amy Edmondson, Google's Project Aristotle, Ron Westrum, and others. One of Deming's main exhortations was to drive fear out of organizations and to empower employees.[21] Deming understood that fear was counterproductive in organizations. Encouraging open communication and reporting of issues without fear of reprisal is essential to identifying and addressing impediments to flow.

The most reliable approach to learning is taking a scientific approach. In brief, the scientific method implies that we develop mental models about the system we're seeking to understand, use those mental models to develop a hypothesis about that system, and then run tests that might invalidate or affirm that hypothesis.

The most reliable tests involve changing just a single variable. This implies creating a stable starting point from which we can make a single change. Thus, it's clear how scientific thinking depends on standardization. Standards create stability. And that stability, in turn, allows us to notice and make sense of differences that might be exposed by running tests.

A second key aspect of the scientific method is the willingness to be wrong. Being right and being wrong feel exactly the same. What feels different is *discovering* that we are wrong. Thus, learning is error correction for the mind, as alluded to by Kathryn Schulz in *Being Wrong*.[22] This is, by definition, uncomfortable. Thus, learning requires patience, humility, and deliberately putting ourselves in situations where we may discover our mistakes.

Most of our mental models are implicit, and we implicitly want them to be true. Our confirmation bias organizes information into these mental models, simplifying the world by ignoring information that doesn't make sense to us. Learning implies letting go of our current models.

This is the purpose behind the idea of "go and see," *genchi genbutsu*, made popular in Lean. Going to the actual place where work is happening allows us to both solicit reliable information and test our hypotheses.

This scientific thinking should not be relegated to just a select few members of the organization. It is something that should be applied systematically by every person in the organization every day. The culture of "stop the line," *jidoka*, means creating a culture of stopping to fix problems on the spot. This means that the pursuit of quality is exercised continually across the organization.

Conclusion

Mapping and creating a Flow Roadmap provides you a solid starting point for improving flow along with specific interventions that address the opportunities you uncover, but from that point on, your actions and decisions need to be guided by clear thinking. The principles we've collected and referenced in this chapter can not only help you navigate your next steps effectively but also improve your mapping practice and uncover new insights as you map and analyze performance.

In the next chapter, we'll take that further, offering specific leadership and control mechanisms that make it easy to do the right thing—and hard to do the wrong thing.

Key Takeaways

- Principles provide scalable, adaptable, and applicable guidance for making decisions that drive effective action within and beyond the practices of Flow Engineering.
- Principles support Flow Engineering by guiding what we do with the information we gain from mapping.
- The Lean stages of specifying value, mapping the value stream, enabling flow and pull, and pursuing perfection provide a valuable framework for key principles.
- Value, clarity, and flow are enabled by shared understanding and applying the principles of Flow Engineering.

CHAPTER 11

Leading
Flow
Engineering

"The ultimate test of practical
leadership is the realization
of intended, real change that
meets people's enduring
needs."

JAMES MACGREGOR BURNS

THE PRINCIPLES OF Flow Engineering provide important guidance for everyone involved in process improvement. But for principles to be effective, they must be put into practice consistently. Consistent practice requires discipline and mindfulness, and this, in turn, requires strong and sustained effort. Strong and sustained effort, in turn, depends on confidence that great results are possible. And confidence, in turn, depends on inspiration and vision.

Changing a team's values, understanding, and behavior is culture change. A primary driver of successful culture change is what is known as transformational leadership. This means to set forth an inspiring vision of what the team is capable of, to encourage and exhort the team in that direction, to provide steady and consistent reminders of the principles, and to repeatedly redirect the team's attention to the outcomes they seek. In this chapter, we'll look at how to lead Flow Engineering efforts.

Cybernetics and Leadership

The five maps you learned in Part 2 are designed to help teams take effective action by fostering value, clarity, and flow. To understand effective action at scale, we need to return to the concept of cybernetics.

If you're an agent of change in your organization, you are responsible for bringing that change about safely. To safely deliver change, you must control risk. And to control risk, you need the ability to respond quickly and effectively when problems emerge so that small problems don't derail the entire initiative.

Leadership just means influence, as John C. Maxwell stated in *The 21 Irrefutable Laws of Leadership*.[1] Leaders, by definition, do not exist independently of those they lead. People follow the example, the inspiration, and the words of leaders. Thus, leaders' control of their own body, speech, and mind indirectly exerts influence on the teams they lead. We call this "leading from the inside out."

The role of leadership is to assume the risk and responsibility of guiding others safely in a beneficial direction in spite of great uncertainty. Flow Engineering involves a special kind of leadership: guiding teams to realize progressively greater personal and collective capacity. Uncovering more and more of our team's potential, rather than just executing on known skills, involves significant uncertainty and significant learning from everyone involved. To know whether we're on track, we must establish feedback loops.

Designing Feedback Loops

The cybernetic approach to leadership involves designing feedback loops that can function as control systems. Control systems are methods to allow one system to control or safely interact with another. Feedback loops are an important aspect of any system. Negative feedback loops in a control system help bring the system being controlled back into a safe range. Positive feedback loops in a control system help encourage desirable behavior.

The simple Value Stream Map in Figure 11.1 depicts multiple feedback loops and acts as a template for understanding the flow of work. The macro feedback loop is defined by customer preferences, while micro feedback loops within and between each stage of work are defined by teams' internal standards.

FIGURE 11.1: A Value Stream Map Depicts Multiple Feedback Loops

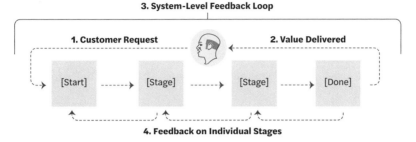

The cycle from customer request (1) to value delivered (2) establishes a system-level positive feedback loop (3) that encourages growth and allows the team to learn and tune performance. Internal feedback loops (4) are typically negative feedback loops that allow for more fine-grained control and learning.

The purpose of an organization is to understand and respond to customer preferences. This requires methods to solicit customer sentiment (the macro feedback loop) since this is a leading indicator of repeat sales and sustainable customer relationships. The feedback loops between individual stages provide methods to control quality within the process to avoid releasing defects to the customer.

Feedback loops must be correctly tuned to the problems they are managing. Reacting to the wrong signal can be costly. Reacting incorrectly can be wasteful. You can also drown in too much low-value feedback. Your target must be clear and valuable, and you need information that guides the flow of activity toward that outcome. Feedback loops must also evolve as target outcomes evolve. Each objective has its unique key results, with specific metrics that provide feedback on progress.

Feedback loops allow us to keep a system under control. Imagine if it were difficult or impossible to control your body or your car. How frightening, dangerous, embarrassing, and frustrating would this be? Control is implicit in everything that we do, and the lack of control poses many dangers. Control isn't about robotic precision and repetition. Dancers have control, and that control enables them to be creative. A group of dancers synchronize and amplify their performance through collective control.

The collaborative mapping exercises shared in this book are a way for teams to gain control of their flow of work by building clarity. This simple act of identifying collective value, building collective clarity, and enabling collective flow aligns with the way living beings naturally bring their worlds under control: through understanding and engaging with it.

Executing on the Flow Roadmap

As Peter Drucker famously quipped, "strategy is a commodity, execution is an art."[2]

Establishing a Flow Roadmap, or any other intended course of progress, is a great start. But life moves fast, priorities change, things take longer than planned, and we get distracted. Many great plans are set in motion but are never accomplished. Here are some approaches to help ensure that the momentum around flow doesn't taper out.

Rhythm: Teams need daily, weekly, monthly, quarterly, and annual rhythms that create opportunities to look back at past progress (or lack of progress) to assess. The simple act of making a plan and reviewing progress at intervals creates a feedback loop. The feedback loop is a human one; our past self sets a reminder that our present self now needs to act on, and our present self is setting reminders to help our future self stay on track. This habit is deeply ingrained in some people and anathema for other people, but it is a habit that can be established, and that is a basic requirement for building an operational cadence at a team or organizational level.

Simplicity: The main failure mode of most improvement initiatives is taking on too much. Our attachment to the idea of accomplishing "all the things" means that we risk not accomplishing any of the things: *Do one thing. Build confidence. Do the next thing.* It's for this reason that we counsel people building a Flow Roadmap to target just one improvement goal. If that's easy for you and the team, great. Take on more. But do it gradually.

Humility: Team learning implies that we do not already know everything. Those who already know everything have nothing to learn. Staying humble helps you stay open to new information, risks, and opportunities.

Amplify Successes: Share progress and successes within the team and with other teams. Process improvement is slow and subject to setbacks, but sharing updates makes others more aware that small improvements are something worth talking about and worth celebrating. Also share failure in the context of learning. The confidence to acknowledge the real state of affairs is an antidote to the exaggerated positivity that some people and teams project as a defensive shield.

Begin Again: The key skill for sustained progress is restarting an initiative after it falters. It's inevitable that improvement efforts will stall from time to time. Starting them back up again requires a distinct determination.

Balancing Prescriptive and Generative Approaches

As mentioned in Chapter 2, there are many common templates for managing business processes. These vary on a spectrum from *prescriptive* to *generative*. Some of the more common ones are shown in Figure 11.2. The primary approach that we emphasize in this book is Value Stream Management, bootstrapped and enabled by the maps created through Flow Engineering.

FIGURE 11.2: Business Frameworks Are Templates for Management

Flow Engineering aims to balance prescriptive and generative approaches. The sequence of maps and the steps within them is the prescriptive aspect of Flow Engineering. It provides a structure that orients teams toward goal-seeking behavior and continuous optimization. It should be clear, repeatable, and relatively consistent, though the outputs are always unique and tailored to each organization and point in time. The informal interaction that unfolds during mapping exercises is the generative aspect of Flow Engineering. We cannot predict in advance what conversations and insights will unfold while others do these mapping exercises. The prompts and practices act to provoke a response, and the response reflects the lived experience of participants.

This is why it is often said that the mapping is more important than the map. The mapping is a living interaction that is shaped by and shapes participants. The map is an artifact spun out from that living interaction. The map may remain a useful conversation starter to provoke further thought, but unless they're referenced regularly over time, the maps themselves have no power.

Governing and Enabling Constraints

To this point, we've used the term "constraint" to refer to the bottleneck that restricts flow through a value stream (as in the Theory of Constraints). But constraints are not always negative; they can be an extremely valuable aid in crafting a system of work for optimal flow.

Dave Snowden, originator of the Cynefin framework, popularized a twofold distinction between constraints: governing constraints and enabling constraints.[3] *Governing constraints* are those that limit or control something; *enabling constraints* are those which encourage or make something possible.

The categorization into enabling constraints and governing constraints is not a characteristic of the constraint itself; it's a description of how the constraint functions. The same constraint can be both governing and enabling. For example, a ship's sail is constrained by the ropes that restrain it. That constraint governs the sail by preventing it from moving too far out of the desired position. But the same constraint also enables the sail to catch winds in a particular direction, which, in turn, can enable movement.

Governing constraints restrict or guide certain types of thinking or behavior; they are most applicable in a complicated domain where solutions can be determined in advance. A constraint in a value stream that limits flow is a governing constraint. Such a constraint is shown in Figure 11.3; it restricts the flow or quality of work downstream, leading to decreased performance. Unblocking flow is our primary target for rapid performance improvement. There can be multiple negative impacts on flow, but there's always one constraint that has the greatest impact.

FIGURE 11.3: The Constraint on a Value Stream

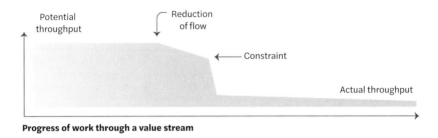

This figure illustrates how a constraint has a distinct, measurable impact on the flow of work on a value stream.

Enabling constraints are those that enable or encourage certain types of behavior; they are most applicable in a complex domain where new solutions are emergent. Generative approaches, often seen in innovative and creative fields, are more about exploration and discovery. They facilitate experimentation, adaptation, and learning. Enabling constraints are designed to empower and enable action. Unlike governing constraints, they don't limit possibilities but rather create a framework within which creativity and innovation can flourish.

Prescriptive management systems emphasize creating governing constraints by allowing or disallowing certain activities. Prescriptive approaches involve setting specific rules, guidelines, and procedures that dictate how tasks should be performed. Governing constraints are akin to these prescriptive rules. They are limits set to control and direct behavior, ensuring adherence to standards, safety, legality, and other essential factors. Governing constraints typically aim to make it hard to do the wrong thing.

Generative management systems emphasize enabling constraints by, for example, soliciting input from contributors to the question, "What should be our main area of focus?" The question itself constrains discussion, but it does so in a way that draws out insights from participants. Enabling constraints might include basic guidelines, principles, or values that provide a starting point or a foundation. However, they leave ample room for individuals to explore various paths and solutions. Enabling constraints typically aim to make it easy to do the right thing.

Enabling and governing constraints make some things easy and other things hard. To illustrate what this means in the context of flow, Table 11.1 provides several examples of each constraint type.

TABLE 11.1: Examples of Enabling and Governing Constraints

Enabling	Governing
Maps/canvases	Service level agreement
OKR/V2MOM structure	Industry regulation
Technology platforms	Organizational structure and hierarchy
Playbooks	WIP limit
Principles	Security policies

Dave Mangot, author of *DevOps Patterns for Private Equity*, illustrates the power of enabling constraints: "If we want teams that are empowered to move quickly and safely, instead of giving them strict instructions on how to perform their jobs, we can make the right way the easy way."[4] Enabling people to effectively and efficiently get to where they want to go is sometimes described as "paving a path."

Chris Matts provided further guidance for how to think about where each constraint is best applied: "Where there is no uncertainty, governing constraints are the most effective approach. Where there is no uncertainty, use of enabling constraints is at best inefficient and at worst destabilizing and destructive."[5] In a flow context, this means that in a stable and consistent value stream, governing constraints can help optimize and improve more effectively than enabling constraints. In a chaotic or less established value stream, enabling constraints can help encourage the right behaviors without becoming too onerous or restrictive. This also implies that we can use constraints to improve consistency (by restricting specific behaviors) or innovation (by enabling specific behaviors). When enabling behavior, we aim to avoid premature optimization (tightening up) while also avoiding a lack of guidance or direction (aimless wandering).

Teaching and Coaching

Peter Senge's 1990 book *The Fifth Discipline* popularized the concept of a learning organization. According to Senge, a learning organization is:

> ...an organization that has adopted learning as an integral element. It is the place where people are constantly expanding their ability to achieve their goals, where new models of thinking are being cultivated. Collective ambition is liberated and people are constantly learning how to learn as members of an organization.[6]

In a world of continual change, such flexibility of mind is a critical adaptive skill. Flow Engineering deals with the challenge of improving value, clarity, and flow by changing how we feel, think, and act individually and collectively. This makes work more meaningful and also more manageable.

Establishing a learning organization, Senge explained, depends on establishing five disciplines: building shared vision, systems thinking, mental models, personal mastery, and team learning.[7] Three of these principles have already been introduced in this book: building shared vision is the primary goal of Outcome Mapping; systems thinking is central to Value Stream Mapping and Dependency Mapping; and each of the mapping exercises is a way of expressing and synchronizing our mental models of work. We now offer some brief thoughts on Senge's remaining two principles: personal mastery and team learning.

Personal Mastery

There are two types of challenges: situations where you don't know what to do and situations where you know what to do but don't want to do it. Addressing the first challenge requires clarity: careful observation, thought, discussion, and creativity. Addressing the second challenge requires subordinating our innate experience of value—our feelings—to what our conscious mind believes to be valuable. In other words, discipline.

Discipline is the equivalent of mental weightlifting. Lifting weights involves applying a physical force to counteract the force of gravity. Discipline involves applying the mental force of conscious intention to counteract the force of distraction and reactivity. The result of continuously applying discipline is that patterns of behavior become ingrained and natural, and thus require less effort to carry out. A wonderful summary of the methods for developing personal habits can be found in *Atomic Habits* by James Clear, and insights into how to cultivate talent in others can be found in *The Talent Code* by Daniel Coyle. A central point in both books is that the key lies in small, continuous improvements compounded over time.

Coaching instills discipline in a team by giving them feedback. Coaches hold a mental model of the target behavior. They observe the team, alert them to mistakes, give guidance, and praise progress. This is an exercise in value, clarity, and flow on a moment-by-moment, day-by-day basis. It makes the difference between success and failure over the long term. Part 2 of this book offered creative exercises that help teams craft a broad vision for progress. But just as navigating on an ocean requires grit and determination, executing on the Flow Roadmap requires patience and continuous effort.

One of the main qualities of a coach or leader is not being scared of their own or others' discomfort. Executing on a plan means encountering confusion, setbacks, and distractions and persevering anyway. This is not a comfortable undertaking, but it is a valuable one.

Team Learning and Potential

Earlier we described leadership as bravely entering the unknown. A key unknown at play here is potential. To sustain confidence while drawing out the potential of others requires sustained optimism and a vision of what is possible. Such optimism has been repeatedly shown to be a self-fulfilling prophecy. Work by Robert Rosenthal in the 1960s first established how teachers who were led to believe their students were on the verge of dramatic intellectual improvements helped those improvements come about: "Expectations affect teachers' moment-to-moment interactions with the children they teach in a thousand almost invisible ways. Teachers give the students that they expect to succeed more time to answer questions, more specific feedback, and more approval: They consistently touch, nod and smile at those kids more."[8]

Adults are less malleable than children, but the same principles apply to coaching adults. When we believe in the potential of our team, we draw that potential out. This implies setting and maintaining high standards while energetically giving targeted support and assistance with building the habits students need.

Both Outcome Mapping and Future State Mapping emphasize a team's potential state, turning attention to what could be. Implicit in both of those maps is a team that is capable of carrying that out. As the team adopts a valuable target outcome and envisions their future state of performance, this vision also changes their self-identity. In becoming a team that can accomplish that goal, they develop higher expectations of themselves.

Team learning implies that teams develop shared understandings of their operating environment and anchor that understanding in visual artifacts such as the five maps of Flow Engineering. In this way, team learning stabilizes individual learning, where each person's understanding supports the understanding of others on the team, and behavioral expectations are clear from the standards around us.

By collaborating in creating the five maps, the entire team has a chance to unify around process improvement. When, for example, teams engage in Dependency Mapping to identify the causes of a particular bottleneck, they build the full mental context (value and clarity) needed to unblock the flow of work at that stage. If people are sincerely motivated to improve a process, problem-solving behavior emerges naturally.

For teams seeking process improvement, there is no substitute for training and coaching the team in principles such as those explained in Chapter 10. In *The Toyota Way to Lean Leadership*, Jeffrey Liker and Gary Convis observed, "It's often said at Toyota that the best measure of a leader's success is what is accomplished by those they trained."[9] The scale of modern enterprises presents enormous challenges that require a combination of training, communication, and automation.

Closing Leadership Gaps

It is important to clearly understand the qualities that leaders need to effectively control risk in their organization. The 2021 *EDA Trends in Executive*

Development Report surveyed leaders from 1,030 medium and large enterprises and identified the following key competencies for effective leadership:[10]

- Leaders who understand the whole company and not just their silos.
- Critical thinkers at every level.
- Increased communication and transparency.
- Ability to lead through change, change, and more change.
- Employees who are empowered to use their critical thinking skills.
- Companies who are genuinely committed to equity and inclusion.

The report also highlighted the following competency gaps in the next generation of leaders:

- Ability to attract, develop, and retain the quality of talent needed to achieve the business objectives.
- Ability to create a compelling vision and engage others around it.
- Ability to inspire others.
- Ability to deliver results or be results-oriented.
- Ability to manage the stress and demands of a real-time overloaded leadership environment.

Flow Engineering offers a minimal, adaptable way to address and satisfy these needs within and across teams. Outcome Mapping facilitates the creation and sharing of a compelling vision that inspires action. Mapping flow and measuring performance facilitates understanding of the full system of work, critical thinking about constraints, and empirical improvement. A Flow Roadmap turns insights into actions that deliver measurable results. As a collection of methods, Flow Engineering includes, engages, and empowers talent to communicate, collaborate, and act more effectively.

Conclusion

Large scale organizational change depends on culture change. The maps of Flow Engineering are an exercise in culture change, in that they help a group align around a shared goal, a shared understanding, and a shared behavior.

Leading Flow Engineering requires transformational leadership: setting a clear and inspiring vision, showing an authentic example, providing personalized coaching, and giving space for the team to practice and experiment on their own.

Flow Engineering aims for a balance between prescriptive and generative approaches. It also requires anticipating and employing countermeasures to address headwinds, which we'll cover in the next chapter. By leveraging the foundational principles that support Flow Engineering and crafting your own enabling and governing constraints, you can aim to make the right way the easy way and maximize your odds of success.

Key Takeaways

- Leading for flow requires the ability to design feedback loops to help a team ensure they are on track.
- Flow Engineering aims to balance prescriptive and generative approaches by helping teams adopt a strategic focus that is generated from their own insights.
- Skillfully applied constraints make it easier for people to do the right thing and harder to do the wrong thing.

| # Traps to Avoid

> "Control the clock, not obey the clock.
> Collaborate, not coerce.
> Commit, not comply.
> Complete, not continue.
> Improve, not prove.
> Connect, not conform."
>
> The mantra from *Leadership Is Language*

THERE ARE MANY conditions and challenges that may impede your progress toward improving flow with Flow Engineering. We include some notable examples here, as well as countermeasures to mitigate their negative effects. The top five headwinds we've encountered are as follows:

1. Neglecting the narrative.
2. Misaligned and conflicting incentives.
3. Not mapping the complete stream.
4. Craving unnecessary precision.
5. Conflict with existing operating models.

Neglecting the Narrative

Every significant change can be seen in a negative context. It's easy to prefer "the devil you know, over the devil you don't." Change requires effort, commitment, time, capacity, flexibility, and tolerance. To overcome all those costs, you need to consider what message is being sent by improvement efforts and how that message is being delivered. It's very easy for folks who learn about an impending (or worse, already implemented) change to fear the worst or make assumptions about how they might be negatively impacted.

It's common to rush into action on a change, heading straight for a tool or an automated solution. If teams don't understand the intention, they can assume the goal is to monitor or micromanage them.

The following behaviors may look like rapid starts taken by decisive actors, but they can easily cause change initiatives to fail:

- Not starting with an experiment or a pilot to test assumptions and place small bets.
- Not making room for failure, learning, and adaptation.
- Heading directly for a target without considering or acknowledging the current state.
- Diving straight into doing things without a plan.
- Adopting a "with us or against us" stance; creating a rift between the carefree and the cautious.
- Not communicating, celebrating, and sharing progress, thus draining momentum as time passes.

A major benefit of Flow Engineering is that by creating maps together, stakeholders and contributors are included from the start. Perspectives are shared and a dialogue is created. Detractors can be assuaged of their fears or, even better, included in planning more positive actions. Instead of inventing reasons why a change is doomed to fail, they can be invited to help it succeed (or at least highlight obstacles in advance).

Outcome discovery and Outcome Mapping sessions, shown in Figure 12.1, can help teams understand current state and opportunities. Based on what you discover, you can direct the conversation more productively as you continue to map.

For example, if several people mention past failed change efforts, you may draw out or draw attention to what could be done differently this time. It's important to send the message that for better or worse, the past is gone, and the present opportunities exist only because of what's gone before. There's nowhere to go but forward to better, together. It's important when measuring flow that focus remains on the system, not the individual. We talk more about this in Chapter 13.

FIGURE 12.1: Outcome Discovery and Outcome Mapping
Help You Craft a Productive Narrative

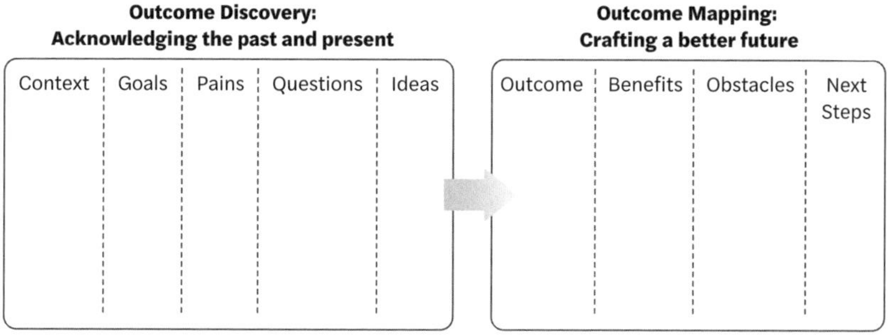

Outcome Discovery: Acknowledging the past and present					**Outcome Mapping:** Crafting a better future			
Context	Goals	Pains	Questions	Ideas	Outcome	Benefits	Obstacles	Next Steps

Whatever you say about your improvement efforts, ensure they fit the language and narrative currently used in the organization. That could mean framing it in the context of a SAFe implementation, OKRs, a Big Hairy Audacious Goal, or the latest "Town Hall" messaging. It's important to meet people where they are—on *their* familiar territory, not yours. This could mean that you don't mention Flow Engineering at first, or ever. It could mean that you rebrand Flow Engineering to better fit your organization. (For instance, GE took Eric Ries's *Lean Startup* and adapted it to become GE FastWorks.[1]) Read the room; play to your audience. As you deliver wins and progress, the narrative can evolve to encompass more of the ideas shared in this book.

"We already know our biggest constraint."

Sometimes the first challenge to address is that teams already have a narrative on what they need to fix. As a change agent, you may run into some variant of this as you work to improve visibility, measurement, or performance. This can also take the form of "We just need to execute," or, "We just need the right people." It can indicate concerns about a lack of flow, a lack of results, or a perceived lack of action.

Even if those statements are true, this rush to action makes a dangerous assumption: that everyone else already shares the same context and aspirations or, worse, that their buy-in is not necessary. Even if there is a shared awareness of a constraint, there's usually more to learn before tackling it. Is the scope of the constraint understood? Are its causes? What are the key obstacles to addressing it? Are leaders, peers, and contributors all aligned? Is there a measured baseline for before/after comparison?

If you can answer those questions with confidence, you may not have to map. If not, there's no reason to wallow in analysis paralysis. Quickly jump into mapping (or at least a conversation) and turn the assumption into a qualified statement. The reason value and clarity precede flow is that action without clarity or value produces waste, which can be worse than not acting at all.

Misaligned and Conflicting Incentives

Flow Engineering is all about solving flow problems. That often requires stepping away from the work to examine the work. This is in conflict with the status quo of "go, go, go!" in organizations. Even if the pace isn't high, it can be challenging simply to pause or even consider how the work is working.

Common conflicts start to emerge when you look for them:

- Short-Term vs. Long-Term Goals: Management might focus on short-term financial targets, leading to decisions that hinder long-term technological innovation or sustainability.
- Quantity vs. Quality: Sales teams might be incentivized by volume rather than the quality of sales, leading to pressure on delivery teams to fulfill unreasonable promises made during the sales cycle.
- Individual Performance Metrics: Incentivizing individual performance in a way that discourages teamwork or collaboration affects overall project outcomes.

- **Growth vs. Stability:** Pushing for rapid growth or market capture without considering technological stability and scalability risks long-term viability.
- **Customer Satisfaction vs. Cost Reduction:** Prioritizing cost-cutting measures might degrade customer experience or service quality.
- **What We Think Is Best vs. What We're Incentivized For:** It's important to consider that even in cases where improvement or change is beneficial, it can be seen as detrimental or disruptive if incentives are motivating current behavior.

Like the connection depicted in Figure 12.2, outcome discovery and Outcome Mapping can serve as a way to bridge the gap between local incentives to establish shared focus on a global target outcome—something of value to everyone involved.

FIGURE 12.2: Outcome Mapping and Discovery Can Bridge Local Incentives by Establishing a Higher-Value Shared Target

Global target outcome

Local incentive

Local incentive

The Utilization Incentive

As we mentioned earlier, the efficiency paradox too often results in decreased performance when resource utilization is maximized. Even so, we often use utilization as a proxy for productivity. It turns out being busy isn't the same as being efficient, and it certainly isn't the same as being effective. That busyness is often a result of too much WIP, unclear priorities, too many dependencies, and a host of other conditions we've discussed, but it can also be a deeply ingrained organizational or cultural habit. Behaviors like arriving early, staying late, always giving 110%, and stacking calendars with meetings are often rewarded by organizations that pay closer attention to activity (or output) than outcomes.

If you find yourself in an environment that seems to be incentivizing behaviors that restrict flow or sabotage improvement efforts, focus on what's within your sphere of influence and control. Seize opportunities to connect improvement investments to high-level objectives you can align to (cutting costs, improving NPS, and increasing retention). Demonstrate quick wins and celebrate actions from others. Ask provocative questions, like "How do you see X (short-term pursuit) helping us deliver on Y (long-term goal)?" Build relationships with those who might support your efforts by sharing your goals and offering your support to theirs.

Even when it seems like you're stuck in the "frozen middle" of middle management and unable to drive change, there's always an effective action you can take to enable flow. The experience of being stuck is created by the tension between the uncertainty, disruption, and investment required for improvement and the relative clarity and ease of maintaining the status quo.

We're typically rewarded based on the status quo (or by not disrupting current performance) but not on change. When you aim to drive change, look for the incentives reinforcing the status quo; they're a more important constraint to influence than individual peers or leaders. One of the most challenging obstacles you'll encounter in your efforts to improve flow is reconciling target outcomes that conflict with existing incentives. If you notice a target outcome that conflicts with what you've revealed in discovery, work with your mapping participants to reconcile the gap before proceeding.

Not Mapping the Complete Stream

In cases where you lack visibility into upstream decisions outside of your control, and in cases where your work has unseen impact on those downstream, you run the risk of micro-optimization within your sphere of visibility and control (see Figure 12.3). This potentially creates waste and may also overburden downstream teams. Local focus is often the enemy of global progress.

Flow Engineering maps can help you drive a productive conversation and invitation to make those invisible upstream and downstream activities visible and measurable. Bring an incomplete map to groups who can help you fill in the gaps. That visibility and measurement will allow you to make flow improvement decisions and changes without the risk of micro-optimization.

FIGURE 12.3: Limited Visibility Enables Limited Focus

Craving Unnecessary Precision

Seeking precision is a common trap when starting to measure value stream performance. When you're aiming to reduce wait times in a value stream, it's essential to adopt a comprehensive approach rather than getting mired in perfectionism or narrow focus.

First, examine the entire process from inception to delivery; focusing solely on one stage without considering upstream delays can be misleading. It's a common pitfall to let the pursuit of perfection hinder data-driven decision-making or, worse, deter attempts to improve the process altogether. For instance, tightening the developer feedback loop is commendable, but it's also crucial to address issues like interruptions and work in progress (WIP) first; it does no good to improve productivity at the cost of developer burnout. Similarly, an overemphasis on detail in the DevOps loop while neglecting significant time wasted upstream just adds to the waste.

Investing substantial time and resources in creating detailed metrics or dashboards that are rarely used is just another form of waste. These tools should aid frequent and meaningful decision-making, not just serve as annual review instruments. Being truly data-driven means consistently integrating data into decision-making processes, not just in occasional, isolated instances.

To effectively increase the customer Net Promoter Score (NPS) or any other key performance indicator, it's important to identify and measure the drivers behind these metrics. This should be done with just enough precision to inform confident decision-making, focusing on readily actionable insights first. Overly precise measurements can be redundant if not matched with the capability to utilize them effectively. In summary, in value stream

optimization, a broad, pragmatic, and purpose-driven approach is more beneficial than an excessively detailed or narrow one.

FIGURE 12.4: Example Value Stream Map with Irrelevant Downstream Precision

When your constraint adds weeks of delay, a few hours difference isn't consequential.

Consider spending eight months building out and debugging the ultimate metrics dashboard, but it only gets used once a year for performance
reviews. This is like measuring with a micrometer and then cutting with a
dull axe. If you often check the weather out of boredom but neglect to check
the weather before you leave the house, are you really data-driven?

If you work backward from the target, the necessary resolution becomes
clear: Do you want customer NPS to go up? What is driving NPS? How do we
know? What's the obstacle to raising it?

Measure progress in whatever way gives you enough signal to make a
decision with reasonable confidence, and worry about detail when the easy
improvements have been accomplished and you're a pro at data-driven
decision-making.

Precision is useless in measuring value stream performance—unless you
are prepared for and capable of using it. If you can swing an axe with micrometer precision, go ahead and invest in a micrometer.

Isao Yoshino summed this up in *Leading to Learn, Learning to Lead*:
"A practical style is more important than precision when setting targets.
Precision doesn't matter in the beginning—you need the direction to go, and
then you can learn and improve it. Spending weeks and weeks of doing nothing is worse."[2]

Conflict with Existing Operating Models

Meeting people where they are means understanding and acknowledging the current state prior to striving for change. This is not just a show of respect. The inertia of the current state operating model is always the primary challenge to bringing about change. Here are some tips to support your efforts leading Flow Engineering in complicated, large-scale environments.

The first thing to remember is that there's bound to be resistance if the context, framing, and value is unclear to any participants. Ensure the narrative is shared and highlights the purpose of the effort: targeting process waste and friction, not individuals and contributions. Outcome Mapping can help establish the right conditions for effective mapping.

Second, if the organization is large enough, the mess will be large. It may be difficult to represent, but any structured effort to visualize is preferable to nothing. You can always check in to see if the representation is reasonably accurate and solicit feedback and adjustment. Remember, precision isn't valuable or necessary. You may not get timing that adds up at all, but perhaps the most valuable information is about the types of activities being performed.

Third, you have a variety of countermeasures available at your disposal, and you have smart stakeholders you can engage. Parallelization may be a great option or not possible. Information flow could lead to the greatest improvement. Sometimes the most important waste to target is simply the most annoying waste.

Fourth, improvement isn't solely the responsibility of the facilitator. You didn't make the mess, so you're certainly not accountable for cleaning it all up. Sometimes the best improvement you can hope for today is visibility and awareness. Keep an open mind, listen to the participants, and challenge them to be creative and resourceful. Make it safe and easy for them to contribute their perspectives and expertise, and you'll see solutions emerge.

Finally, unless you find yourself in a generative culture where participants are comfortable talking about value-adding and non–value-adding activities in a constructive way, focus on the less sensitive and subjective information and work up to more sophisticated measurements over time.

CASE STUDY | ## Agile Release Train Improvement in a Financial Services Firm

The Scaled Agile Framework (SAFe) is one of the most widespread approaches to bringing order to software development at scale. SAFe's program increments (PIs) represent large-scale (eight to twelve week) delivery involving a great deal of planning and dependency reconciliation. Standard PI planning can take two full days. In many organizations, it can take a week or two, with the work often hidden in parallel and fractional activities conducted by a variety of stakeholders.

In their efforts to create order at such a massive scale, it's easy to lose the concern for end-to-end flow in the details and entrenched concerns of the many groups involved. This scale of time and team size makes mapping challenging and significantly complicates improvement efforts. Sometimes it seems like you may be opening a can of worms by mapping, but in our experience, even the messiest current state has a better future state hiding just out of plain sight.

Consider one of the world's largest financial institutions, in the midst of a large-scale SAFe implementation, struggling with delays, friction, lack of visibility, and no clear opportunity to improve. Steve was brought in to cut lead time in their core Agile Release Train (ART, which is near identical to a value stream in the SAFe world) lead time by 50%. This was a tough sell to begin with, since most stakeholders only cared about and measured their own segment of the value stream, often based on best-case scenario timing.

The problem with the best-case scenario is that it rarely resembles the common experience and it leaves little room for improvement. Excessively optimistic estimates often indicate a culture where realistic assessments are punished in some way, leading to what's often referred to as "the watermelon effect," where measures look green on the outside, but they're red on the inside. None of these effects are a result of SAFe specifically. Any large-scale effort lacking visibility and alignment can foster challenging conditions. Despite the hurdles, there seemed to be a huge opportunity to rapidly improve lead time performance.

This mapping effort would be the first time the organization ever looked at the entire end-to-end flow of work across the ART. The scale also made it extremely difficult to get any kind of representative data. Nobody could recall how much time passed between stages or any particular detail. When your lead time is longer than a year, the details tend to get blurry.

FIGURE 12.5: The Current State Map Depicting the Full Agile Release Train (ART)

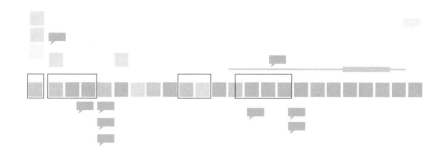

Mapping relied on participants' rough recollection of activity stages and timing but drove an extremely productive and engaging conversation on how time in the value stream was spent. Tackling value-adding and non–value-adding time is a sensitive topic in what Ron Westrum would classify as pathological or bureaucratic environments.[3] In order to shine a light on how time is spent without creating a false dichotomy of "good" and "bad," the time was classified across categories, as listed in Table 12.1. The classification provided a simple added dimension of context to a map with imprecise timing in order to identify the target constraint with higher confidence.

TABLE 12.1: Visual Activity Classification Legend, Depicting Non–Value-Adding, Testing, Value-Adding, and Coordinating Activities

Activity Class	Definition	% of Lead Time	Color
Non–value-adding	Doesn't add stakeholder value to the outcome	58%	Pink
Testing	Validating work (non–value-adding)	14%	Purple
Value-adding	Creates or enhances value from a stakeholder perspective	18%	Blue
Coordinating	Planning, organizing, scheduling, not including 3–6 months of pre-planning (non–value-adding)	10%	Green

When Value Stream Mapping, recall the 5 Rs presented in Part 2: recent, real, reach, representative, and road-tested. We want to focus on representative flow: What does activity typically look like? In this case, more than 90% of the work in this ART involved changes to the mainframe. Despite this, the improvement efforts targeted only the development segment of the stream and only non-mainframe changes.

Their micro-optimizations within development were showing good performance, but the true lead time for the value stream was getting worse and worse. All this context arose during the mapping sessions; these hidden dynamics were brought to the surface so they could be addressed directly. It became clear why performance wasn't improving along with the metrics and why work seemed to be getting slower and more onerous over time.

FIGURE 12.6: Example Future State Map Depicting Non-Critical and Non–Value-Adding Activities

= Primarily Non-Value Adding   = Primarily Value Adding   = Coordinating   = Testing

The Future State Map depicts non-critical and non–value-adding activities executed in parallel rather than blocking flow.

This reality was difficult to address, but it was the only way to begin to truly improve performance. There was a great deal of friction, uncertainty, and discomfort in the mapping process and the conversations it evoked, but it all would have gone unseen and unsaid were it not for the effort to map and improve. Mapping provided the time, a safe space, and encouragement to discuss waste, collective responsibility, and organizational performance measurement.

Mapping a future state value stream provided a vision of what was possible, even with little to no influence over the broader system of work. The Future State Map in Figure 12.6 shows what was possible by simply focusing on the critical path to value delivery without modifying existing processes. Even without significant changes to activities within the value stream, it was radically redesigned to meet the performance goal, and the design could be implemented immediately, without disruption to individual contributors.

Table 12.2 outlines the key differences depicted between the current and future states, but it only alludes to the potential for high ROI improvement. Having the Value Stream Map and discussion provided visibility into exactly which stages could be significantly improved with simple changes, which would rapidly drive costs and lead time down while improving customer and employee satisfaction and allowing for faster feedback and adaptation.

TABLE 12.2: Current State Flow Performance vs. Future State

Current State	Future State
Unclear improvement opportunities	Single constraint to target
Optimized for edge cases	Optimized for common cases
$2M per release	$1M per release
64-week lead time	32-week lead time (with no stage modification)
Non–value-adding stages blocking progress	Non–value-adding stages executed in parallel
Value-adding activity: 17% of lead time	Value-adding activity: 53% of lead time

Even within a highly complicated and large-scale SAFe implementation, Value Stream Mapping can provide a complementary approach that dramatically improves visibility, collaboration, and performance without disruption or significant investment of time or money.

Conclusion

Flow Engineering may seem simple, but it's not easy. We pointed out tips and traps throughout the mapping practices, but leading change is a larger challenge. You'll encounter situations that seem impossible to depict as a simple flow of activity. You will always be working within an existing narrative, or confronted with several, and needing to craft your own. You'll encounter misaligned and conflicting incentives that threaten to derail or sabotage improvement. You'll be forced to map an incomplete system with incomplete information and make trade-offs in service of your target outcome. Outcome Mapping prompts the team to anticipate obstacles such as these. These can seem insurmountable when you actually encounter them. Stay focused on the overarching goal by regularly reminding yourself and the team of the benefits of breaking through.

Key Takeaways

- Seek to understand the existing narrative and craft an effective narrative to fuel your progress. Effective leadership requires effective storytelling.
- Identify misaligned or conflicting incentives so they can be addressed and mitigated. Look for a north star that everyone can align to.
- There is an art and science to establishing effective scope. Leverage the principles and guidance we've shared to map a scope that reveals the key constraint.
- Precision can be an obstacle in the early stages. Make sure you consider your target objective and focus on only what's needed to act effectively.
- Just like the existing narrative and incentives, the present operating model needs to be considered and navigated. Remember to always meet people (and systems) where they are.

CHAPTER 13

Value Stream Management

> "One of the interesting outcomes from clients that adopt value stream management, is that they realize how inefficient silos have made their organization, and that by drawing the lines through the organization, they found out that they have product teams."
>
> CHRIS CONDO, Principal Analyst, Forrester

What Is Value Stream Management?

PETER HINES DEFINED Value Stream Management in 1998 as "a new strategic and operational approach to the data capture, analysis, planning and implementation of effective change within the core cross-functional or cross-company processes required to achieve a truly lean enterprise."[1] Value Stream Management has come to be associated with tools for monitoring value stream performance, but Value Stream Management remains primarily a management practice, *something you do*. It centers on two primary activities: (1) optimizing the flow of work that delivers customer value and (2) measuring those delivered outcomes to make better decisions.

If you think of an organization as a network of value streams (discussed further in Chapter 14), Value Stream Management includes the design, operation, and optimization of that network, though the practice is often focused on one stream at a time. Because Value Stream Management is a process of ongoing optimization, it is helpful to begin by looking at the transition from *project* thinking to *product* thinking.

The Movement from Project to Product

Project management has long been the dominant model for managing major technology initiatives. The problem is that it applies a finite solution to an infinite opportunity. Once delivered, a project is largely forgotten and transitioned into a maintenance state of minimal investment and attention.

FIGURE 13.1: Focus on Project Leads to Ignoring Longer Term Impact

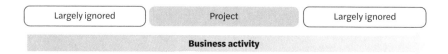

Because of the massive opportunities afforded by technology, software, and global networks, the value of long-lived systems that can grow massively in scale and be continuously improved has driven a need for a focus on continuous and sustained flow.

The value stream model acknowledges that most business needs and opportunities have a long life cycle—a continuous flow—that can't be satisfied with a singular or even periodic effort in relative isolation. Figure 13.2 illustrates the continuous improvement possible with the stability, continuity, and iteration of delivery across an established value stream.

FIGURE 13.2: Each Cycle of Continuous Improvement Builds on the Previous One

Thinking of your teams in the context of delivering products via value streams allows you to effectively mitigate the three Ds of scale. The stable team membership and investment in continuous improvement avoids disengagement. The orientation to a clear and sustained customer value relationship avoids disorientation. The continuity provided by working toward long-term, sustainable outcomes avoids distraction. The transition from projects to products is a transition from disengagement, disorientation, and distraction to flow.

CASE STUDY	**Rapid Improvement from Projects to Products**

In 2020 an agency was looking to add predictability, scale, and consistency to their process. Their ultimate goal was to begin to develop their own specialized products and create sustainable value streams to replace their volatile project-based workflow.

The agency was looking to scale without adding headcount or burning out staff. In the short term, they wanted a way to boost margins on repeated activities, which we identified as return business from existing clients. In the long term, they wanted to productize their offerings to maximize margin, stability, and scalability. Primary challenges we identified were consistency, strategy, and clarity.

FIGURE 13.3: Current State Map: Steps, Timing, Roles, Tools, Artifacts

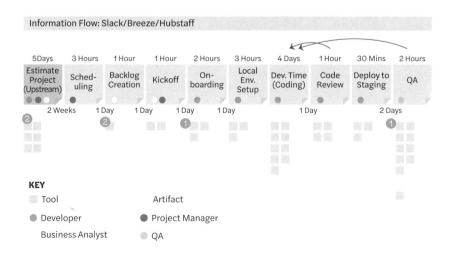

In total, the process went from a current state of thirty-three days with two-thirds of that consumed by handoffs and delays to a target state of seven days with minimal delays via increased process visibility (Kanban), minimal automation (Slack notifications), and an estimation playbook. As a side benefit, the team characterized the effort as an Empathy Quest since it provided a way for the team to understand the work and value provided by unfamiliar roles, as well as the relationships between upstream and downstream contributors.

Flow Engineering helped quickly kick-start their project-to-product transition, and the simple improvements discovered through mapping demonstrated dramatic impact with little investment.

The transition from project to product is a story of flow. The need for increasing performance, continuous value delivery, and sustainable operations has driven product orientation. But this product operating model is not without costs.

FIGURE 13.4: Project or Product Orientation Lies on a Spectrum

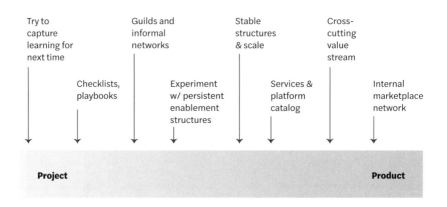

Try to capture learning for next time	
Checklists, playbooks	
Guilds and informal networks	
Experiment w/ persistent enablement structures	
Stable structures & scale	
Services & platform catalog	
Cross-cutting value stream	
Internal marketplace network	

Project   **Product**

Project	Product
• Initial value bet	• Adaptive value bets
• Bring people to the work	• Bring work to the people
• Temporary organization	• Continuous, iterative
• Single batch	• Small batches
• Output oriented	• Outcome oriented
• Customer validated	• Customer collaborative

The behaviors and opportunities of continuous product delivery demand an investment in management infrastructure and practices capable of facilitating that flow over a long term at large scale. Smaller batches, continuous iteration and feedback, adaptation, and sustainability all require information, visibility, and clarity to manage effectively and avoid being overwhelmed. This need has been addressed by the practice and tooling of Value Stream Management. Value Stream Management builds upon disciplines like service management, application life cycle management, and Lean management to focus on the complete value stream, as well as the interactions and interdependence across streams. It requires sustained performance monitoring, trend analysis, and large-scale observability of work performance to enable better product outcomes. It's a key component in scaling and sustaining your Flow Engineering efforts.

Value Stream Mapping vs. Value Stream Management

Value Stream Mapping sits as a single method within the overall practice of Value Stream Management. Where Value Stream Mapping helps you understand flow of a single stream as it exists in a single point in time and then design a future state, Value Stream Management is a continuous practice that tracks value stream performance over time, revealing historical patterns and increasingly providing trend analysis and prediction capabilities. Table 13.1 contrasts the two across a number of dimensions.

TABLE 13.1: A Comparison of Value Stream Mapping
and Value Stream Management

Value Stream Mapping	Value Stream Management
Iterative and periodic practice	Continuous practice
Easy to start	Difficult to start
Human-centric, storytelling, and narrative	Tool- and data-centric, automated insights

TABLE 13.1: A Comparison of Value Stream Mapping
and Value Stream Management *cont.*

Value Stream Mapping	Value Stream Management
Perspective and qualitative focus	Perspective and qualitative focus
Visual collaboration	Visibility and continuous inspection
Walls and sticky notes (also virtual)	Integrations, dashboards, and data
Creates and recreates business case	Ongoing incremental optimization
Highlights waste and assumptions	Automates for continuous compliance
Defines present and future	Records past and present
Facilitates creativity, reinvention	Facilitates improvement, iteration
Future opportunity: living representation	Future opportunity: simulation & prediction
Enabling constraint	Governing constraint

Why Not Dive Straight into Value Stream Management?

We've spent most of this book talking about value, clarity, and flow because without considering these factors, efforts to improve performance can quickly fail. Contributors are very familiar with performance measurement, and a new name or new tool to accomplish it is likely going to be regarded with a lot of skepticism. Eli Goldratt highlighted a key insight for driving change when he stated, "Tell me how you'll measure me and I'll tell you how I'm going to behave."[2]

Consider typical testimonials from engineers involved in a Value Stream Management adoption initiative:

Senior Engineer 1: This Value Stream Management thing feels like Agile™ 2.0. What I've seen has been very hand-wavy and vague, without many specifics. I am still not clear what actual data is going to be input (other than ticket state) into this system and what actually is going to be done with that data. I want to see concrete examples and not hand-waving about "value."

Senior Engineer 2: Generating metrics from ticket state sounds good in theory, but ultimately, I don't think it makes sense. They want to analyze the software development process the same way you would analyze an assembly line. I'm sure there are some things that carry over, but overall, I just don't think you can apply methods that work for managing an assembly line to knowledge work. Once we start getting pressure for those metrics to look a certain way, we will game them and continue on with the real work on our own. That first Value Stream Management meeting we had as a team, a lot of it felt like a normal retrospective but with more ceremony, fluff, and buzzwords. Even about 90% of the items that were brought up for improvement were just things we had brought up in previous retros but never had a chance to prioritize. Maybe the next session will have more meat.

Formal studies like "Can Performance Metrics Harm Performance?" by Berend van der Kolk and Wesley Kaufmann have identified other risks. They highlight two common effects:

> First, professionals attempted to reduce cognitive dissonance by focusing on quantifying performance in a broad sense. The interviewed professionals changed their behavior by focusing on easily measurable parts of their tasks, hence adapting to the "result-driven" organizational reality.[3]

This first behavior is known as the streetlight effect, characterized by a parable: A policeman encounters a drunk man searching for his lost keys under a streetlight, despite losing them in the park. The policeman asks why he's searching in this area, to which the drunk man replies, "That is where the light is." We tend to look for things where it's easy to look.

The second effect described by van der Kolk is that,

> Some professionals chose to pay less attention to other activities that were not easily measurable. For instance, it was indicated in the study that some professionals did not "connect" anymore to colleagues because of the introduction of performance measurement, indicating the erosion of the important organizational practice of "collegiality." In other words, we begin to ignore the things we can't easily measure.[4]

In *The Principles of Product Development Flow*, one of Don Reinertsen's first principles highlights the common mistake of performance measurement and an upstream cause of these types of reactions: "The Inactivity Principle: Watch the work product, not the worker."[5] It's easy to attribute delays to the contributors within a value stream, but it's more accurate to look at the system and watch the work product move through it. This requires visibility and accurate information flow, but it's also the only way to see the forest for the trees.

| CASE STUDY | **Evolving Measurement from Individual Metrics to Team-Level Metrics at Parchment** |

Many organizations are still grappling with a necessary evolution of how they measure performance and apparently learning what not to do for the first time, firsthand. Systems thinking has called attention to the impossibility of measuring a whole by its parts, yet it continues across seemingly every organization.

Phil Clark, VP Head of Application Engineering at Parchment, shared a common journey from individual measurement to more holistic measurement in a presentation at Flowtopia in 2023.[6]

Phil had been with the company when the transformation began in 2012 and during the shift to product-aligned cross-functional teams in 2015, and he has witnessed this full evolution toward more holistic measurement. In terms of his own journey, he recalled pivotal moments that embodied the three phases laid out in Figure 13.5.

FIGURE 13.5: Phil's Journey at Parchment

More Gamification

1999–2014   **Cost Center and Individual Metrics**

- Focus on individual output.
- Measuring individual development activities, lines of code, utilization, and stack ranking based on such metrics.
- Individuals are treated as units of cost and fungible resources being moved from project to project.

2015–2020   **Focus Shift to Teams**

- Focus on team outcomes and capabilities.
- Recognized as knowledge workers creating solutions in a world of known- and unknown-unknowns.
- Collaborative, cross-functional teams, non-fungible, having long-lived team members.

2021–today   **Team Metrics**

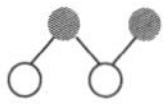

- Insights into team performance and the flow of work.
- System-measurable metrics that foster team conversations and empower teams to review and experiment with improvements.
- Incorporated surveys to capture team sentiments.

Less Gamification

Phil's metrics journey includes eleven years with Parchment. It showcases a twenty-four-year evolution from individual metrics to a combination of team and system metrics, along with team sentiment.

His experiences with individual metrics may seem familiar to you:

- He recalled a senior executive in the early 2000s stating, "Good engineers should produce 5,250 lines of code in six months' time."
- His individual target for utilization was set at 85%, which he "frequently gamed for weekly time entry to make the numbers look good."
- He recalled stumbling on the information showing his place at four out of twenty in the team's stack ranking of engineers.

Phil's journey follows a learning and implementation evolution that may be familiar to you as well:

- 2018: Read *The Phoenix Project, The Goal,* and *Making Work Visible.*
  - Began transitioning Scrum teams to Kanban.
- 2019: Read *Accelerate, Project to Product,* and *The Principles of Product Development Flow.*
- 2020: Read *Team Topologies, Sooner Safer Happier;* researched and learned about Value Stream Management.
  - Introduced Value Stream Management platform.
- 2021: Delivered Value Stream Mapping and discovered the Value Stream Management Consortium.
  - Launched internally developed metrics dashboard.

This mix of theory, practice, and tooling (in that order) provided Phil a strong foundation on-ramp to useful performance measurement, as well as a resource that informs better conversations with leaders still using legacy and mechanistic mental models. He learned "to tell them the why in their language." It's not enough to have what you think is a better way to measure performance; it has to be sold to the leaders looking for answers. Their measurement shifted from individual focus to collective focus, as laid out in Table 13.2.

TABLE 13.2: The Parchment Measurement Journey

Individual Scrutiny	Collective Flow
Lines of code	Outcomes over output
Utilization	Team metrics
Comparing individuals based on individual output	Projects to products
	Value Stream Management
	System metrics: Flow, DORA
	Sentiment metrics: SPACE, DX, etc.

His approach espouses a focus on bottlenecks and conversations to enable performance at the team level. By focusing on value streams rather than individual contributors, Phil was able to build a measurement context that not only avoids the negative consequences of individual focus, but also puts performance in the context of teams, flow, and outcomes.

Mapping to Enable Value Stream Management

The three gaps in solutions to the problem of scale we introduced in Part 1 also apply to Value Stream Management: alignment gap, visibility gap, and on-ramp gap.

Alignment Gap: Value Stream Management platforms often cost hundreds of thousands of dollars to effectively pilot and millions of dollars to fully implement. That can be a hard sell in an organization that's only just hearing about value streams or wondering if this is just the latest trend. In order to effectively define the value of the investment, the benefits to multiple stakeholders, the obstacles to address, and a clear plan of implementation, Flow Engineering can be leveraged to assist in making a strong, clear, and relevant case linking a Value Stream Management investment to performance objectives and business goals. By including stakeholders in mapping or sharing clear maps, it's far easier to align the decision-makers to a compelling opportunity.

Visibility Gap: The map is not the territory, and data doesn't give you the full picture. By mapping first, you can establish a shared mental model of what the pilot stream looks like and how it behaves. This makes it far easier to instrument and understand where the gaps in the data may lie. Data is often segmented or incomplete; it needs context to bridge gaps. Mapping provides you with a wealth of context from multiple stakeholders, inside or outside a team.

On-Ramp Gap: Value Stream Management implementation is easier and less risky if you start small, demonstrate value, and grow using positive results. It should be applied to an ideal candidate stream (which requires context from Flow Engineering analysis). You need access to data, which means you likely need to engage dependent teams. That data must be high quality, which means you will benefit from analyzing the percent complete and accurate (%C&A) of the pilot stream activities and the state of that data across the flow of activities.

Tackling the On-Ramp Gap by Reducing Uncertainty

There are several key factors that create the on-ramp gap in organizations:

- **Delay:** There's too often a significant delay between deciding to do something and seeing any results. This makes everyone nervous and can lead to a lot of distracting "are we there yet" status requests.
- **Visibility:** Compounding the delay problem, progress is not easily visible.
- **Uncertainty:** When you start anything, you have significantly less confidence and clarity than when you're nearly at the finish line.

To counteract the delay, visibility, and confidence factors, teams will often invest in elaborate planning, slide decks, documentation, meetings, prototypes, etc. These aren't necessarily waste, but they can be extremely time intensive and are rarely collaborative efforts, leading to clarity issues and misalignment. This planning paradox—that planning reduces uncertainty but delays delivery—plagues implementation efforts, since "just enough" planning is both an art and a science.

FIGURE 13.6: Waiting for Data Availability and Quality Means Uncertainty Remains High for Longer and Outcomes Are Later to Arrive

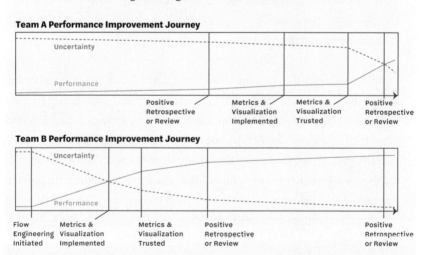

Rapid mapping with Flow Engineering reduces uncertainty and delivers early outcomes versus the delay and cost of waiting until Value Stream Management is fully implemented.

Consider the uncertainty of the two teams in Figure 13.6.[7] Team A follows a typical implementation journey. They may invest in training, certifications, planning, and documentation—very little of which impacts uncertainty. In fact, it can easily increase it. Many certifications and large-scale frameworks are parts of complicated, comprehensive bodies of knowledge and can quickly become daunting as known-unknowns pile up. They'll have to cross hurdles of data availability (siloed tools and ownership of data) and data quality (incomplete, incorrect, corrupt, unlabeled, uncorrelated, and misleading data), all before they can see any semblance of Value Stream Management manifested in their organization. They'll likely start with a small group to minimize disruption and cost (and having too many chefs in the kitchen), which means they'll have to bring others up to speed later, likely when they're needed at full speed. Even when data is integrated and made available, it likely won't be trusted, and fear of individual evaluation was most likely not assuaged in the communication plan. (There was a communication plan, right?) As a result, uncertainty remains high, and results remain minimal for nearly the entire implementation journey. *On-ramp = months.*

Team B begins with Flow Engineering. As a result, a valuable target outcome for implementation is defined, well-considered, and shared from the very start. Many contributors from multiple domains can be included as a result of minimal time requirements. The group can easily select an ideal candidate stream and quickly collect a baseline of performance, as well as quick wins for performance improvement. They can map out dependencies for data access and quality concerns and share those maps with groups involved and affected. They can take all the insights they collect in a few hours mapping and craft a Flow Roadmap that lays out the implementation in clear terms for everyone to share. Uncertainty and delays are low, visibility and outcomes are high. *On-ramp = days.*

To mitigate the risks of diving right in, you can bootstrap your Value Stream Management implementation journey with Flow Engineering by starting small and scrappy and implementing it where it's most relevant and valuable, as well as where the data, access, and practice are most readily available. Mapping can help you understand the value of implementation, the scope and shape of a candidate stream, and where the data resides (and the quality of it), as well as plan the implementation with a Flow Roadmap.

Conclusion

Value Stream Management provides a method to enable ongoing performance improvement of a value stream. A common mistake is attempting to dive straight into Value Stream Management without first doing the preparatory work needed to align the team around outcomes, map the full end-to-end value stream, etc. The ability to effectively increase flow by managing a value stream depends on establishing value and clarity using the mapping process.

Developing this level of rigor is a great accomplishment but requires continuous work. If you are not getting better, you are getting worse; there is no remaining still. But experiencing success in Value Stream Management builds confidence that similar approaches can be shared throughout the organization. This brings us to the subject of the next chapter: scaling Flow Engineering.

Key Takeaways

- Value Stream Management includes mapping, observability, tooling, data, and, most of all, people.
- Value Stream Management takes us beyond org charts as the structure of organizations to stream alignment and operation.
- Value Stream Management includes operations, collaboration, incentives, funding, and more.
- Value Stream Management encompasses individual contributors, value streams, and value stream networks.
- There is a growing ecosystem of Value Stream Management tools that are providing key capabilities to manage streams at large scale.

CHAPTER 14

Scaling Flow Engineering

"Finally, enacting new systems
is not about getting 'the
answer,' it is about developing
networks of engaged and
trusting people who are guided
by a common understanding
of the current system and a
commitment to create new
systems."

PETER SENGE, *The Fifth Discipline:
The Art and Practice of the Learning
Organization*

FLOW ENGINEERING COUNTERACTS the disengagement, disorientation, and distraction costs of scale. But to have a large-scale impact, you must achieve this effect across an entire organization. That's neither feasible nor affordable one value stream at a time. We've worked with organizations composed of tens of thousands of contributors, with giant portfolios of products distributed across regions, divisions, and lines of business. Even in a few hours per stream, the task of mapping it all is immense. Luckily, you'll never have to map it all to have a dramatic impact on the overall system.

Just like Figure 14.1 depicts, it's often simple to see that dependencies are common, and by addressing them for one stream, you can address them across the entire organization. As you learn information about where else the dependency is utilized (change advisory boards, security testing), you can estimate the broader impact of improvements.

FIGURE 14.1: Value Streams Sharing a Common Constraint

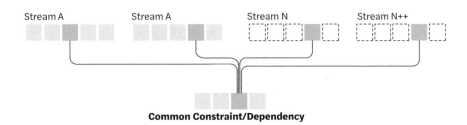

Many value streams share common constraints. Once a common constraint is identified, it can be improved for all dependent streams.

This obviously has dramatic implications for the ROI of mapping and improvement. It's not uncommon for a few hours of mapping to uncover a week of easily addressed delay or waste shared by a dozen or more teams. That represents an ROI of multiple orders of magnitude.

In other cases, a dependency will be internal to the team or not linked to a shared team or stream (tooling, capability, information flow, data quality), and either by estimation or by mapping a similar team or stream workflow, the commonality emerges. For example, each team may be copying data from one system to another, and a single integration could address it across all teams. Without the visibility across streams, the global impact would likely go unnoticed or unaddressed because the local impact seems small.

To achieve global impact from locally discovered constraints, waste, and friction, there are a few simple and rapid methods to reach out beyond a single stream and assess larger-scale opportunities:

- Sharing Maps: You can easily share the maps you create with other teams and groups to share progress and learning, validate your understanding from their perspective, or enlist them to help fill in gaps. This can also spark their interest in creating their own maps or joining your efforts.

- **Surveying:** Sending out a survey, poll, or even a discussion thread on a chat platform like Slack can help you quickly and asynchronously gather information from a variety of perspectives and form a larger-scale understanding. You can ask any of the questions captured in Flow Engineering, such as "What's your current target outcome?" or "What's having the biggest impact on your lead time?" or "What's your most impactful dependency?" Answers can be compiled and synthesized to inform key areas of focus and where you may want to dig deeper.
- **Communities of Practice:** We discuss the role and operation of communities of practice later in the chapter.

The Value Stream Network as a Map of the Enterprise

James Martin illustrated in *The Great Transition* how "an enterprise is a collection of value streams."[1] Any given organization today may look a lot more like a loosely or tightly coupled collection of teams. It is this coupling that creates an interconnected network. As that network is formalized and stabilized, stable value streams emerge.

As organizations shift from project to product, they focus less on disruptive reorganization to tackle individual deliverables and instead organize to continually improve how they deliver customer value. Mik Kersten's book *Project to Product* covers this transition and introduces the concept of the value stream network in the context of measuring and improving flow.[2] The ultimate impact of Flow Engineering is to improve flow across the entire value stream network.

Identifying Value Streams across Your Organization

Once you've begun to map your value streams, you'll need to start organizing and creating a holistic understanding of streams within the larger context of your organization. We've found it helpful to consider the behavior and characteristics of value streams as they lie across two dimensions:

1. Developmental to Operational
2. Core to Supportive

Understanding these dimensions provides a structure to think and talk about the purpose and attributes of different value streams and how you can design and adapt them over time.

1. DEVELOPMENTAL VS. OPERATIONAL VALUE STREAMS

Value Streams are frequently categorized as either developmental or operational, depending on whether they focus on delivering a consistent product or developing something new each time. But this binary categorization hides a useful and more flexible spectrum of identification.

There are many reasons why strictly categorizing streams into developmental or operational works against you, but here are three important aspects:

1. Binary categorization only works for things that are either/or, but streams always have a mix of focus and obligations. They have to both improve and maintain stability, operate and develop, execute and innovate. What matters is the degree to which they satisfy each of the conflicting demands.

2. Binary categorization creates an "us-versus-them" scenario where streams are at odds by default. It forces you to do more work to compensate for a model that doesn't work for you. DevOps is the response to an unhelpful separation between development and operations in software development. Repeating the same issue with value streams will create the same problems DevOps has worked to address for over a decade. If you separate developmental and operational concerns into distinct silos, you immediately raise truly challenging questions: What do developmental and operational streams have in common? How does each leverage the strengths of the other? How might they speak the same language and collaborate? What's the common ground they should meet on?

3. Binary categorization makes it difficult to think about how to balance the necessary ingredients for performance. You can't exclusively focus on only development or only operations, but binary focus implies you have to, or at least demands some form of compromise. This results in compromised decision-making since the inherent flaw in the

separation has to be continuously reconciled. This reconciliation may be easy for some, but if DevOps is an example we can reference, it's rarely accomplished. What you have in reality is a spectrum of focus and investment with development and operations as opposite poles. An individual, team, or team of teams can focus more on innovation, a developmental pursuit, with its own set of metrics and measures to indicate progress while still maintaining an aspect of stability and efficiency. They don't choose one or the other; they simply choose one *over* the other. This has implications for management and adaptation over time. The focus becomes a decision filter, which can be used to identify value, build clarity, and enable flow.

Consider an operational value stream, such as a team of teams managing infrastructure and providing services to internal stakeholder value streams and contributors. You can see it plotted in Figure 14.2 as Stream B. It may have a current focus on efficiency and predictability and monitoring metrics that reflect that focus: cost of operations, incident recovery lead time, mean time between failures, etc. If some external condition arises to disturb the focus or priority of the stream, the stream leadership and contributors can act accordingly and shift along the spectrum.

FIGURE 14.2: The Spectrum of Flow Investment

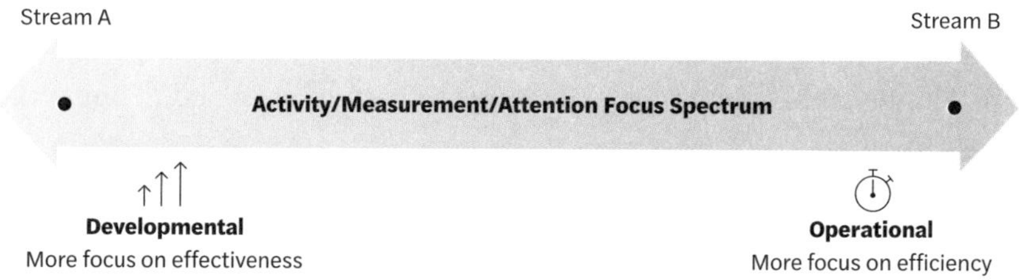

Stream A   Stream B

Activity/Measurement/Attention Focus Spectrum

Developmental   **Operational**
More focus on effectiveness   More focus on efficiency

Say operational AI reaches a level of capability that allows them to improve their target metrics, they could temporarily shift further toward developmental activities to evaluate it, adopt it, and implement it.

On the other end of the spectrum, consider a product development value stream, like Stream A in Figure 14.2. They're facing criticism for high costs, low predictability, and rising production defects. They primarily measure effectiveness and customer outcomes, but their lack of operational capability and focus is beginning to jeopardize their sustainability. They can shift focus further toward operational metrics, capabilities, and investment.

TABLE 14.1: Developmental and Operational Focus Implications

Enabling	Developmental	Operational
Focused on:	Effectiveness	Efficiency
	Design	Execution
	Innovation	Stability
	Novelty	Maintenance
	Value creation	Value maximization
Characterized by:	Variation	Consistency
	Uncertainty	Certainty
	Investigation	Measurement
	Experimentation	Optimization
Function of constraints:	Enablement	Governance

The potential to shift along this spectrum provides flexibility for value streams to find and adjust their position as needs or opportunities arise. It provides another method for evaluating the current state and defining the future state.

2. CORE VS. SUPPORTIVE VALUE STREAMS

Just like we have a spectrum of operational and developmental focus for value streams, it's helpful to think about value streams as they relate to core and supportive concerns. This can make it easier to share a common language about streams and stream behaviors that impact flow, as well as aid decision-making when it comes to value stream design and performance improvement.

Core streams are tied to the strategy and business model of the organization, while supportive value streams ensure core streams have access to resources, capabilities, and information required to operate effectively and efficiently. Core streams are any flow of work that directly contributes to revenue or value creation for the business. Core value streams contribute directly to external customer value. There is a value-experiencing or purchasing customer or user at the end of the stream. Every company has at least one core stream and can have many, often connected to each other in some way. Core streams are *why you're in business.*

Core value streams leverage supportive streams. Supportive streams provide services and capabilities to core streams. Supportive value streams contribute value to the core streams by enabling or enhancing their performance. Supportive streams are *how you stay in business.* The ideal model for this interaction is a "pull" from the core stream to the supportive stream, which is providing its value as a self-service capability to the core.

Core streams can be supported by multiple supportive streams. Supportive streams can then be supported by further supportive streams. And, supportive streams can also support multiple core streams. For example, the same supportive stream can provide automated testing and building capabilities to two separate product teams.

Each value stream has at least one defined customer (internal or external) and consumes the products and services of others as their customer. Figure 14.3 (see page 234) shows how a core stream relies on a supportive stream for an infrastructure platform and how that platform team relies on a build pipeline provided by another stream. If these streams are creating self-service capabilities, the dependent streams can leverage those capabilities on demand without an interruption to flow.

This is how a company like Amazon builds loosely coupled services that can be used individually and interchangeably while providing services to other services and products like Amazon.com or customer applications atop that. A platform team providing services to product teams, who consume a design system from a design team and get approvals via an accessible self-service legal system, provides an agile, high-velocity network without hard dependencies.

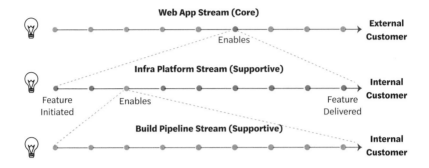

FIGURE 14.3: Interdependence of Core and Supportive Value Streams

Amazon Web Services (AWS) is an example of supportive streams becoming core streams. After an initial experiment in 2002, Amazon assessed its infrastructure capabilities as a viable business in 2003 and officially spun AWS out as a core set of public-facing capabilities in 2004.[3] AWS's capabilities remained a supportive function for Amazon.com, became a core function for Amazon Web Services, and is a supportive function underpinning its customers' infrastructure capabilities.

Classification across the core to supportive spectrum, like developmental/operational, can be helpful for considering relative investment (e.g., in marketing, branding, pricing, cost management, etc.), but it can also be detrimental in the wrong environment. If core streams hold relatively higher prestige than supportive, there will be negative downstream effects as contributors will become aware of a stratification that often breeds conflict or resentment. There can't be first-class and second-class value streams in a coherent value stream network.

The value of these classification spectrums is in gaining a clear understanding of streams throughout your organization to enable better conversations and decisions. Because digital value streams are invisible without a proper model to represent them, it's crucial we have a productive set of terms to talk about and think about that model. Even more important for our purposes with Flow Engineering, we need to be able to improve the performance of value streams, so using a model that allows for and enables change is essential.

We'll now illustrate how the developmental/operational spectrum along with the core/supportive spectrum can be used to visually plot streams as a connected value stream network. This allows you to visualize your organization as interconnected value streams and better understand and communicate dependencies and cross-organizational flow.

Value Stream Network Mapping

We can create a simple map of the value stream network without getting into the details of each value stream, as depicted in Figure 14.4. This shows how interdependent organizations are and can help identify structural opportunities or inefficiencies. In a Value Stream Network Map, we show value streams as interconnected points in a basic diagram to understand how and where streams interconnect and to show supporting services like legal, HR, procurement, etc. Creating a Value Stream Network Map gives you a clear, visual artifact that can help clarify high-level conversations and planning.

FIGURE 14.4: A Value Stream Network Map

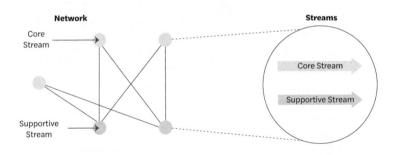

The value stream network can represent interconnected streams at macro scale.

To map the Value Stream Network, we use the two dimensions of developmental to operational and core to supportive to create a map of the larger value stream network. Plotting streams on a graph in this way is similar to a Wardley Map, typically used to show capabilities along a value chain.[4] But our focus is not on *what* is consumed and produced by the organization. We're concerned with the *how*; the value streams. For the purposes of illustrating flow, each node on the map represents a value stream that can shift along these dimensions, rather than capabilities that evolve toward commoditization. These allow us to show interconnections and to visualize the full organization. This type of large-scale map can help us visualize dependencies between streams, but it can also help us define, plan, and discuss larger-scale strategy.

To create a value stream network, begin by identifying the streams or services that you want to include in the map. We recommend starting small rather than trying to map the entire enterprise. If you intend to progress through all the maps of Flow Engineering, it will be easier to focus on a relevant section of the network rather than the entire organization. Distribute these streams as nodes along the vertical axis from *core* at the top (value streams delivering the reasons external customers choose you) to *supportive* at the bottom (value streams that provide internal support and enable sustained success), as shown in Figure 14.5.

FIGURE 14.5: The Y Axis of a Value Stream Network Map

Supportive to core denotes proximity to external customers.

Next, position these value streams horizontally based on where they fall on the *developmental* to *operational* spectrum, as shown in Figure 14.6. This dimension reflects the amount of inevitable variation and the performance focus in the value stream. Value streams that perform the same activity consistently, again and again, are operational and should emphasize efficiency by minimizing variation. Those that involve creatively conceiving new ideas are developmental and necessarily include significant variation. Developmental streams should emphasize effectiveness rather than efficiency.

FIGURE 14.6: The X Axis of the Value Stream Network Map

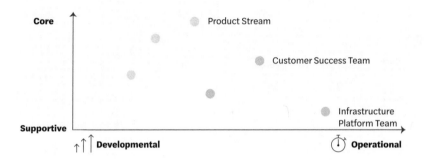

Developmental to operational denotes the performance focus of the stream.

Next, show the main interdependencies in the value stream by linking these nodes together. To keep the diagram simpler, only show the main dependencies, as per Figure 14.7.

FIGURE 14.7: Connections Show Dependencies between Value Streams

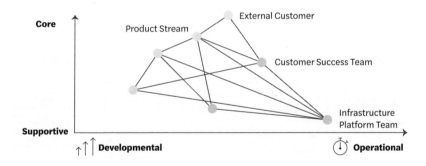

Figures 14.8 and 14.9 (see page 238) are value stream networks showing part of an organization's interconnected value streams. These diagrams provide a way to strategize about how changes to the organization would impact activity and outcomes. For example, Figure 14.8 shows how the organization may shift its focus and investment to further operationalize its

internal development platform. This may be motivated by needs that can be described directly on the map for clarity, such as reduced costs and variability, or decreasing disruptive incidents and improving stability.

FIGURE 14.8: Example Value Stream Network Map Showing Shift in Internal Dev Platform

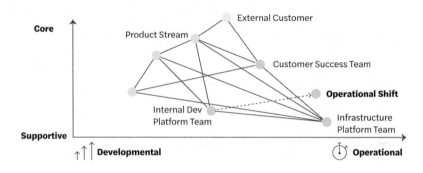

Streams can shift performance focus to respond to needs or conditions, such as an increase in stability or cost reduction.

The Value Stream Network Map can help you illustrate and discuss plans for, and the impact of, shifting along the developmental/operational spectrum. Figure 14.9 shows how a seemingly standard capability provided through a customer success platform could shift to adopt AI technology.

FIGURE 14.9: Example Value Stream Network Map Showing Developmental Shift

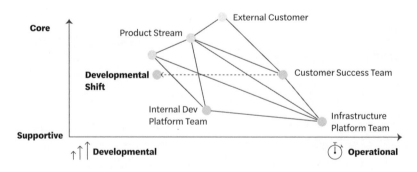

Streams can shift to focus more on innovation or new capabilities, which has implications for how they're measured and managed.

The experimental nature of these technologies would require a shift to the left to behave more developmentally. Using the map, you can discuss what this might require in terms of new measurements or methods to drive, support, and sustain the shift.

A value stream network is a map of your company, a set of relationships between value streams and their dependencies. Compared to the typical organizational chart, it's a depiction of how work is performed and supported throughout the organization. Rather than a hierarchical representation of roles and responsibilities relative to leadership, it represents activity relative to internal and external customers.

Thinking back to the Checkbox Project mentioned in Part 1, a value stream network could help you define and disentangle the necessary interactions involved in that effort. Thinking back to Sharon's case at Bolt Global, the network view could help her illustrate a larger-scale opportunity to improve flow across the organization. Having a spectrum of mapping techniques at your disposal as you work to engineer flow across organizations allows you to zoom out to the macro view and zoom in to the micro view where you see value.

Learning Communities

Dojos

As explained in the paper "Getting Started with Dojos," dojos are "a space that is designed to host an immersive learning experience where full-stack teams come together to learn."[5] Ross Clanton summarized the power of dojos to improve a team's performance: "The purpose of the dojo is learning, and we prioritize that over everything else. That means you have to slow down to speed up. Over the six weeks, they will not speed up. But they will get faster as an outcome of the process."[6] A dojo experience can be more or less intensive depending on the needs and expected return on investment, but the value of stepping away from the work and learning new skills pays off considerably over time. The flow-related learning conducted in a dojo could involve working through a fictional end-to-end case or doing a real-life application within the organization. It can present opportunities to learn facilitation skills, adopt more sophisticated mapping techniques, improve data collection and synthesis, apply countermeasures, or even design a custom-tailored version of Flow Engineering that best fits the local organizational culture.

Communities of Practice

Along with value streams, one of the networks that can reach across your organization are communities of practice, groups that assemble to share learning, ideas, and challenges. These were popularized as Guilds in Spotify's 2012 article "Scaling Agile @ Spotify."[7] This can start as small as two individuals meeting on an informal basis and grow into a large group with regular meetings and formalized deliverables like standards, playbooks, and documentation.

While you're starting out with Flow Engineering, you can leverage communities of practice outside the walls of your organization to ask questions, hear experience reports, and connect with like-minded individuals. The Flow Collective is one such community dedicated to improving collective flow across organizations, and it's a resource you can leverage as you start your journey with Flow Engineering.

CASE STUDY | **The Flow Collective**

The Flow Collective is a public community founded during the lockdown periods of the COVID-19 pandemic response. It was created as an online venue for conversations about flow among friends who would otherwise discuss the topic (and others) over a drink or a meal.

The platform is simple: Slack for asynchronous communication, a weekly Zoom call to talk in real time, and a Mural board to serve as a Lean Coffee platform. The Flow Collective emphasizes several key aspects in its approach to fostering creativity and learning:

- Stepping Away from Your Context: It provides a space separate from the traditional work environment, allowing for free and innovative thinking without the constraints of workplace norms and expectations. This separation encourages creativity and sharing ideas without the fear of judgment or the need to adhere to specific workplace behaviors.

- **Share and Listen:** Members of the Flow Collective engage in open, dynamic conversations every week where diverse ideas and perspectives are shared. This open dialogue brings together a variety of experiences and viewpoints, sparking new insights and realizations.
- **Support from Experienced Peers:** The collective consists of individuals with significant experience and knowledge, offering a rich environment for learning and growth. The sharing of ideas among these experienced peers not only fosters a sense of community but also provides a platform for mutual support and encouragement.
- **Learn in Public:** The concept of learning in public is central to the Flow Collective. Members are encouraged to share their developing ideas in a supportive community, allowing for exploration, feedback, and refinement. This process of public learning and sharing facilitates a continuous cycle of improvement and innovation.
- **Collect Learning as a Shared Reference:** The knowledge and insights gained through the collective's discussions and interactions are not just for individual benefit; they are collected and shared among members. This shared pool of learning not only serves as a valuable reference for everyone, enhancing the collective's overall knowledge and understanding over time but also provides a crowdsourced body of knowledge.

Communities like the Flow Collective foster a culture of open communication, continuous learning, and creative collaboration. By making a space to step into, away from traditional workplace structures and dynamics, members can share, learn, and develop their understanding of flow with a group of like-minded supporters. You can follow the example of the Flow Collective to craft your own community inside or outside your organization. And if you're reading this, you're officially invited to join the Flow Collective as a forum to learn, share, and grow at FlowCollective.org.

Flow Enabling Teams

To foster, support, and scale Flow Engineering practices throughout an organization, we encourage the model of enabling teams defined in *Team Topologies* by Matthew Skelton and Manuel Pais: "Enabling teams have a strongly collab-orative nature; they strive to understand the problems and shortcomings of stream-aligned teams in order to provide effective guidance."[8]

By pairing with and supporting stream-aligned (and platform) teams, flow-enabling teams can help teams and streams realign, refocus, reveal con-straints, and unblock flow. Despite the value of these activities, busy teams struggle to take time away from the work to improve the work.

Stephen Covey used the analogy of sharpening the saw to illustrate the value of taking time for improvement efforts: "They take some time, but in the long run, they save us a great deal of time. We must never get too busy sawing to take time to sharpen the saw, never too busy driving to take time to get gas."[9]

A flow-enabling team that works with multiple teams across an organi-zation gradually builds skill and insight from seeing many teams, scenarios, and issues. They can also invest in learning from peer networks to develop a heightened sense of common and shared challenges across the organization and across other organizations.

FIGURE 14.10: Flow Enabling Team Interactions with Product Streams

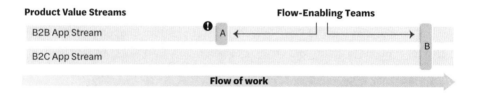

A flow-enabling team works with value stream aligned teams to help them learn, map, and address flow issues. It can support either reactively (A) or proactively (B).

Flow-enabling teams can work either reactively or proactively with streams and stream-aligned teams. Reactive interventions could be triggered by events like the loss of a team member, reorganization, new needs arising, or a realiza-tion that metrics are moving in the wrong direction. The flow-enabling team can work to stabilize the team or elevate their performance depending on the need. Proactively, the flow-enabling team can engage with teams for regular baselining, sharing insights from other parts of the organization, sharing new learning and techniques, or training and building Flow Engineering capabilities within the engaged team. A Flow Engineering team can assist teams across the organization to improve performance in a number of ways:

- The Flow Engineering team can facilitate mapping workshops under a full or partial program, as well as train and coach improvement efforts. This is a primary mode of interaction with other teams.
- Working together for a period of time, the teams could develop and test new methods and practices, including new mapping techniques or countermeasures. These can be incorporated in the portfolio of offerings and capabilities provided to other teams.
- The Flow Engineering team can publish templates and other resources, as well as documentation, training, case studies, videos, etc. that enable other teams to perform Flow Engineering activities within their own teams or with others.

A dedicated Flow Engineering team does not need to be formalized from day one, and it could begin as just one person's periodic investment in better performance. It can also become a powerful and permanent capability that can scale its impact throughout your entire organization.

Dependency Management

Many of the issues you'll encounter in current state flow are linked to dependencies, and their impact is significant. Troy Magennis, who has produced extensive work on data, forecasting, and measurement, calculated the odds of on-time delivery in a team with five dependencies (other teams, approvals, etc.) at one in thirty-two and stated, "Every dependency you can remove DOUBLES your chances of successful on-time delivery."[10]

Piloting Flow Engineering (Bridging the On-Ramp Gap)

Everyone wants improvement, but it's not easy to justify investment, especially when it involves change. Leading from the inside out means that the approach has to meet people where they are and align to where they want to go. To effectively get improvement efforts off the ground, it's not enough to simply propose Flow Engineering or any approach—regardless of how compelling—if there's no capacity or cognitive load to invest in it. We've aimed to make it as easy as possible to see a path to and through Flow Engineering. But we know that easy and valuable is often not enough to drive change.

There are two powerful and easy ways to get started with Flow Engineering.

1. Conduct a conversational Outcome Map: As the Lean decision filter stated in Chapter 10, "Value trumps flow." It's critical to repeatedly reestablish the valuable target you're seeking to achieve and to do so together with everyone involved to ensure alignment and shared clarity. In either one-on-one or group conversations, you can establish whether Flow Engineering could help address needs by taking notes and categorizing them into the outcome discovery categories explained in Chapter 5. If the conversation raises issues with throughput, friction, misalignment, visibility, etc., you may have an opportunity to leverage Flow Engineering as a countermeasure.
2. When a desired outcome is clear, talk through what it might look like, the benefits to stakeholders, obstacles, and next steps. You can mentally, physically, or digitally create a conversational Outcome Map in a single thirty-minute meeting that helps you get on track, get back on track, or stay on track. The advantage of a conversational map is that you can present it to your counterpart and ask, "Did I hear this right?"

To maximize your odds of progress and success, remember the following:

- Everyone has their own obligations and incentives. Make sure your efforts clearly align to a high-value business goal, initiative, target, or objective.

- Make it clear how improving flow, quality, or value directly contributes to what the business values. You can use an Outcome Map to plot and share this.
- Use the map as a reference to either guide a conversation with peers and leaders or share it directly in a conversation to serve as a visual asset.
- Create an Outcome Map together with key stakeholders in order to gather direct perspectives and leverage the IKEA effect.

You can also use Flow Engineering to get started with Flow Engineering. First, define a target outcome: Let's say we aim to improve lead time for a single pilot team by 30%. If a thorough mapping process takes six to eight hours, that's a modest investment of time to deliver that level of improvement. This can be a way to start the adoption of Flow Engineering and scale the impact of improvement efforts.

Begin by identifying a pilot team and working through the maps. By starting with a single pilot team at first, we can demonstrate value and success quickly. Notice that our target outcome is *not* to implement Flow Engineering. Why not? Flow Engineering is a means to an end, rather than an end in itself. The best way to pilot Flow Engineering is to use it to benefit your business. Pick a real problem, a real opportunity, and something that aligns to high-level objectives. Put the maps to work and then pick another target. Flow Engineering isn't something you implement and roll out; it's something you do and practice.

One of the first challenges for the pilot team is understanding how high-level streams of workflow through the organization today. Examples of high-level streams include a major version release workflow, partner engagement flow, or any other key sequence of activities that delivers on the company's primary business model. Even if individuals believe this is well understood, the exercise of making this visible opens opportunities for new discoveries about how the organization delivers value. Visualizing one work stream within the org will often lead to identifying adjacent work that may form an extension of the same value stream or another related stream.

The next objective of the pilot team is to identify obvious constraints and waste to generate quick wins. These quick wins will not only feed our motivation and sense of progress but also fuel inspiring communication with others who can join, support, and expand the efforts.

When we talk about the changes being introduced, they could be of many types, but they are often disruptive, and their value can be hidden by delayed feedback. We need to work with the teams to identify how to make the change valuable and visible for them. Having maps available to share for visibility, input, and feedback can spark and build momentum that can lead to mapping other streams, other outcomes, and larger impacts. This is the start of the flow flywheel.

Starting the Flow Flywheel

The challenge of investing time in Flow Engineering is that most teams operate at or above full capacity, making it challenging to step away and try something new. This is why we suggest fitting mapping into existing time boxes like retrospectives or off-site meetings. With a minimal initial investment, you can create a quick win that provides enough capital (time, space, enthusiasm) to invest in the next one. Once progress has begun, you can continue to reinvest and grow the impact. Flow Engineering can prepare the conditions to grow substantial flow improvement capabilities and, once started, can serve as a flywheel for continued and larger-scale change. Figure 14.11 shows the stages of building momentum, described next.

FIGURE 14.11: The Flywheel of Flow Engineering

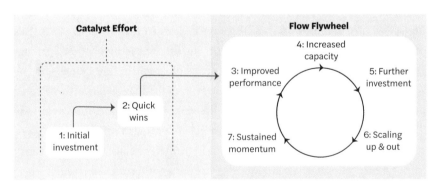

I. Initial investment: Stepping away from the work is the best way to understand and improve it. This stage is often the most challenging, as it requires overcoming inertia and resistance to change. Flow Engineering mapping is intended to be fast (and thus cheap) and interactive (and thus engaging). It can also be an exercise incorporated in other team improvement activities, such as retrospectives. Outcome Mapping can be useful to connect your efforts to benefits that the larger organization is seeking.

2. Quick Wins: Your first victories of increased alignment and visibility can power your initial progress. Often, Current State Mapping reveals opportunities that can eliminate huge amounts of waste overnight, just by minimizing non–value-adding activity or delays. Future State Maps serve as an artifact to build support and alignment. Mapping builds cohesion and engagement within and across teams.

3. Improved Performance: The initial investments start to pay off, leading to enhanced efficiency, productivity, or quality. This improvement is the first sign that the flywheel is starting to spin. Celebrating early wins and sharing learning can build support and progress. Measures of progress in the Flow Roadmap become metrics and milestones you can share to demonstrate the value of your efforts. The clarity of tight-scope improvement actions makes it easier to focus, execute, and deliver change.

4. Increased Capacity, Capability, and Time: As performance improves, it can lead to more available capacity and time. This might be due to more efficient processes, less rework, or fewer interruptions. The organization can do more with the same or fewer resources.

5. Further Investment: With more available time and capacity, the organization can invest further in innovative improvements, data collection, and the development of new capabilities. Available capacity can be dedicated to repaying technical debt, playbooks, platform development, and other enabling capabilities.

6. Scaling Up and Out: Learning can be shared more broadly with other teams, partners, and dependencies. Focus can be expanded to new constraints and new target outcomes. Value Stream Management can enable more sophisticated measurement, greater visibility, and greater impact.

7. Sustained Momentum and Growth: As this cycle continues, the organization experiences sustained momentum, where each improvement

fuels further improvements. This is the flywheel effect in full swing, where initial hard work leads to a self-sustaining cycle of growth and advancement. At this point, improvement is a natural part of work. Work item profile (flow) distribution tracks time spent on each distinct type of work, and metrics capturing throughput and value realization track ROI. This allows for continued adaptation and evolution.

Conclusion

Part 3 has covered a broad range of concepts and techniques to enable your first steps with Flow Engineering and to support deeper learning and broader application over time. Chapter 10 began by sharing guiding principles for engineering flow. We worked through the practical application of leading flow improvement, beyond the maps and mapping, in Chapter 11. Common traps that teams are likely to encounter were the focus of Chapter 12. In Chapter 13, we looked at Value Stream Management as a practice of ongoing performance improvement. With Chapter 14, we revisited our initial problem of scale by exploring how to effectively scale your efforts with Flow Engineering. Together, these provide a portfolio of concepts and practices that we hope will support your efforts to improve flow across your organization. We appreciate the great challenge you're taking on, tackling the problem of scale in your organization. With these tools, you're ready to kick-start your flow flywheel and foster value, clarity, and flow, even within a challenging enterprise environment.

Key Takeaways

- Quick wins with Flow Engineering may span multiple teams with common flow challenges, amplifying the impact of mapping with a single pilot team.
- Dojos and communities of practice can allow you to rapidly develop and improve Flow Engineering skills and capabilities on a large scale.
- A Flow Engineering enabling team can work across a large organization to facilitate, intervene, and share learning at scale.
- With minimal initial investment, Flow Engineering can power a flywheel that continually improves flow across the organization.

Conclusion

"We can't impose our will on a system. We can listen to what the system tells us and discover how its properties and our values can work together to bring forth something much better than could ever be produced by our will alone."

DONELLA H. MEADOWS, *Thinking in Systems*

BEYOND ANY SPECIFIC PROGRAM, practice, or set of principles, Flow Engineering is an effort to improve the conditions and performance of one of the most challenging work environments: complex, global, increasingly digital enterprise organizations. Enterprises at such a scale lead to distance between people, perspectives, and purposes. This distance creates disengagement, disorientation, and distraction. These conditions make it difficult to align and collaborate and to do our best work.

Many approaches, systems, frameworks, and programs exist to address these conditions, but few find an actionable balance between prescriptive and generative. Many solutions leave gaps that make it difficult to onboard, visualize, and align with the current state or future targets. We draw inspiration from cybernetics, a view that applies at any scale, from individuals to ecosystems. To enable effective action under these conditions, we must enable the elements of action: value, clarity, and flow.

Flow Engineering provides a means to develop these elements of action through the enabling constraints of five sequential collaborative mapping practices:

1. Outcome Mapping: Defining a clear target outcome.
2. Current State Mapping: Identifying the constraint in the current state.
3. Dependency Mapping: Analyzing the constraint preventing the target outcome.
4. Future State Mapping: Defining what will deliver the target outcome.
5. Flow Roadmap: Prioritizing key action items to deliver the target outcome.

When we know the constraints and complexity affecting our capacity for change and improvement, Flow Engineering is easy to start. It leverages the best of prescriptive and generative approaches. It works at small and large scale and is easily tailored, open, extendable, and adaptable. We hope by this point you've put it into practice, but if you haven't, you're welcome to join us at FlowCollective.org to start at any time.

The simplest representation of Flow Engineering traces the cybernetic loop of value, clarity, and flow with three questions:

1. What is our most valuable target?
2. What is holding us back from it?
3. What will we do to address that?

If you're thinking of these questions, you've already started to improve flow across your organization. Simple, but not easy. The structure of Flow Engineering is there to make the process straightforward, clear, and actionable.

There's a great deal that needs to go your way to succeed with a large-scale change effort. There's very little you need to gain a quick win, demonstrate success, and start the flywheel of progress. Write up a simple conversational Outcome Map in your next meeting and share it to validate your understanding. Remix OKRs into an Outcome Map to see them from a different perspective. Map the flow you spend most of your time in and see if you find delay or waste you could address yourself. Once you do, make sure you step back and celebrate your efforts and your learning—and while you're at it, tell us how it went and what you learned!

Writing this book has revealed how much more there is that we don't yet know. There's far more beyond the horizon of this book: knowledge and practices to expand the depth, breadth, and impact of your efforts. To continue your pursuits, explore and dig deeper—you may find a great deal of value in the following areas we couldn't accommodate in the limited scope of the book:

- Cost of Delay: Don Reinertsen has proposed this as an über metric for flow along with Throughput Accounting.[1]
- Wardley mapping (Simon Wardley) for large-scale strategic understanding and evolution of architecture and capabilities.
- *Leading the Transformation* and *Engineering the Digital Transformation* by Gary Gruver for specific technical and practice interventions for continuous delivery.
- "The Project to Product Transformation" to illustrate changes to operating models, incentives, and priorities.[2]
- Cynefin (Dave Snowden) to inform ways of approaching various operating environments and conditions.
- Hoshin Kanri (policy depoloyment) to strategically deploy Value Stream Management and align tactics and operations.[3]
- Look to the Poppendiecks, Meadows, Capra, Deming, Senge, etc. to delve deeper into systems thinking, flow, and performance improvement theory and practice.

We hope that with this book we've not only enabled you to improve flow, but inspired you to explore further, in turn inspiring others to join your journey. Thank you for joining ours.

Key Takeaways

- Flow engineering is a human activity. The goal is to deliver value continuously, sustainably, and collaboratively.
- To grow the influence and effects of flow engineering, you need to consider the impacts, incentives, and systems at play across the organization.

- You can leverage proven Lean and scalable change-adoption methods to grow Flow Engineering.
- You can effectively scale Flow Engineering via enabling teams, dojos, and communities of practice.
- FlowCollective.org is a global community of flow-focused individual changemakers who can support your individual journey.

Appendix

Value, Clarity, and Flow Detail

Figure A.1 presents a more detailed view of the three elements of action: value, clarity, and flow.

FIGURE A.1: Value, Clarity, and Flow

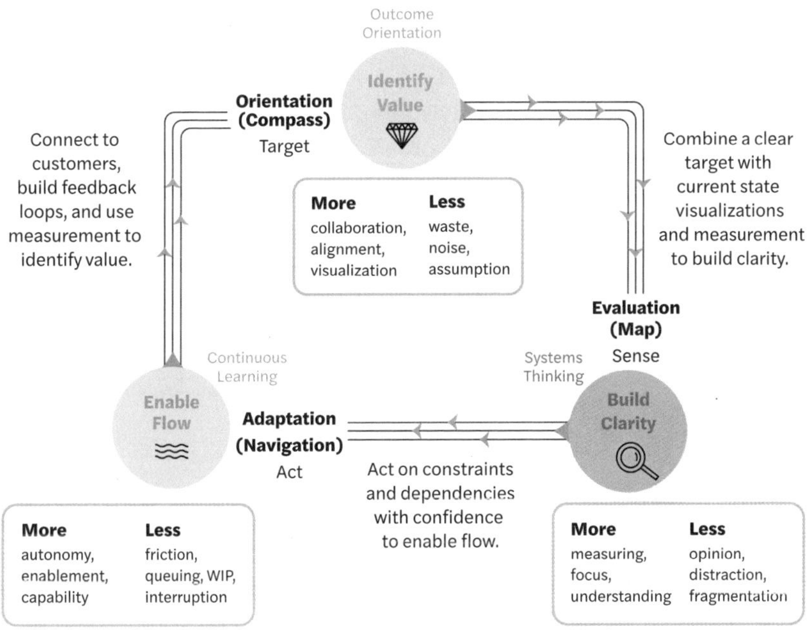

Applying Little's Law

Little's Law is a principle from queue theory that provides a simple calculation to evaluate flow in value streams. It helps you understand, for example, how long you can expect to wait for items in your backlog to be delivered based on current performance. Little's Law relates the number of items waiting to be processed (L) to the average arrival/departure rate (λ) and the average wait time of an item within the system (W). The law is expressed as $L = \lambda W$.

In knowledge work, it can be used to relate the amount of work in progress (WIP) to the time to complete this work. It can help you calculate optimal WIP throughout your value streams by showing the combined impact of ingress work, WIP, and throughput. To calculate this correctly, you must ensure you are familiar with the average values for your value stream prior to performing calculations: lead time (W), work in progress (L), and throughput (λ).

As Daniel Vacanti pointed out, being able to use it reliably requires consistent measurement and "looks at the past, not the future."[1] Little's Law represents a mathematical ideal that depends on a number of assumptions:

- This law holds only for value streams operating at a relatively steady state. As an example, the WIP at the start of the week should match the WIP at the week's end.
- The average rates of both incoming and outgoing work through the value stream should be equal, otherwise throughput can't be accurately quantified, i.e., work items can't be injected or abandoned midstream.

Due to the high amount of variability in knowledge work, these assumptions rarely hold true. But the general relationship between WIP, lead time, and throughput is directionally correct: if you want to increase throughput, work to reduce WIP and/or lead time.

Components of Little's Law
- L: Average number (load) of work items (features, bugs, improvements, etc.) in process (WIP) in the value stream.
- λ: Throughput of work items through (initiated and completed) the value stream.

- W: Average time a task spends in the value stream, from being initiated to being enabled for use. You can think of W here as customer wait from request to fulfillment.

Scenario: Applying Little's Law in a Value Stream Context

- Observation Period: 1 month.
- Work Items Completed: 60 work items.
- Work in Progress: On average, 15 work items are in different stages of the value stream at any given time.

STEPS

- Calculate the arrival rate (λ): If 60 items are completed in a month, the arrival rate λ is 60 items/month.
- Calculate the average time an item spends in the system (W): Little's Law can be rearranged to $W = L/\lambda$. With (load) $L = 15$ items and (arrival) $\lambda = 60$ items/month. $W = 15/60$ months $= 0.25$ months.
- This means, on average, a work item takes about 0.25 months (or about 7.5 days) from start to finish in the system.

INSIGHTS AND ACTIONS

- **Backlog Completion:** Knowing throughput can help you think about a backlog in terms of when it could be delivered: If each work item takes 60 days to be delivered (W), and you have five items in progress at a time (L), it will take you 6.5 years to clear out a 200-item backlog.
- **Bottlenecks:** If the team finds the average time (W) too long, they can investigate the constraint in the process. Are items getting stuck in code review? Is there a delay in testing?
- **Capacity:** If W is high, it might indicate a need for more capacity or a change in the development process.
- **Predictability:** Knowing W helps predict delivery times, improving the team's ability to make commitments, but only if flow remains consistent.
- **Process Improvement:** If the team aims to reduce W, they can experiment with different approaches, like limiting work in progress, to see how it affects the average completion time.

Applying Metrics to Value Stream Management

FIGURE A.2: Calculating Speed: Lead, Wait, and Active Times

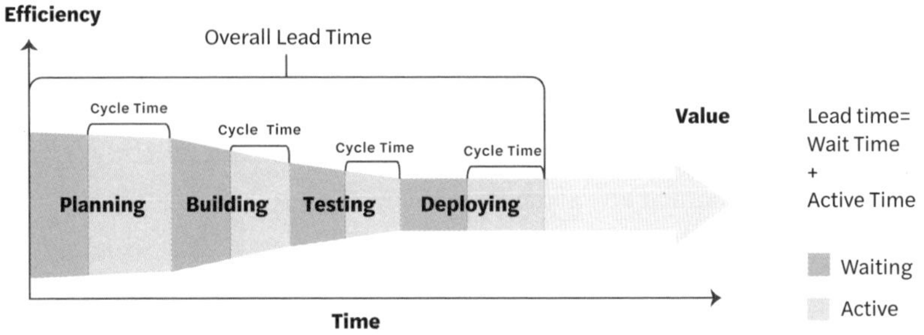

Lead time is the most critical metric in flow improvement for three key reasons seldom discussed:

- Time is the one dimension of work you have the least control over. Lead time is the most complete representation of the fact that time is always passing, for you and your customers.
- Lead time encourages collaboration. It encompasses every cross-functional group involved in value creation, unifying each individual contributor under a collective metric.
- Lead time represents the most complete closed loop of learning from customers. It allows you to understand the earliest point you could deliver value based on an insight gained from your last customer-impacting change.

The biggest misconception of lead time is that it's just the total time that you spend doing the work, which is incorrect. Lead time, by standard definition, actually includes the time that the work waited plus the cycle time for each stage that you worked on that item. So, if you had a user story that was waiting for eight months, and you only spent two months actually developing it, your total lead time ends up being ten months, because we are taking the wait time and the cycle time of each stage together to give you the actual lead time because we are thinking in terms of customer outcomes.

FIGURE A.3: Cycle Time Includes All Value-Added and Non–Value-Added Time Composing Each Stage

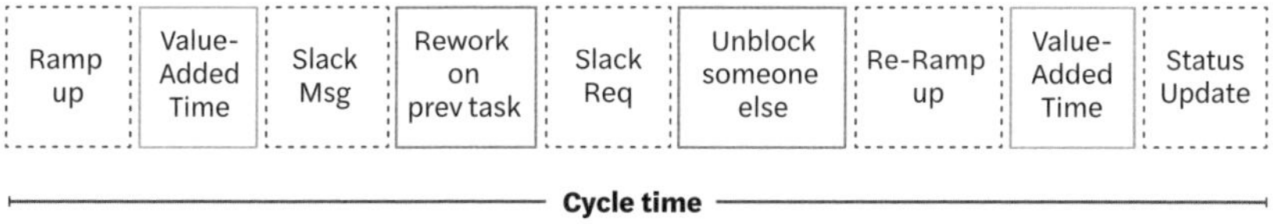

Ramp up	Value-Added Time	Slack Msg	Rework on prev task	Slack Req	Unblock someone else	Re-Ramp up	Value-Added Time	Status Update

⊢————————————— **Cycle time** —————————————⊣

Cycle time actually includes the time actively developing the work item along with all the delays, rework, distractions, and operational activities conducted in the course of each stage. A lot of waste can hide in there, but we rarely invest in zooming in to that detail because it's not necessary or valuable. We simply ask contributors what percentage of the time in each stage is value-added time. Time they're able to actively develop the value of the work item.

It's not uncommon for this percentage to be very low, and it should be expected to be low at first. The reason to measure it isn't to evaluate it at its current level but to establish a baseline for improvement and an understanding of the ROI potential of improvement.

FIGURE A.4: Calculating Quality: Percent Complete & Accurate

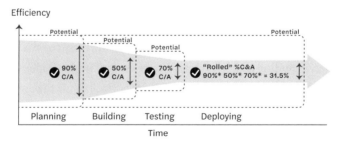

% Complete & Accurate: How many items passed through one stage without needing to be returned for rework or clarification?   **KEY** ✓ Actual

The image above illustrates how we calculate quality, which is the percent that is complete and accurate. If we break down the definition of this metric, it's really how complete and accurate the work was that passed through the various stages, or how many items passed through one stage without needing to be returned for rework or clarification.

At the very beginning of the development process, a product owner or business analyst is typically responsible for gathering requirements and writing user stories. These become work items, which are what the development team then ends up working on. Even an excellent business analyst may only manage to write a user story that hits about 95% of all of the various scenarios and edge cases that need to be addressed. It then gets handed off to a developer. About 5% of the time there are not enough requirements or there's information that is fundamentally missing from the story. At that point, the developer is blocked, and the work actually has to go back to the business analyst.

This happens very often in the DevOps space. The problem that we have is how to measure that and keep track of how often work is being sent back. That scenario can take place not only in the development stage but sometimes even at the testing phase, where someone's completed development, but from a testing perspective, there have been major issues found, so the work gets sent back.

That is where percent complete and accurate (%C&A) comes into the picture and why it is so important. This measure shows what percentage of the work in each of your stages was completed correctly and accurately and did not need to be returned. Ideally, each piece of work would pass from one stage to the next without introducing a defect, but we know that in real-life scenarios and in practice, defects can be introduced at any stage.

The later stages are dependent on the quality of the work in the earlier stages, which means that business analysts really need to be writing clear user stories, including all of the various edge cases. The developer then has to make sure that they are developing the story accurately so that when it gets to testing there are no major issues. As such, we need to make sure that the quality of work is up to par at every single stage.

Let's take one more look at that last image (Figure A.4). You'll see we have our actual percent complete and accurate for planning, which is about 90%; for building, it's at 50%; and then for testing, it's at 70%. So, how do we read that number, which indicates the likelihood that a single piece of work will never have to be reworked in its journey? We can see that our final complete and accurate metric is 31.5%, which is the product of the actual complete and accurate metrics of the planning, building, and testing stages.

With customers who are effectively using Value Stream Maps today, that final number lives somewhere around 15% to 20%, although it's not uncommon to see teams new to Value Stream Management with rolled %C&A under 5%.

Calculating the ROI of Flow Engineering

If you don't currently have clear performance data on your workflow, a clear picture of what it looks like, and a clear path to better, wouldn't you like to have that ASAP? Let's say after mapping you identify three high-priority, relatively simple improvements to implement right away. It will likely take at least three months to see measurable progress. Then, with three more months of progress and operation, you'll have enough data and experience with the current state that you can map it again and look to a new outcome. In six months, you'll have made enough progress that you'll have a new desired outcome, and will have found new bottlenecks to identify and tackle.

FIGURE A.5: Example Map Board in Progress

In practice, Outcome Mapping requires at least one two-hour session to go from scratch to a fully formed map ready for action. We can see in Figure A.5

a very extensive Outcome Map, which covers goals and pains, values and principles, prioritization, and experiment definition. As you go from the raw input toward insight, you can rearrange the maps as you like and easily export them to be shared throughout the organization.

Since knowledge work is increasingly done across time zones rather than shared offices, collaborative online mapping has moved from a bonus to a necessity. With Flow Engineering we're concerned with improving the flow of work in the next three to six months within a specific value stream. Our aim is to not only improve operations but outcomes. Common desired outcomes we've seen in Flow Engineering efforts with clients and partners include:

- Deliver software three times more often.
- Deploy changes to test environments ten times faster.
- Recover from production issues five times faster.
- Reduce production defects by half.
- Reduce variability by half.

One reason that teams (especially remote teams) may hesitate to carve out time for a mapping exercise is that they are afraid to set aside or request sufficient time for the teams to meet. This is a perfect example of false economies, and we need to counter that tendency clearly.

The highest-paid members of any organization are the executive leadership team. But those are also often the teams that most regularly have long team off-sites for thinking and planning and multi-hour meetings each week to plan and strategize. Thinking takes time. Communication takes time. Time costs money. But the cost of inadequate thinking and communication vastly outweighs the up-front cost of thinking correctly from the outset.

The amount of time, money, energy, and goodwill that are burned through ineffective organizational activity is certainly hundreds of billions, if not trillions, of dollars globally. This effect is often described as expending organizational energy as heat instead of as work. Terms like "thrashing" are also used to describe the activity of staying busy without having an optimal impact.

A perfect example of thrashing is people whose calendars are filled with thirty-minute meetings pertaining to a huge number of parallel initiatives. Such meetings leave little time to accomplish real work, and even with buffer time, it takes an average of twenty-three minutes and fifteen seconds to effectively "get back to work."[2] Parallel projects invariably drag on for far longer and yield far lower quality than selectively taking up projects and completing them as quickly as possible before taking on new work.

We can estimate direct and indirect costs of a member in an IT organization being brought into a meeting at $125 an hour (opportunity cost could be higher). For the mapping exercises described in this book, it's reasonable that they might involve eight people each. Some exercises, like Dependency Mapping, may not be required depending on what's discovered in the earlier stages. This allows us to estimate a cost of $1,000 per hour of Flow Engineering exercises.

To estimate the benefits, we can imagine that we are influencing the activities of twenty knowledge workers who are each doing work valued at $200,000 per year (value delivered should be greater than salaries paid). Our goals in Flow Engineering are to help the team increase their throughput, improve quality, reduce attrition by increasing job satisfaction, and reduce the chances of a project being unsuccessful. Assuming they are all working full time, that team should be bringing $4 million of value per year.

TABLE A.1: Estimated Costs of Flow Engineering Exercises

Activity	Typical Initial Duration	Subsequent Time Required	Estimated Annual Cost
Outcome Mapping	3 hours	1 hour	$4,000
Current State Mapping	3 hours	1 hour	$4,000
Dependency Mapping	2 hours	1 hour	$3,000
Future State Mapping	2 hours	1 hour	$3,000
Flow Roadmap	3 hours	1 hour	$4,000
Total	13 hours	5 hours	$18,000

If we can help the team to increase their throughput by 20% (the common average improvement impact delivered by mapping[3]), that $18,000 investment brings an equivalent of $800,000 benefit per year. Similarly, if we can prevent 20% of their work from being wasted or ineffective, that's worth $800,000 per year. Reducing attrition also brings financial benefits by averting the need to rehire, retrain, and burden the team with disruption.

That back-of-the-envelope estimate shows a 44x benefit from these activities. This cost accounting approach is obviously an oversimplification, but it can be a useful way to illustrate the cost benefit. What's also notable is that improvement in one stream is typically replicable across multiple streams, magnifying the impact for far less investment. Even if the costs were scaled by several times or the benefits reduced significantly, this represents a remarkably positive effect from investing this time.

Glossary

The most critical aspect of language is that everyone involved uses and understands it the same. We encourage you to discuss what critical terms mean in your context and adjust them as needed. These are provided from our context and can serve as a baseline if you need a reference.

Customer: An entity that receives and perceives value from the value stream's outputs. This encompasses a broad range of recipients, including external clients, internal stakeholders, and partners, highlighting the diverse perspectives of value reception.

Cycle Time: The duration a stage requires for completion, including any inherent delays or waiting periods.

Flow Efficiency: The proportion of active time (or touch time) compared to overall lead time within the value stream, offering a gauge for assessing the stream's operational efficiency. This metric should be placed in the context of blocks, interruptions, rework, and other detrimental factors affecting performance. It can be refined to emphasize the contribution of direct value-generating activities to the stream's performance.

Lead Time (or Flow Time): The comprehensive duration required for a work item to traverse the value stream from start to finish. This metric encapsulates all stages, including production, pauses, and corrections, summarized simply as "hypothesis-to-happiness," signifying the journey from initiation to customer satisfaction.

Percent Complete and Accurate (%C&A): A quality metric indicating the proportion of work that progresses through a stage that meets requirements, without the need for rework or clarification.

Stage: A single distinct activity within the value stream, typically bounded by handoffs. For our purposes, analogous to step, process, or set of tasks.

Segment: A subset of the value stream consisting of multiple stages.

Throughput (or Flow Velocity): The measure of a value stream's output over a given period, indicating the efficiency of delivery to customers. The Theory of Constraints places this in relation to costs. Little's Law places this in the context of input relative to output.

Value: Ultimately defined by the recipient. The benefit that a product or service provides to the customer.

Value-Added Time: The duration spent on activities that directly contribute to the final product or service's value from the customer's perspective.

Value Stream: An integrated series of activities designed to deliver a specific outcome for a *customer* who might be the final consumer, stakeholder, or user. This stream encapsulates the journey of work from initial need to the delivery of value.

Wait Time: The interval of inactivity between stages, characterized by delays and queuing.

Waste: Activities within the value stream that consume resources without enhancing the product or service's value.

Work in Progress (WIP, Flow Load, or Work in Process): The quantity of work items currently under process within the value stream, from the inception of effort to completion. This is often tracked per stage to highlight accumulation and reveal a constraint.

Work Item Profile (or Flow Distribution): The classification of work items within the value stream, aiding in the assessment of work type distribution and flow characteristics. Common profiles include features, experiments, bug fixes and issue remediation, flow improvement, technical debt payment, and risk mitigation.

Bibliography

"A Brief History of AWS." Media Temple (blog). August 31, 2017. https://origin-blog .mediatemple.net/cloud-hosting/brief-history-aws/.

"Accelerating Change." The Natural Step (website). Accessed December 8, 2023. https://thenaturalstep.org/approach/.

"Amazon: Number of Employees 2010-2023 | AMZN." Macrotrends. Accessed November 30, 2023. https://www.macrotrends.net/stocks/charts/AMZN/amazon/number-of -employees.

"The Biggest Startup: Eric Ries and GE Team Up to Transform Manufacturing." GE News (website). December 9, 2013. https://www.ge.com/news/reports/the-biggest-startup -eric-ries-and-ge-team-up-to.

"Churchill and the Commons Chamber." UK Parliament. Accessed December 1, 2023. https://www.parliament.uk/about/living-heritage/building/palace/architecture /palacestructure/churchill/.

"Peter F. Drucker Quotes." QuoteFancy. Accessed November 29, 2023. https://quotefancy.com/quote/888106/Peter-F-Drucker-The-purpose-of-an -organization-is-to-enable-ordinary-humans-beings-to-do.

Ackoff, Russel L. *The Democratic Corporation: A Radical Prescription for Recreating Corporate American and Rediscovering Success.* Oxford: Oxford University Press, 1994.

Anderson, David, Mark McCann, and Michael O'Reilly. *The Value Flywheel Effect: Power the Future and Accelerate Your Organization to the Modern Cloud.* Portland, OR: IT Revolution, 2022.

Anderson, Katie. *Learning to Lead, Leading to Learn: Lessons from Toyota Leader Isao Yoshino on a Lifetime of Continuous Learning.* Integrand Press, 2020.

Arnold, J. J., and Ö. Yüce. "Black Swan Farming Using Cost of Delay: Discover, Nurture and Speed Up Delivery of Value." Paper presented at the 2013 Agile Conference, Nashville, TN, 2013. https://ieeexplore.ieee.org/document/6612885.

Atkinson, John. "Manpower Strategies for Flexible Organisations." *Personnel Management* 16, no. 8 (August 1984): 28–31. https://www.stonebridge.uk.com/uploads/courses/566.pdf.

Barry, Quintin. *Moltke and His Generals: A Study in Leadership.* Solihull: Helion & Company Limited, 2015.

Beck, Kent et al., "Manifesto for Agile Software Development." AgileManifesto.org (website). Accessed December 20, 2023. https://agilemanifesto.org/.

Blanchard, Ken. "No One of Us Is as Smart as All of Us." Ken Blanchard Books. May 25, 2022. https://www.kenblanchardbooks.com/no-one-of-us-is-as-smart-as-all-of-us/.

Bongers, F. J., W. A. Kosters, and B. G. Husslage. "How Long Does It Take To Refocus After Being Interrupted? A Systematic Review and Meta-Analysis of Resumption Lag In Complex Cognitive Activities." *Human Factors*, 61 no. 3 (2019): 420-439.

Boston Consulting Group. "Flipping the Odds of Digital Transformation Success."
    October 2020. https://web-assets.bcg.com/c7/20/907821344bbb8ade98cbe10fc2b8
    /bcg-flipping-the-odds-of-digital-transformation-success-oct-2020.pdf.

Brooks, Frederick P. *The Mythical Man-Month,: Essays on Software Engineering.* Boston:
    Addison-Wesley Professional, 2010.

Bryar, Colin, and Bill Carr. *Working Backwards: Insights, Stories, and Secrets from Inside
    Amazon.* New York: St. Martin's Press, 2021.

Buckingham, Marcus, and Curt Coffman. *First, Break All the Rules: What the World's
    Greatest Managers Do Differently.* Washington, DC: Gallup Press, 2016.

Burrows, Mike. "#2MBM: Meaning before Metric, Measure before Method." Agendashift.
    July 2, 2020. https://blog.agendashift.com/2020/07/02/2mbm-meaning-before
    -metric-measure-before-method.

Capra, Fritjof, and Pier Luigi Luisi. *The Systems View of Life: A Unifying Vision.* New York:
    Cambridge University Press, 2016.

Carpentier, Chantal Line. "New Economics for Sustainable Development Attention
    Economy." United Nations Economist Network. Accessed December 1, 2023.
    https://www.un.org/sites/un2.un.org/files/attention_economy_feb.pdf.

Clanton, Ross, et al. *Getting Started with Dojos.* Portland, OR: IT Revolution, 2019.
    https://itrevolution.com/product/getting-started-with-dojos/.

Clanton, Ross, et al. *The Project to Product Transformation: Practical Guidance from
    Fourteen Enterprise Journeys.* Portland OR: IT Revolution, 2019.
    https://itrevolution.com/product/project-to-product-transformation/.

Clark, Phil. "Inspect." Presentation at the 2023 Flowtopia Conference in Las Vegas.

Cote, Michael. *Monolithic Transformation.* O'Reilly Media, April 2019.

Cottmeyer, Mike. "LK2009 Anderson, Scotland, and Hathaway." Leading Agile (website).
    2009. https://www.leadingagile.com/2009/05/lk2009-anderson-scotland-and
    -hathaway/.

Covey, Stephen. *The 7 Habits of Highly Effective People: Powerful Lessons in Personal Change.*
    New York: Free Press, 2004.

Criscuolo, Paola, Ammon Salter, and Anne Ter Wal. "The Role of Proximity in Shaping
    Knowledge Sharing in Professional Services Firms." Paper presented at the Summer
    Conference 2010 on "Opening Up Innovation: Strategy, Organization and
    Technology" at Imperial College London Business School, June 16-18, 2010.
    https://www.researchgate.net/publication/228681027_The_role_of_proximity
    _in_shaping_knowledge_sharing_in_professional_services_firms.

Cutler, John. "TBM 7/52: Two Bets." *The Beautiful Mess* (blog). January 26, 2023.
    https://cutlefish.substack.com/p/tbm-752-two-bets.

Cutler, John. "TBM 34/52: Words Matter—Strategy & Certainty." *The Beautiful Mess* (blog).
    August 3, 2022. https://cutlefish.substack.com/p/tbm-3452-words-matterstrategy-and.

Cutler, John. "TBM 245: The Magic Prioritization Trick." *The Beautiful Mess* (blog).
    September 30, 2023. https://cutlefish.substack.com/p/tbm-245-the-magic-prioritization.

Cynefin.io. "Constraints." Accessed December 20, 2023. https://cynefin.io/wiki
    /Constraints.

DeGrandis, Dominica. *Making Work Visible: Exposing Time Theft to Optimize Work & Flow.*
    Portland, OR: IT Revolution Press, 2017.

Deming, W. Edwards. *Out of the Crisis*. MIT Press, 1982.

Duhigg, Charles. "What Google Learned from Its Quest to Build the Perfect Team." *New York Times*. February 25, 2016. https://www.nytimes.com/2016/02/28/magazine /what-google-learned-from-its-quest-to-build-the-perfect-team.html.

Forsgren, Nicole PhD, Jez Humble, and Gene Kim. *Accelerate: The Science of Lean Software and DevOps: Building and Scaling High Performing Technology Organizations*. Portland, OR: IT Revolution, 2018.

Gabbert, Fiona, Lorraine Hope, and Ronald P. Fisher. "Protecting Eyewitness Evidence: Examining the Efficacy of a Self-Administered Interview Tool." *Law and Human Behavior* 33, no. 4 (August 2009): 298–307. https://doi.org/10.1007/s10979-008-9146-8.

Gallup. "Employee Engagement." Accessed October 14, 2023. https://www.gallup.com /394373/indicator-employee-engagement.aspx.

Gallup. "State of the Global Workplace: 2023 Report." Accessed November 7, 2023. https://www.gallup.com/workplace/349484/state-of-the-global-workplace.aspx.

Gilbreth, Frank, and L. M. Gilbreth. *Process Charts*. New York: The American Society of Mechanical Engineers, 1921. https://www.thegilbreths.com/resources/Gilbreth -Process-Charts-1921.pdf.

Goldratt, Eliyahu. *The Goal: A Process of Ongoing Improvement*. North River Press, 2012.

Goldratt, Eliyahu. *The Haystack Syndrom: Sifting Information Out of the Data Ocean*. North River Press, 2006.

Grant, Adam. "Are You a Giver or a Taker?" TED Talk. Posted on January 24, 2017. 13:28. https://www.youtube.com/watch?v=YyXRYgjQXXo.

Greene, Jay. "Amazon's Big Holiday Shopping Advantage: An In-House Shipping Network Swollen by Pandemic-Fueled Growth." *Washington Post*. November 27, 2020. https:// www.washingtonpost.com/technology/2020/11/27/amazon-shipping-competitive -threat/.

Hagemann, Bonnie, et al. *Trends in Executive Development 2021–2024: A Benchmark Report*. EDA Inc., 2024.

Hagger, M. S., et al. "Autonomous and Controlled Motivational Regulations for Multiple Health-Related Behaviors: Between- and Within-Participants Analyses." *Health Psychology and Behavioral Medicine* 2, no. 1 (2014): 565–601. https://doi.org/10.1080 /21642850.2014.912945.

Hern, Alex. "The Two-Pizza Rule and the Secret of Amazon's Success." *The Guardian*. April 24, 2018. https://www.theguardian.com/technology/2018/apr/24/the-two -pizza-rule-and-the-secret-of-amazons-success.

Hines, Peter. "Value Stream Management." *The International Journal of Logistics Management* 9, no. 1 (January 1998): 25–42.

Humble, Jez, Joanne Molesky, and Barry O'Reilly. *Lean Enterprise: How High Performance Organizations Innovate at Scale*. Sebastopol, CA: O'Reilly Media, 2015.

Kalbach, Jim. *Mapping Experiences: A Complete Guide to Customer Alignment Through Journeys, Blueprints, and Diagrams*. O'Reilly Media, 2021.

Katz, Judith H., and Frederick A. Miller. *Opening Doors to Teamwork and Collaboration: 4 Keys That Change Everything*. San Francisco: Berrett-Koehler Publishers, 2013.

Kazempour, Kamran, et al. "The Checkbox Project: Learnings for Organizing for Outcomes." *The DevOps Enterprise Journal* 5, no. 2 (Fall 2023). https://itrevolution.com /product/the-devops-enterprise-journal-fall-2023/.

Kersten, Mik. *Project to Product: How to Survive and Thrive in the Age of Digital Disruption with the Flow Framework*. Portland, OR: IT Revolution Press, 2018.

Kim, Gene. *The Unicorn Project, A Novel about Developers, Digital Disruption, and Thriving in the Age of Data*. Portland, OR: IT Revolution, 2019.

Kim, Gene, and Steven J. Spear. *Wiring the Winning Organization: Liberating Our Collective Greatness Through Slowification, Simplification, and Amplification*. Portland, OR: IT Revolution Press, 2023.

Kniberg, Henrik, and Anders Ivarsson. *Scaling Agile @ Spotify with Tribes, Squads, Chapters & Guilds*. October 2012. https://blog.crisp.se/wp-content/uploads/2012/11/SpotifyScaling.pdf.

Lewis, Michael. *Moneyball: The Art of Winning an Unfair Game*. New York: W.W. Norton & Company, 2003.

Liker, Jeffrey, and Gary Convis. *The Toyota Way to Lean Leadership: Achieving and Sustaining Excellence through Leadership Development*. McGraw Hill, 2011.

Lipmanowicz, Henri, and Keith McCandless. "15% Solutions: Discover and Focus on What Each Person Has the Freedom and Resources to Do Now (20 min.)." Liberating Structures (website). Accessed December 9, 2023. https://www.liberatingstructures.com/7-15-solutions/.

Magennis, Troy. "How Does Utilization Impact Lead-Time of Work?" Observable HQ (blog). November 9, 2020. https://observablehq.com/@troymagennis/how-does-utilization-impact-lead-time-of-work

Magennis, Troy. "Impact of Multiple Team Dependencies in Software Development." Observable HQ (blog). July 29, 2019. https://observablehq.com/@troymagennis/impact-of-multiple-team-dependencies-in-software-developm.

Mao, Andrew, et al. "An Experimental Study of Team Size and Performance on a Complex Task." *PLoS ONE* 11, no. 4 (April 2016). https://doi.org/10.1371/journal.pone.0153048.

Mangot, Dave. "Make the Right Way the Easy Way." CIO. October 24, 2019. https://www.cio.com/article/217754/make-the-right-way-the-easy-way.html.

Mark, Gloria, Victor Gonzalez, and Justin Harris. "No Task Left Behind? Examining the Nature of Fragmented Work." *CHI '05: Proceedings of the SIGCHI Conference on Human Factors in Computing Systems* (April 2005): 321–330. https://doi.org/10.1145/1054972.105501710.1145/1054972.1055017.

Martin, James. *The Great Transition: Using the Seven Disciplines of Enterprise Engineering to Align People, Technology, and Strategy*. New York: AMACOM Books, 1995.

Martin, Karen. *Clarity First: How Smart Leaders and Organizations Achieve Outstanding Performance*. New York: McGraw-Hill Education, 2018.

Martin, Karen, and Mike Osterling. *Value Stream Mapping: How to Visualize Work and Align Leadership for Organizational Transformation*. New York: McGraw-Hill Education, 2013.

Matts, Chris. "Constraints that Enable." The IT Risk Manager (website). December 9, 2018. https://theitriskmanager.com/2018/12/09/constraints-that-enable/.

Maxwell, John C. *The 21 Irrefutable Laws of Leadership*. Thomas Nelson, 2007.

McGilchrist, Iain. *The Master and His Emissary: The Divided Braise and the Making of the Western World*. New Haven, CT: Yale University Press, 2019.

Modig, Niklas, and Par Ahlstrom. *This is Lean: Resolving the Efficiency Paradox*. Rheologica Publishing, 2012.

Panagiotopoulos, Georgios, Constantine Zogopoulos, and Zoe Karanikola. "The Learning

Organization According to Senge: Recording and Validation of the Park Research Tool in Primary Education Schools in the Prefecture of Ilia." Global Journal of Human Resource Management 6, no.5 (November 2018): 1–19. https://www.eajournals.org /wp-content/uploads/The-Learning-Organization-According-to-Senge.pdf.

Parkinson, Northcote. "Parkinson's Law." *The Economist*. November 19, 1955. https://www.economist.com/news/1955/11/19/parkinsons-law.

Pereira, Steve. "Principles of Value Stream Identification." Value Stream Management Consortium (website). May 22, 2023. https://www.vsmconsortium.org/blog /principles-of-value-stream-identification.

Pink, Daniel H. *Drive: The Surprising Truth About What Motivates Us*. Edinburgh: Canongate Books, 2010.

Reinertsen, Donald G. *The Principles of Product Development Flow: Second Generation Lean Product Development*. Redondo Beach, CA: Celeritas Publishing, 2009.

Ring, Matt, et al. "Measuring Value: Navigating Uncertainty to Build the Right Thing for Our Customers and Our Business," *DevOps Enterprise Journal* 5, no. 2 (2023). https://itrevolution.com/product/the-devops-enterprise-journal-fall-2023/.

Romanukha, Andriy. "Stop Starting, Start Finishing with Agile." ReadWrite. Last modified March 23, 2023. https://readwrite.com/stop-starting-start-finishing-with-agile.

Rosenblueth, A., and N. Wiener, "The Role of Models in Science," *Philosophy of Science* 12 (1945).

Rother, Mike. *Toyota Kata: Managing People for Improvement, Adaptiveness, and Superior Results*. New York: McGraw-Hill, 2009.

Rother, Mike, and John Shook. *Learning to See: Value Stream Mapping to Add Value and Eliminate Muda*. Cambridge, MA: Lean Enterprise Institute, 2003.

Saldanha, Tony. *Why Digital Transformations Fail: The Surprising Disciplines of How to Take Off and Stay Ahead*. Oakland, CA: Berrett-Koehler Publishers, 2019.

Senge, Peter M. *The Fifth Discipline: The Art & Practice of the Learning Organization*. New York: Doubleday, 2006.

Sheth, Bhavin R., and Ryan Young, "Two Visual Pathways in Primates Based on Sampling of Space: Exploitation and Exploration of Visual Information." *Frontiers in Integrative Neuroscience* 10, no. 37 (November 2016). https://doi.org/10.3389/fnint.2016.00037.

Schulz, Kathryn. *Being Wrong: Adventures in the Margin of Error*. Ecco, 2011.

Sipser, Michael. *Introduction to the Theory of Computation*. 3rd ed. Boston: Cengage Learning, 2012.

Skelton, Matthew, and Manuel Pais. *Team Topologies: Organizing Business and Technology Teams for Fast Flow*. Portland, OR: IT Revolution, 2019.

Slater, Daniel. "Powering Innovation and Speed with Amazon's Two-Pizza Teams." Amazon Web Services Executive Insights. 2023. https://d1.awsstatic.com/executive -insights/en_US/two_pizza_teams_eBook.pdf.

Smith, Adam. *The Wealth of Nations*. Edited by Andrew Skinner. New York: Penguin Publishing Group, 1999.

Spear, Steven J. *The High-Velocity Edge: How Market Leaders Leverage Operational Excellence to Beat the Competition*. New York: McGraw Hill, 2010.

Spiegel, Alix. "Teachers' Expectation Can Influence How Students Perform." NPR. September 17, 2012. https://www.npr.org/sections/health-shots/2012/09/18/161159263 /teachers-expectations-can-influence-how-students-perform.

Sproule, Michael J. "Organizational Rhetoric and the Public Sphere." *Communication Studies* 40, no. 4 (1989): 258–265. https://doi.org/10.1080/10510978909368279.

Stickdorn, Mark, et al. *This Is Service Design Doing: Applying Service Design Thinking in the Real World*. Sebastopol, CA: O'Reilly Media, 2018.

Sussna, Jeff. *Designing Delivery: Rethinking IT in the Digital Service Economy*. Sebastopol, CA: O'Reilly Media, 2015.

Thrasher, Paula. "Interactive Virtual Value Stream Mapping - Visualizing Flow in a Virtual World." Presentation at the 2020 DevOps Enterprise Summit in 2020. 35:54. https://videos.itrevolution.com/watch/466912411/.

Vacanti, Daniel. "Little's Law and System Stability." Interview by Klaus Leopold. LEANability, June 8, 2017. https://www.leanability.com/en/blog/2017/08/littles-law-and-system-stability/.

van der Kolk, Berend. "Can Performance Metrics Harm Performance?" Insights. November 9, 2018. https://www.ie.edu/insights/articles/can-performance-metrics-harm-performance/.

van der Kolk, B., and W. Kaufmann. "Performance Measurement, Cognitive Dissonance and Coping Strategies: Exploring Individual Responses to NPM-Inspired Output Control." *Journal of Management Control* 29 (2018): 93–113.

Vas, Zsófia. "Role of Proximity in Regional Clusters: Evidence from the Software Industry." In *Regional Competitiveness, Innovation and Environment*, edited by Zoltán Bajmócy and Imre Lengyel, 162–182. Szeged: JATEPress, 2009.

West, Geoffrey B. *Scale: The Universal Laws of Growth, Innovation, Sustainability, and the Pace of Life in Organisms, Cities, Economies, and Companies*. New York: Penguin Books, 2017.

Wiener, Norbert. *Cybernetics: Or Control and Communication in the Animal and the Machine*. Cambridge, MA: MIT Press, 1948.

Wiener, Norbert. *The Human Use of Human Beings: Cybernetics and Society*. New York: Hachette Books, 1988.

Wikipedia. "Abilene paradox." Accessed December 1, 2023. https://en.wikipedia.org/wiki/Abilene_paradox#cite_note-Harvey-3.

Wikipedia. "IKEA effect." Accessed December 1, 2023. https://en.wikipedia.org/wiki/IKEA_effect.

Wikipedia. "Metcalfe's law." Accessed December 1, 2023. https://en.wikipedia.org/wiki/Metcalfe%27s_law.

Wikipedia. "Ringelmann effect." Accessed December 1, 2023. https://en.wikipedia.org/wiki/Ringelmann_effect.

Wikipedia. "Six sigma." Accessed December 8, 2020. https://en.wikipedia.org/wiki/Six_Sigma

Wikipedia. "Teleology." Accessed December 8, 2020. https://en.wikipedia.org/wiki/Teleology.

Wikipedia. "Time and motion study." Accessed December 1, 2023. https://en.wikipedia.org/wiki/Time_and_motion_study.

Womack, James P., and Daniel T. Jones. *Lean Thinking: Banish Waste and Create Wealth in Your Organization*. New York: Simon & Schuster, 1996.

Womack, James P., Daniel T. Jones, and Daniel Roos. *The Machine That Changed the World*. New York: Free Press, 2007.

Notes

Introduction

1. Blanchard, "No One of Us Is as Smart as All of Us."
2. Sheth and Young, "Two Visual Pathways in Primates Based on Sampling of Space."
3. Saldanha, *Why Digital Transformations Fail.*
4. Martin, *Clarity First.*

Chapter 1

1. "Peter F. Drucker Quotes."
2. West, *Scale*, 32.
3. "Amazon: Number of Employees"; Greene, "Amazon's Big Holiday Shopping Advantage."
4. Mark, Gonzalez, and Harris, "No Task Left Behind?"
5. Katz and Miller, *Opening Doors to Teamwork and Collaboration*, 87.
6. "Employee Engagement."
7. Gallup, "State of the Global Workplace: 2023 Report."
8. Pink, *Drive.*
9. Duhigg, "What Google Learned from Its Quest to Build the Perfect Team."
10. Criscuolo, Salter, and Wal, "The Role of Proximity."
11. Vas, "Role of Proximity in Regional Clusters," 162–182.
12. Kim and Spear, *Wiring the Winning Organization*, xxviii.
13. Wikipedia, "Ringelmann effect."
14. Mao et al., "An Experimental Study of Team Size."
15. Mao et al., "An Experimental Study of Team Size."
16. Slater, "Powering Innovation and Speed with Amazon's Two-Pizza Teams."
17. Hern, "The Two-Pizza Rule and the Secret of Amazon's Success."
18. Sproule, "Organizational Rhetoric and the Public Sphere."
19. Sipser, *Introduction to the Theory of Computation*, 348.
20. Carpentier, "New Economics for Sustainable Development Attention Economy."
21. Atkinson, "Manpower Strategies for Flexible Organisations."
22. Wikipedia, "Metcalfe's law."
23. Brooks, *The Mythical Man-Month*, 25.
24. "Churchill and the Commons Chamber."
25. Kazempour et al., "The Checkbox Project."
26. DeGrandis, *Making Work Visible*, 43.
27. Wikipedia, "Time and motion study."
28. Brooks, *Mythical Man-Month*, 7.

Chapter 2

1. Wikipedia, "IKEA effect."
2. Martin, *The Great Transition*, 16.
3. Martin, *The Great Transition*, 104.
4. Rother, *Toyota Kata*, 18.

Chapter 4

1. Wikipedia, "Abilene paradox."

Chapter 5

1. Wikipedia, "Teleology."
2. Rosenblueth and Wiener, "The Role of Models in Science," 320.
3. Boston Consulting Group, "Flipping the Odds of Digital Transformation Success."
4. Bryar and Carr, *Working Backwards*, 98–120.
5. Lewis, *Moneyball*, 59.
6. "Accelerating Change."
7. Grant, "Are You a Giver or a Taker?"
8. Hagger et al., "Autonomous and Controlled Motivational Regulations."

Chapter 6

1. Rother and Shook, *Learning to See*, 26.
2. Pereira, "Principles of Value Stream Identification."
3. Gilbreth and Gilbreth, *Process Charts*, 4.
4. Rother and Shook, *Learning to See*, 13.
5. Thrasher, "Interactive Virtual Value Stream Mapping."
6. Womack and Jones, *Lean Thinking*, 29.
7. Reinertsen, *The Principles of Product Development Flow*, 35.
8. Kalbach, *Mapping Experiences*.
9. Gabbert, Hope, and Fisher, "Protecting Eyewitness Evidence."
10. Cutler, "TBM 34/52."
11. Martin and Osterling, *Value Stream Mapping*, 72.
12. Jim Benson, personal conversation with the authors, 2023.
13. Lipmanowicz and McCandless, "15% Solutions."

Chapter 7

1. Parkinson, "Parkinson's Law."
2. Covey, *The 7 Habits of Highly Effective People*, 66.

Chapter 8

1. DeGrandis, *Making Work Visible*, 2.
2. Romanukha, "Stop Starting, Start Finishing with Agile."

Chapter 9

1. Stickdorn et al., *This Is Service Design Doing*, 139.
2. Martin and Osterling, *Value Stream Mapping*, 27.

3. Kersten, *Project to Product*, 90.
4. Burrows, "#2MBM: Meaning before Metric, Measure before Method."
5. Cutler, "TBM 245."

Chapter 10

1. Capra and Luisi, *The Systems View of Life*, 316.
2. As quoted in Kim, *The Unicorn Project*, 3.
3. Beck et al. "Manifesto for Agile Software Development."
4. Cottmeyer, "LK2009 Anderson, Scotland, and Hathaway."
5. Womack and Jones, *Lean Thinking*, 29–90.
6. Ring et al. "Measuring Value."
7. Ring et al. "Measuring Value."
8. McGilchrist, *The Master and His Emissary*, 47.
9. Deming, *Out of the Crisis*, 22.
10. Sheth and Young, "Two Visual Pathways in Primates."
11. Liker and Convis, *The Toyota Way*, 149.
12. Liker and Convis, *The Toyota Way*, vi.
13. Modig and Ahlstrom, *This is Lean*, 9.
14. Ackoff, *The Democratic Corporation*, 23.
15. Magennis, "How Does Utilization Impact Lead-Time of Work?" This site provides an excellent calculator to illustrate the mathematics of high utilization.
16. Deming, *Out of the Crisis*, Chapter 2.
17. Wikipedia, "Six sigma."
18. Goldratt, *The Goal*, Chapter 17.
19. Goldratt, *The Haystack Syndrome*.
20. Spear, *The High-Velocity Edge*, 183.
21. Deming, *Out of the Crisis*, Chapter 8.
22. Schulz, *Being Wrong*, 5.

Chapter 11

1. Maxwell, *The 21 Irrefutable Laws of Leadership*, 11.
2. Quote is commonly attributed to Peter Drucker.
3. Cynefin.io, "Constraints."
4. Mangot, "Make the Right Way the Easy Way."
5. Matts, "Constraints that Enable."
6. Panagiotopoulos, Zogopoulos, and Karanikola, "The Learning Organization According to Senge."
7. Senge, *The Fifth Discipline*, 12
8. Spiegel, "Teachers' Expectation Can Influence How Students Perform."
9. Liker and Convis, *The Toyota Way to Lean Leadership*, 41.
10. Hagemann et al., *Trends in Executive Development*.

Chapter 12

1. "The Biggest Startup."
2. Anderson, *Learning to Lead, Leading to Learn*, 171.

3.   Forsgren, Humble, and Kim, *Accelerate*, Chapter 3.

Chapter 13
1.   Hines, "Value Stream Management."
2.   Goldratt, *The Haystack Syndrome*, 26.
3.   van der Kolk and Kaufmann, "Performance Measurement, Cognitive Dissonance and Coping Strategies."
4.   van der Kolk, "Can Performance Metrics Harm Performance?"
5.   Reinertsen, *The Principles of Product Development Flow*, 33.
6.   Clark, "Inspect."
7.   Inspired by Cutler, "TBM 7/52: Two Bets."

Chapter 14
1.   Martin, *The Great Transition*, 63.
2.   Kersten, *Project to Product*, 111.
3.   "A Brief History of AWS."
4.   Anderson, McCann, and O'Reilly, *The Value Flywheel Effect*.
5.   Clanton et al., *Getting Started with Dojos*, 4.
6.   Ross Clanton, as quoted in Cote, *Monolithic Transformation*
7.   Kniberg and Ivarsson, *Scaling Agile @ Spotify*.
8.   Skelton and Pais, *Team Topologies*, 130.
9.   Covey, *The 7 Habits of Highly Effective People*, 38.
10. Magennis, "Impact of Multiple Team Dependencies."

Conclusion
1.   Arnold and Yüce, "Black Swan Farming Using Cost of Delay."
2.   Clanton et al., *The Project to Product Transformation*.
3.   Womack and Jones, *Lean Thinking*, 320.

Appendix
1.   Vacanti, interview.
2.   Bongers et al., "How Long Does It Take To Refocus," 420–439.
3.   Based on personal experience reports and from multiple practitioners we've spoken to.

Acknowledgments

We're incredibly grateful to so many who have inspired, informed, and improved the ideas and practices collected in this book. We've been tremendously fortunate to leverage the collective learning of great thinkers from across the Lean, cybernetics, systems thinking, collaboration, Agile, and DevOps communities. We've also been lucky to have the opportunity to test and implement the material in this book across organizations large and small, with leaders who were courageous and trusting enough to try something different.

Thanks to our friends Karen Martin, Dominica DeGrandis, Jez Humble, and Mik Kersten for their pioneering contributions to our understanding of mapping and improving flow, sharing their experience and their generosity as guides. To our friends Adam Hawkins, Carmen DeArdo, Courtney Kissler, Fritjof Capra, Gary Gruver, Gene Kim, Helen Beal, Jeremy Akers, Jim Benson, João Rosa, John Cutler, John Willis, Jon Smart, Manuel Pais, Matthew Skelton, Mixel Kiemen, Nicole Helmerich, Patrick Debois, Paula Thrasher, Peter Maddison, Steve Spear, and Vera Hofmann for sharing experience, support, and brilliant thinking to improve this book and its practices.

Andrew owes a special debt to Meredith Bell and Sandrine Olivencia for helping and inspiring AutoRABIT on the journey to becoming a lean organization.

Thank you to our patient and supportive families for making space and energy for this book to grow.

Thank you to our Flow Collective community and to all the other people who inspired and collaborated with us on so many ideas, concepts, and practices over the years.

Finally, huge thanks to our editorial team, Anna Noak and Leah Brown, who shepherded us through this journey with incredible skill and patience.

About the Authors

Steve Pereira has spent over two decades improving the flow of work across organizations. He's worked through tech support, IT management, platform and infrastructure engineering, product management, and as a founding CTO for enterprise SaaS. He serves as CEO of Visible Consulting, as COO to the Value Stream Management Consortium, Chair of the OASIS VSM Interoperability technical committee, and co-founder of the Flow Collective to bring flow-focused professionals together. Since 2017, he has been developing and facilitating Flow Engineering to make flow improvement in large organizations accessible, collaborative, and actionable.

Andrew Davis is Chief Product Officer at AutoRABIT and the author of *Mastering Salesforce DevOps*. He's a Salesforce architect, developer, and product leader with a focus on the human side of software development. He's been the leading figure in introducing DevOps concepts to the Salesforce world. Trained as an engineer, he spent fifteen years as a Buddhist monk, teaching meditation and personal transformation and helping develop communities of practice. These days he studies the intersection of business, technology, and psychology through systems thinking. He is co-founder of the Center for Harmonious Living with his wife, Ashley, to promote healthier ways of approaching work and life.